Thoughts for sports educators working with pole vaulters

"It is not the critic who counts, not the man who points out how the strong man stumbled or where the doer of deeds could have done better.
The credit belongs to the man who is actually in the arena: whose face is marred by the dust and sweat of blood, who strives valiantly; who errs and comes short again and again
… who knows the great enthusiasms, the great devotions and spends himself in a worthy cause.
Who at the best, knows in the end the triumph of high achievement and who, at the worst, if he fails, at least fails while daring greatly, so his place shall never be with those cold and timid souls who know neither victory nor defeat."

Theodore 'Teddy' Roosevelt. 1904

" …what a pity it is that an art so important, so difficult, and so intimately concerned with the invariable laws of mechanical nature, should be so held by its possessors that it cannot improve but must die with each individual. Having no advantages of previous education they cannot arrange their thoughts; they can scarcely be said to think. They can far less express or communicate to others the intuitive knowledge which they possess, and their art, acquired by habit alone, is little different from an instinct. We are as little entitled to expect improvement here as in the architecture of the bee or the beaver. The species cannot improve."

Patrick O'Brian, "The Ionian Mission".
Commenting on the skill of captaining a sailing ship in battle at the turn of the eighteenth century.

This book is dedicated to all the sports educators around the world who give their time, energy and enthusiasm to helping young people chase their dreams.

Acknowledgements

Simon Arkell and all of the other orphans upon whom we have practised and learned our trade over the last forty five years. We hope the experience we have gained has not been wasted.

The Bailey Family of Nampa, Idaho: for their whole hearted acceptance of a heretic.

Larry Berryhlll for his support and friendship along with a chance to work with his athletes at BYU.

Graham Boase: for his support and friendship over many years and his contribution to the editing of this book.

Peter Bowman: for providing much of the pole vault equipment we desperately needed at a crucial period in the development of the group..

Sean Brown: for being a pole vault 'tragic' and his work in developing and maintaining his website 'Neovault'.

Sergey Bubka: for being the inspiration for this book..

David Butler: for the generous use of some of his illustrations.

Steve Chappell: for a friendship which has lasted over forty years

Herbert Czingon: for permission to use material from his superb website, "Stabhochsprung".

Lauren Eley: for her perceptive editing and accurate proof reading, and just for being a nice person.

Coach Bob Fraley of Fresno State for his open minded approach to a bloody Aussie.

John Hamann: without 'St. John of Hallett Cove', the task of developing pole vaulters in South Australia would have been infinitely more difficult.

Jess Jarver: for the immense contribution to the professional development of generations of Australian coaches, including the authors of this work.

Lane Maestretti: For providing an example of what a true American patriot should be.

Tom McNab: for providing a major stimulus for Alan to become a coach of athletics.

Wilf Paish: for providing a model of what a sports educator should be.

Vitaly Petrov: for sharing his knowledge, wisdom and friendship.

Tony Rice: for unstinting support and encouragement over a period of thirty years.

Brian Roe: for his friendship, for improving officiating in Australia, for his support in improving the competition program for young vaulters and, most importantly his willingness to be a sponge for much of Alan's angst.

Mark Stewart: for being a true 'gentile homme', a world class coach and for providing moral support through thick and thin.

Finally to our families, especially Alan's long suffering wife, Jennifer, who has absorbed much of his frustration as he attempted to take this project from a dream to reality.

CONTENTS

Foreword

This book is the expression of many years of experience as an outstanding educator, teacher and coach. Alan and I shared our early years as teachers of Physical Education in England, rivals on the track but great friends off it, sharing a passion to help perfect the knowledge, the communication skills of educators and coaches charged with the success of their young athletes. Having spent over half a century involved with all aspects of track and field from the novice child to a range of Olympic Champions, I can believe that it would be difficult for any coach in the world to match the all round ability of Alan Launder. An association with Alan is a life changing experience.

Pole vaulting is the most challenging of all track and Field events. Challenging to the athlete in that the skills partly satisfy man's oldest desire of unaided flight. Challenging to the teacher who needs to safely introduce the skills of purposeful flight to those so fascinated. Challenging to the coach who needs to accommodate the new skills forced upon us by changes in technology and the desire to scale barriers others are yet to meet. This book will help ALL of those involved in the process of educating such an intricate and complex series of skills. From the novice athlete who holds a pole, be it rigid or flexible, for the first time, through to the world record holder and associates, all will find "Pearls of Wisdom" hitherto not recorded in any text on the event.

Alan Launder is an inspired and gifted teacher, an even more inspired coach and without doubt one of the world's leading pedagogues. I have the most profound respect for his knowledge of sport and sport pedagogy and I have frequent cause to admire the unique way in which he handles all of the physical and psychological skills involved in every aspect of skill perfection.

It is clear that Alan has found an equally professional colleague with a range of skills, especially in gymnastics and illustration, to complement his own. John Gormley graduated Magna cum Laude from Loughborough College and has had considerable experience as a teacher, coach and teacher educator. He brings a unique combination of skills to the production of this work.

I know that this text will be a must for any person involved with the mastery of pole vaulting and there will be lessons, within its pages, for anyone closely involved with educating the Physical.

WILF PAISH
I.A.A.F. tutor. International Coach. Formerly National Coach for the North of England.

Useful Websites

beginnertobubka.com
polevaulterducation.org
neovault.com
stabhochsprung.com
pocketvideos.com
pvscb.com
polevaultworldaccordingtogus

PREFACE

"The day a book comes off the printing press, it needs to be rewritten.

Anonymous

The aim of this book is to contribute to the improvement of teaching and coaching in the pole vault. Its objectives are to clarify the fundamental nature of this event and to present an Australian approach to developing pole vaulters. While it will be particularly valuable for sports educators at the beginning of their careers, it may also prove to be a useful resource for experienced teachers and coaches.

Why is a book of this kind needed? After all, the proliferation of Websites, CDs and DVDs devoted to the pole vault ensures that there is a vast amount of information available about the event. Unfortunately, despite this abundance of information, wisdom is often in short supply!

While it is true that watching video images of pole vaulting is usually entertaining, especially when they are hyped up by loud rock music, it is rarely educational! The fact is, that to learn anything worthwhile from this kind of material, you must know what to look for in the first place! This becomes a kind of 'Catch 22' since if you learn nothing from the first images you watch, you are not ready to learn anything from the next!

One of our major objectives therefore is to give readers a clear understanding of what is really important in the pole vault. While the images we provide through photographs and illustrations may seem to be old fashioned, they have the advantage of focussing a reader's attention on the critical aspects of modern pole vault technique. The supporting text then provides a clear explanation of all aspects of that technique and shows how each element fits in to the whole efficient pattern of movement.

A work of this kind forces the reader to interact with it, to think, to consider, to debate and perhaps even to disagree. This process is essential if sports educators who choose to coach this challenging event are to begin to develop the cognitive, visual and verbal 'pictures' of pole vaulting which are essential if they are to be effective.

This book has been produced by two committed sports educators with a combined total of over seventy years of highly successful experience of teaching and coaching on three Continents, including North America. Both have also had lengthy experience in Physical Education Teacher Education and have broad ranging expertise in the areas of Child Growth and Development, Anatomy and Physiology, Skill Acquisition, Sports Pedagogy, Biomechanics as well as coaching physically impaired athletes..

They have studied with great coaches like Andrzei Krzesinski in Warsaw, Poland, Maurice Houvion in Vincennes, France, Dr. Jean Claude Perrin of Colombes, Paris and Vitaly Petrov of the Ukraine in Formia, Canberra and Adelaide. All were mentors to Olympic Champions. In addition Alan and John have worked alongside Roman Botcharnikov and Alex Parnov in Adelaide for extensive periods.

Between them, the authors have attended Olympic Games, World Championships and Commonwealth Games as assistant coaches or as personal coaches to competing athletes. They have written numerous papers on the pole vault, including one which may have been the first to present Petrov's most innovative idea, the 'Pre jump' take off, in English.

Alan has attended three of the immensely popular and valuable Pole Vault Summits in Reno, Nevada, and in 2004 was an invited keynote speaker. He has been involved in camps for young athletes in Salt Lake City, Utah, Nampa, Idaho, and at UCLA in California. He has also been an invited coach at Brigham Young University in Provo, Utah.

Valuable inputs have come from informal contacts with other Australian coaches and from observation of their methods and of their athletes. Dr. Mark Stewart is a world class coach from Melbourne who has already produced a World record holder in Emma George and an Olympian in Steven Hooker. Working as a hobby coach with little support, he has developed a stream of young vaulters.

Steve Rippon, who produced Paul Burgess (1994 World Junior Champion) in the athletic backwater of Perth in Australia, was also an excellent coach who found and developed a large number of young athletes. This included James Miller, a 5.75 metre (18'8"1/2) vaulter, who just missed making the 1996 final in Atlanta.

Finally there is Sergey Mirishnichenko, another Russian coach who worked in Adelaide for two years before taking up a coaching position on the Gold Coast of Queensland. He has already had an impact, with two girls qualifying for the 2003 World Juniors in Italy and one, his daughter, making the final.

However the most significant factor is that the authors have themselves taken many young athletes from absolute beginner to international level. They have done this while working in an environment not conducive to developing track and field athletes in any event, far less the demanding and complex discipline of pole vaulting.

They have drawn on all of this experience and combined it with their theoretical knowledge to create a learning resource which provides wisdom, not mere information. However even wisdom has little value unless it can be applied. The primary objective of this book therefore is to show how it is possible to teach beginners to employ the same principles of pole vaulting which enabled Sergey Bubka to become the greatest vaulter in history. This may seem to be a revolutionary idea but we hope that readers will find much of the information, knowledge and wisdom needed for them to begin the fascinating task of coaching their athletes 'to vault like Bubka'.

To this end;

Part One first challenges coaches to consider the Petrov/Bubka technical model of vaulting. It then goes on to outline the Role of the track and field coach and the fundamental processes of coaching, before examining the question of risk management in the pole vault.

Part Two begins by attempting to clarify the relationship between an athlete's style, their technical model and the principles of biomechanics. It then analyses the Petrov/Bubka technical model and shows that not only have many other elite athletes used this technical model with great success, but that young Australian athletes have also mastered key elements of this advanced model of pole vaulting.

Part Three outlines the principles which underpin the Adelaide approach. It provides important principles of sport pedagogy and then details how young athletes can be introduced to the key elements of modern technique.

Part Four initially focuses on the Process of technical coaching and the use of drills in the development of pole vaulters. It goes on to detail the principles of training and conditioning for young pole vaulters and outlines the role of gymnastics in the training program. Finally it suggests that the use of Field tests can assist coaches.

Part Five introduces the basic principles of sports psychology and suggests the routines vaulters and coaches can use to cope with the pressure of competition.

Section Two of the book deals with issues which even highly experienced coaches may find of interest. It examines common myths and misunderstandings in the event, the close relationship between stiff pole technique and modern technique and provides a more detailed outline of the fundamental elements of the Petrov/Bubka technical model.

Finally there are four appendices which deal with
The calibration and rating of pole vault poles.
The thoughts of one of our young athletes on the value of the pole vault experience.
The specific influences on the development of Adelaide approach.
An example of the process of technical coaching.

Footnote: We realise that this cannot be **THE** definitive statement of how to develop pole vaulters. However we have done our best to clarify some of the most important principles for developing young athletes in this challenging event. We have learned a great deal from the process and hope to continue to be students of the event in the future. If nothing else we hope we have contributed to the ongoing debate which is essential if there is to be real progress in any field of human endeavour.

CHAPTER ONE

Introduction

"Praestabilus esse nonnunquam unicum habere consilium, id sit verum et efficax".

Erasmus 1551

The past fifty years have seen an explosion of interest in sport around the world. This has been accompanied by an enormous increase in efforts to improve sporting performance as individuals and teams try to find an edge over their opponents. Science and technology now impact on sport in myriad ways; indeed in some sports the depth of analysis borders on the ridiculous, especially given the more pressing problems this planet faces.

It is therefore surprising to find that in the pole vault, perhaps the most complex of all the disciplines of track and field, some coaches still base their methods on myths and misunderstandings which have their roots in the pioneering phase of fibreglass vaulting. In the "Information age" this is almost inexcusable. Almost but not quite! The fact is that the vast majority of coaches have little time for study or reflection, they are too busy getting on with the tasks of teaching, coaching and living. This can lead them into the trap of simply watching video film, CDs or DVDs, in search of the Holy Grail. The problem here is that unless coaches have a sound conceptual model of the event in the first place, these video images are likely to provide more entertainment than education.

One of the objectives of this text therefore is to attempt to provide a definitive statement of modern technique. This is a challenging task because many coaches believe that "There are many ways to skin a cat". In other words they feel there really is no ONE best way to pole vault and that an athlete's technique depends almost entirely on their physical qualities. This is a difficult argument to counter, especially when the coach concerned is highly experienced and their athletes are achieving good results. However we believe that some coaches take this position because they do not have a clear conceptual model of modern technique in the pole vault, while others are confusing the notion of 'Style' with 'A Technical model'.

Another factor can best be described as 'short termism'. This is common in the USA where coaches typically have four years or less to work with their athletes in a society which only under-stands winning. As a result, coaches often trade long term development for short term gain. An obvious example is a tendency to have young vaulters gripping too high. This may produce a regional or state high school title but may prevent a young athlete from ever reaching their full potential. Another symptom of 'short termism' is coaches who try to 'paper over' major technical weaknesses. They deal with the symptom instead of the cause of a problem, in order to achieve a better result at the Conference or National Championships. Unfortunately instead of admitting this, they hide behind the old furphy, "There are many ways to skin a cat".

Here it might worth noting the words of Erasmus quoted above. In 1551, when considering the strategies of the fox and the hedgehog to get out of danger he observed

"Perhaps it is better to have one way of wisdom provided that it be true."

Every vaulter does have a distinctive 'Style', which is mainly determined by their unique physical qualities and previous movement experiences. For example athletes with a gymnastic background will usually be much neater and tighter on the pole during the inversion phase; good examples of this are Yelena Isinbyeva, Svetlana Feofanova and Anzela Balakhonova. However their 'Style' overlays a 'Technical model', which in turn is based on the principles of biomechanics, about which there should be no debate!

We believe that the first coherent biomechanical solution to the challenge of vaulting with a flexible pole was provided by coaches from the former Soviet Union. Vitaly Petrov outlined all of the key elements of this 'Advanced technical model' in the presentation he gave at the European Coaches Conference in Birmingham, England in 1985. Perhaps because of the problems inherent in a situation where complex concepts were passed through the filter of translation from Russian to English, many of the 'pearls' in his presentation went unnoticed or were misunderstood. Indeed the revolutionary ideas he put forward seem to have challenged almost everything the vast majority of coaches believed about effective pole vaulting at that time, so it is perhaps

Figure 1.1

World Cup in Canberra, Australia in 1985 when Petrov explained his ideas in great detail with copious hand drawn diagrams – which Alan stupidly did not retain! This experience encouraged us to really study what he was saying and to try to apply his ideas with young athletes. This was an important step because, like many other coaches, we initially believed that Bubka's performances could be attributed to his unique physical qualities and his steely determination to be the best.

There is little doubt that there has been a widespread tendency to view Bubka as unique, a one of a kind, who achieved superb performances simply because of his special physical qualities. As a result many saw Bubka's 'style' but did not SEE the Petrov 'technical model' which underpinned that 'style'. However it is becoming increasingly difficult for anyone, no matter how obtuse, to ignore reality. Without exception, the Men's World Championship has been dominated by athletes who exploit this model.

Bubka's sixth and final World Championship win in Athens in 1997 was followed by Maxim Tarasov in 1999, Dimitri Markov in 2001 and Giusseppi Gibilisco in 2003.

Among American athletes it is clear that Lawrence Johnson, World Indoor Champion in 2001 and with a personal best of 5.98 metres (19'7½"), who was coached by Petrov disciple, Roman Botcharnikov, employed this technical model. In addition there is anecdotal evidence to suggest that Nick Hysong was also influenced by the Petrov model at least in the early days of his career, while Stacey Dragila has been making a transition towards it under the guidance of Greg Hull. We have no doubt that if she is successful and can avoid injury, Stacey can continue to be a major factor in women's pole vaulting for some time to come. Here is must be said that Stacey represents all that is best about this marvellous event. A steely determination to succeed that matches Bubka, a tremendous competitive ability and a tough resilient attitude, all wrapped up in a delightful personality. Her impact on the imagination of young female athletes with potential in the pole vault, must be enormous.

It is also interesting to note that Svetlana Feofanova and Yelena Isinbyeva, who have been pushing each other to new heights over the last few years while sharing the World and Olympic titles, use the Petrov model as does Annika

understandable that his ideas were not immediately taken up and widely applied. Another factor may be that this apparently revolutionary approach to pole vaulting leapt ahead of the understanding of most, if not all, sports scientists.

Figure 1.1 shows Bubka setting yet another World Record!

However it is quite astonishing that twenty years on, many vault coaches around the world have either not heard of the Petrov/Bubka model of vaulting, or what is even more amazing, have rejected it! As a result it is still not widely understood nor accepted by all coaches. There are several reasons for this. Among the most powerful are xenophobia and egotism, both of which can prevent otherwise intelligent and professional individuals from taking up new ideas. We are all products of our own experience and it is usually the most powerful force in our belief system. Over 150 years ago the German philosopher/writer Goethe observed that when a person subscribed to a particular school of thought, their adherence to those beliefs blinded them to accurate observations. It seemed to him that the more one 'knew' the less they were able to 'see'.

In fairness it must be pointed out that it was only through serendipity that we had the opportunity to learn more about this advanced technical model at an early stage. This occurred during the

Figure 1.2

Becker of Germany, also a medallist in Paris 2003 who is shown in Figure 1.2. In fact we believe that the rapid improvement in female performances since the formal introduction of the pole vault for women, can be attributed to the fact that many of them learned to vault using the modern technical model. In this way they bypassed the baggage of mythology which continues to affect many levels of male pole vaulting.

Without wishing to denigrate the performance of any athlete, we believe that many have underachieved because of a reluctance to seriously consider the Soviet technical model. This is especially the case in the USA. This is strange because when the Soviet "Sputnik" went into orbit in 1957 there was an immediate and concerted US response which lead very quickly to Aldrin and Armstrong's historic moon walk in 1969, only twelve years later. One coach who did take up the new ideas as soon as he learned of them, was Larry Berryhill of Brigham Young University. Larry visited Australia in the early 1990s and was exposed to Petrov's ideas second hand through the author. He immediately began to try to implement them with the young athletes he was helping at the time, including Nick Hysong.

Although many younger coaches have taken up the gauntlet, there has been no similar concerted American response to the challenge Bubka threw out in the pole vault. This despite the best efforts of super enthusiasts Bob Fraley of Fresno State and Steve Chappell of UCS Spirit who have invited Petrov to speak at the Reno Pole Vault Summit twice in recent years! Perhaps a reluctance to accept this new approach to pole vault-

ing was because it came from the former USSR, which had no real tradition of pole vaulting compared to the USA.

These are challenging statements, given that the U.S.A. recently gained two Olympic titles with Nick Hysong in 2000 and Timothy Mack in 2004 and a third with Stacey Dragila in 2000. However it should not be forgotten that the United States had dominated the event almost since its inception until the arrival of the Petrov driven flow of athletes from the Soviet Block countries. Countries like France have also been guilty of ignoring the new methods while even in Germany, a country where there was a national policy to adopt the Petrov/Bubka approach, it would seem that some coaches still ignore it. In Australia, with a very small number of vault coaches who see each other on a regular basis, Petrov's ideas were rapidly taken up and applied. Unfortunately a small population base, inferior infrastructure and limited opportunities for competition has meant that knowledge has not always been translated into performance.

Perhaps the last word on this issue should go to Bubka, who, even in retirement, is committed to improving standards in the pole vault. At the European Championships held in Munich in 2002, in response to a question from Alan, he indicated that he was completely mystified by the unwillingness of many coaches and athletes to adopt Petrov's ideas. Bubka was adamant that it was his technique which was responsible for his success and not his physical parameters, excellent though those were. He believed that many of the athletes we were watching that day, along with many many more in the USA, had physical ability equal or superior to his own and he was certain that the reason these vaulters were not jumping higher was simply because of the limitations their technique imposed!

His views were totally vindicated the following year when Giusseppe Gibilisco jumped a personal best of 5.90 metres (19'31/2") to win the 2003 World Championships. Two points should be made. First, to date, no one has suggested that Giusseppi achieved this result because of exceptional physical ability. Secondly, he has been coached for the previous seven years by Vitaly Petrov!

Here it might be worth adding that although Bubka's official World Record of 6.14 metres (20'1") has stood since 1994, it is clear that but

Figure 1.3

for two factors he could have achieved much better performances. The lure of US $50,000 for every world record which encouraged him to improve it by only one centimetre at a time, clearly slowed his progress towards his ultimate performance. Indeed he once famously rejected an offer of US$160,000 from a French meet promoter to break the record by two centimetres! Then at the point where financial independence

would have allowed him to find out what his potential really was, injury prevented him from taking the world record to a level where it might never have been approached.

This is not merely hypothetical. Many of his forty plus 6.00metre(19'7) jumps would probably have cleared much higher bars and as long ago as 1986, Petrov affirmed that Bubka was clearing 6.20 metres (20'3") regularly in training. Then in 1996 Alan was one of a number of onlookers to see him clear a soft bar set at 6.30 metres (20'7") on the warm up track in Atlanta. Figure 1.3. We also saw him walk over and immerse his foot in a bucket of ice water immediately after that jump in an attempt to control the pain of a damaged Achilles tendon, an injury which prevented him from competing in the Games.

However the final evidence is even more convincing and dramatic. The bar cam view of his winning clearance of 6.01 metres/19'7", at the 1997 Athens World Championships shows what may well be the highest jump in history. When the author raised the matter at the Jamaica clinic in 2002, Bubka, with a smile broadening his face, responded that Japanese sports scientists had calculated that on this particular jump he would have cleared 6.40 metres (20'10")! He also said that two other vaults in that series would have cleared 6.34 metres (20'8")and 6.32 metres (20'7½") respectively.

The thesis of this book therefore is that the Petrov/Bubka technical model should provide the basis for teaching and coaching the pole vault at every level of performance.

Readers should note that the quote at the beginning of this introduction was deliberately chosen to suggest that wisdom can come from anywhere, any time and in any language.

CHAPTER TWO
Track and field and the role of the coach

"A coach has a thousand careers, the athlete only has one".

Alan Launder 1990

The varied and challenging events of track and field make up one of the great sports of the world. Every year millions of people of all ages around the world take part in athletic competitions, which culminate every four years in the spectacle and drama of the Olympic Games.

One of the great advantages of this sport is that individuals of vastly different ages, physiques, physical capacities and psychological traits can participate enjoyably and successfully from beginner to elite level. The attraction of athletics, as with other great sports, lies paradoxically both in its simplicity and its complexity. At one level, track and field is merely a series of physical challenges based on the natural play activities of running, jumping and throwing. At this level it is the purest of sports in which participants try to find out how fast they can run, how far they can jump or throw and how high they can jump or vault, as they continually strive to improve their performance.

At another level these apparently simple tests become challenges which stretch competitors to the extremes of their ability. They can place enormous stresses on the physical and mental toughness of athletes as they strive not only to better their own previous best performance but to best their opponents in competition. At this level the disciplines of track and field examine the human being in extremis and in doing so remind us of the qualities which have been crucial to the survival of our species. Physical and moral courage, self reliance, skill, speed, power, endurance, dedication and striving for excellence are qualities valued in all cultures throughout history. All are necessary for success in track and field.

The role of the coach

The role of the coach is to help athletes meet the challenges of the sport and to fulfil their potential. Many coaches believe that their role goes far beyond mere performance and into the realms of personal growth and development. They believe that they are in the business of changing people's lives, not merely chasing medals.

The true complexity of the coaching task is still barely understood and has rarely been accurately articulated. It is not quite a science, although scientific principles underpin much of what a coach does, nor is it an art. It is therefore more productive to see coaching as a "Craft" in which science and art are seamlessly melded.

Many vocations and professions, including coaching, are essentially practical. They are about doing, about applying knowledge in real situations, not merely about 'knowing'. Practitioners in many fields are often faced with complex situations where they must respond instantaneously and effectively in both a professional and a personal way to help their client. They work in what Donald Schon called the ".. complex, unstable, uncertain, conflictual world of practice" where there is often little time for the reflection needed to make the perfect 'theoretical' response. Here mere knowledge is of little value because the situation usually calls for immediate action, often with little or no time for reflection.

Schon suggested that there are two alternatives. The first he calls "knowing in action". This describes what is essentially intuitive behaviour where an individual's 'knowing' is demonstrated by what they do, not by what they 'know'. In fact these individuals often cannot explain why they acted in a certain way, even when their response is perfect.

The second level of knowing is "Knowing in reflection". At this level the individual knows why they did what they did, and can objectively assess why they succeeded or failed. We have developed the notion of coaching as a "Craft", where science and art are melded so coaches become more 'reflective' of what they do.

With a "Craft" perspective, coaching can be viewed as a series of distinct but linked 'Processes' which can be clearly identified, analysed and understood. These processes can be presented to novice coaches in a manner which will help them better understand their role. It will also enable them to appreciate the relevance and possible application of essential theoretical principles. Experienced coaches on the other hand may find that their vision of the coaching task will be clarified and that they can now identify and improve those elements which may be preventing them from achieving their full potential.

Figure 2.1 Alan Launder coaching his first pole vaulter, Paul Dove, at Wymondham Secondary School, in Norfolk, England in the summer of 1958. Note the primitive conditions!

Coaching is a highly complex craft in which information, knowledge and wisdom are brought to bear on an unending array of problems which can encompass virtually all aspects of an athlete's personal, professional, academic and sporting life. Coaching is about believing and about doing, about action and interaction where decisions must be made and acted upon, often on the basis of less than complete information. Most importantly, the coach must be a master of "the instantaneous response", that moment when they fuse professional knowledge with interpersonal skills to deal with an issue or a problem. In coaching there are many stressful situations; how these are handled can be critical because it is at these instants of interaction that an individual's real values are exposed. It is when trust – a crucial factor in effective coaching – is built and even when lives are changed.

The coaching task is becoming increasingly complex so the ambitious coach has to be a "performance manager" who can draw on a wide ranging base of knowledge and skill. To be really successful the modern coach must have a working knowledge of human growth and development, biomechanics, exercise physiology, sports medicine, massage, nutrition, pharmacology, audio visual technology, training theory and sports psychology. They must be able to communicate with, and coordinate the efforts of, professionals in each of these fields.

Naturally the coach must also understand the demands of each event in terms of physical shape, skill, power speed, flexibility, energy systems and psychology. In addition, they must be able to carefully observe and analyse an athletes performance. Based on this analysis and a careful assessment of the problems the coach detects, they put together a program designed to eliminate weaknesses and maximise the strengths of the specific athlete. This training program may be geared to short term improvement as with school children readying themselves for a competition three or four weeks later or the long term preparation of an elite athlete planning to compete successfully at an Olympic games in four or even eight years time. It will have clear objectives and planned training tasks to ensure improvement in all elements of performance; it will also take into account the other important aspects of the athletes life and be geared to maximising training loads while minimising the risks of injury.

The coach and author, Tom McNab, believes that the ultimate aim of coaching is to help an athlete develop their own internal 'feeling' (Kinaesthetic) model of performance and understand why they are doing what they are doing. Sergey Bubka made the same point in Jamaica when he said "… the athlete must be knowledgeable of his event with a high level of motor awareness". Yet again we have an issue which has rarely been articulated despite its importance in the Feedback Process. In essence what both are saying is that coaching is only likely to be effective when athlete and coach are speaking the same 'language' and that a crucial aspect of that language relates to the athlete's 'body feel'. Sergey went on to say

"(In competition) What happens if the coach at a given moment, sends a message which has nothing to do with what the athlete felt? What does the athlete do? Follow their own kinaesthetic feelings? Or follow the message sent by the coach from the stands?"

He went on to say

"As coaches we must work beforehand and have less participation during competition."

While this observation may be true, the complexity of coaching is such that even the views of two experts such as these do not cover all of the situations or the different athletes, coaches must deal with. In the first place beginners have very little awareness of what they are doing or why they are doing it; they only gain this understanding over time so they are likely to need considerable input from coaches during competition, especially in the early stages of their career.

However our experience also suggests that not all athletes WANT to have any cognitive level of understanding. They simply want to just 'do it', with as little conscious effort as possible. This has major implications for the coach/athlete relationship. A coach who believes that it is important for an athlete to understand how the model works, how the elements fit together and how various drills are used to develop or improve aspects of technique will find it difficult to work with an athlete who does not want or even need to 'know'.

In the final analysis the good coach needs leadership skills of the highest order. They must be a skilled teacher, an avid student and be able to act as a confidante and counsellor in personal, academic, financial and career matters affecting their athletes. The great coach goes a little further.

An unknown sage once said, **"A Teacher gives knowledge, a Guru gives their life".** This statement captures the essence of great coaches, because there is little doubt that many coaches do indeed give their lives to helping others achieve their potential. The great coaches are philosophers who understand what is really important in sport as well as in life! They bring a sense of balance and perspective to what is an essentially pointless activity, for what intelligent person can really believe that jumping over a bar using a pole is important in the overall scheme of things? For these coaches the attraction of the pole vault is that it tests the whole person, not merely their physical ability.

Clearly the role of a Track and Field coach is immensely complex. That of the pole vault coach arguably the most difficult of all. However that role can bring immense rewards, if only through the friendships one makes. Figure 2.2 shows Steve Chappell vaulting at Dr. Challoner's Grammar School in England, where he was introduced to the pole vault, along with the one hundred other 11 year old boys in his year group by Alan Launder in 1963. Not only did this create a lasting friendship but it may also have had a major influence on Steve's subsequent career path.

Figure 2.2

CHAPTER THREE

The Processes of coaching

"In Australia, Track and Field is almost entirely 'Coach driven'."

Alan Launder

One way to make the complex craft of coaching more understandable and approachable is to identify the key processes which underpin success. We believe that the key "Processes" of coaching track and field are -
* Talent Identification
* Recruiting
* The integration of new athletes into squad
* Athlete assessment
* Instruction
* Technical coaching
* Conditioning
* Psychological Management
* Preparing for competition
* Coaching during competition
* Performance analysis
* Planning
* Organization
* Administration

Each of these processes may involve a range of competencies, knowledge and skills. This confirms the complexity of the overall task of coaching track and field – a complexity which has rarely been recognised. This clearly indicates that coaches must become permanent students of their event, for there is always something new to learn.

The "Context" of coaching

The relative importance of each process will vary for every coach and will depend on the "Context" in which they are working. The "Context of coaching" is another concept which has not been previously articulated, even though it is the key to understanding coaching effectiveness.

The "Context" in which a coach operates is influenced by many factors. Sometimes socio-economic and socio-cultural factors coalesce to produce an environment which is favourable to sport in general and certain sports in particular. So we find rugby critical to the national psyche of New Zealand, soccer in Brazil, cricket in India, javelin throwing in Finland, ice hockey in Canada, distance running in Kenya, skiing in Austria, baseball in Cuba and swimming in Australia – perhaps the most sport crazy country of all! At a local level we find basketball impor-

tant in Kentucky and Indiana, gridiron in Pennsylvania, wrestling in Iowa and pole vaulting in Donetsk!

The notion of the "Coaching context" can be best illustrated by considering a few examples. Compare
* The task of a middle distance coach working in Kenya with one working in a high school in inner city Chicago.
* The role of a sprints coach at a University in Texas with one in New Zealand.
* A coach working with female javelin throwers in Finland with one trying to coach women in Iran.
* A pole vault coach in Donetsk during the 1970s with one working in a remote Wyoming high school in that same era!

It is important to remember that the demands on a coach working primarily with young athletes will differ markedly from coaches working with athletes of Olympic calibre.

The 'Perfect' environment

The critical elements of a **perfect** coaching environment for track and field are -
* Athletes with great physical talent, mental toughness and a determination to succeed which borders on obsession.
* An appropriate training environment.
* Time to train.
* Financial support to enable athletes to make the necessary commitment.
* Medical support – this includes doctors, physiotherapists, masseurs, as well as access to saunas and spas.
* Sports Science support – this can vary from simple video analysis to a completely computerised training facility. It may also include blood testing.
* Sports psychology support.
* A varied and challenging competition program.
* The chance to begin a career path outside sport.
* A great coach.
* A supportive community.

In recent history, political imperatives ensured that coaches and athletes in the German Democratic Republic enjoyed every advantage, as that country pursued sporting success at International level. Proceeding on the basis that while there was only one gold medal for each team game but many in individual sports such as track and field and swimming, this nation invested heavily in those sports. As a result track and field in East Germany had access to many of the most physically talented youngsters in the country; this undoubtedly is one reason for their great success. Unfortunately the other reason was that the desire to succeed encouraged, or perhaps forced, East German coaches to resort to the systematic use of illicit ergogenic aids.

While politics 'drove' track and field in the former East Germany, other factors operate in different countries. In Great Britain the sport has been driven by a good all round competition structure, good levels of financial support from Government and excellent media coverage, particularly television. In Australia the sport is almost entirely 'coach driven' while in the U.S.A. an excellent High school and College competition structure linked to a scholarship system are the major factors in the great success this nation has enjoyed. In Finland so many positive factors have come together so that it could be said that the sport there is 'culturally driven', as a result they have enjoyed success at international level out of all proportion to the size of their population, especially given their less than perfect climate. However in almost all Western Nations the lure of the fully professional sports drains away thousands of talented athletes, even when conditions are apparently favourable.

It may come as a surprise to many coaches that great coaching environments for the pole vault do indeed exist, although without the same access to talented individuals who, as in many countries, are drained off to team soccer. The Italian Olympic training camp in Formia is an excellent example and well worth visiting. It should also be no surprise that the 2003 World Champion in the pole vault, Giuseppe Gibilisco, trains there under the supervision of Vitaly. However it is ironic that the funding for this centre comes from a tiny percentage of the profits of the Italian Soccer Lottery, which is of course well supported by fanatical supporters of that game. However it now appears that even this ideal situation is under threat.

Donetsk!

Readers may also be interested in the "coaching context" from which Bubka emerged. The city of Donetsk in the Ukraine has three indoor track and field halls; each has two run ways for the pole vault as well as a weight room, horizontal bars, rings and ropes. The outdoor stadia in the city all have basic gymnastic equipment.

At the centre where Bubka trained there was a team of eight coaches lead by Vitaly Petrov. Two of those coaches had worked with athletes of international junior standard and one had considerable experience in gymnastics. They worked as a team so that all aspects of training for the pole vault, including the biomechanics of the event, were discussed. Inevitably this lead to improved methods and a deeper understanding of the fundamental principles of pole vaulting. It is also interesting to note that this group of coaches was only a tiny element of the estimated 11,000 professional track and field coaches working in the former Soviet Union at that time.

There was a well developed talent identification system in Donetsk which involved all of the primary school physical education teachers in the city. Gifted children identified at that point, went to sports schools which specialised in soccer, boxing and pole vaulting; the screening process continued for the next two years and lead as many as 200 children a year to try the pole vault. Eventually the most talented of these finished up in the Donetsk centre. Here approximately 300 young athletes trained in ability and age groups as indicated below

Ten training groups of 15 –20 students aged 10 and 11

Six training groups with 10 – 15 students aged 12 and 13 (2.40m – 3.80m)

Four training groups with 10 athletes aged 14 and 15 (3.40m – 4.60m)

Two training groups with eight athletes aged 16 and 17 (4.40m – 5.10m)

One group of 8 athletes aged 18 and 19 (5.00m plus)

It is also important to understand the cultural context at that time in the USSR. First of all great importance was attached to sports performance and there were many ways in which success was recognised. For example an Olympic level sports star was financially better off than a doctor in that system because they could go to the West, under control naturally, and earn American dollars. Of course even at a lower level, good athletes could gain access to a scarce items such as an apartment or a car; equally important they were given special privileges during their mandatory military service.

Secondly there was an emphasis on the Olympic sports. Young people did not have the great range of activities to choose from that Australian youngsters, for example, had during that period. A final critical component of this 'context' was the exceptionally high quality of the coaches. While it was advantageous for anyone to join the Communist Party if they wanted to advance their career, it was possible to avoid this commitment if one was a good enough sports coach. Many individuals who might have chosen other career paths became track and field coaches; Vitaly Petrov was one such person.

Clearly there was a high drop out rate from the Donetsk program, despite the great incentives to becoming even a mid level performer. While this could be attributed to many causes, it is likely that the ever increasing intensity of training required to stay in the program was a factor.

The reality is that the vast majority of pole vault coaches around the world operate in less than perfect contexts. Indeed some face opposition as they try to create a good environment in an area where there is no tradition of pole vaulting. This is the reason why the vault is usually driven by hyper enthusiasts who are prepared to do everything possible to develop the event.

The implication of all of this is that coaches must do everything possible to improve the context in which they work. While this is not always easy, many simple things can help.Make sure that the poles are well marked and easy to access, make sure that training aids such as an outdoor gym are positioned close to the track, as in Adelaide and at Fresno State. Have a box with medicine balls, shot, tape measures and a small selection of weight discs and bars. Most importantly ensure that you have a large sand pit close by the training area

The pole vault coach and the processes of coaching

While all of the "Processes" of coaching are important, some are critical to success in coaching the pole vault. Three of them

- **The Instructional process**
- **The process of Technical coaching**
- **The psychological process**

will be dealt with in later Chapters but other processes which are especially important to the vault coach include -

Talent Identification

We believe that the ideal candidate is a tall long jumper who has had some gymnastic experience and who understands that the pole vault offers them the opportunity to achieve their dreams. One of the critical factors here is the "athletic age" of an athlete because this provides a clue to their long term potential. An athlete who has been competing for several years under the guidance of a good coach in an established program is 'athletically older' than a self taught athlete in their first year of competition. Clearly the former has used up more of their potential than the novice.

Coaches can use field tests to confirm their original eye ball assessment. However the ability to see the diamond in the rough stone is a critical aspect of coaching. Here coaches would do well to remember the story of the "Three spoons diamond" held in the Topkapi Palace in Istanbul, Turkey. This huge diamond got its name because its original owner traded it to a more perceptive individual for three wooden spoons!

The process of talent identification is complicated by the fact that many children between the ages of twelve and fifteen are going through rapid physical changes so their real potential is often hidden. Coaches need a sound background in 'growth and development' if they are to find this hidden talent.

Recruiting

Note that we are not concerned here with the process by which American Universities induce young athletes to attend their institution but with the much earlier process of bringing youngsters into the world of pole vaulting. While talent identification is not easy, recruiting talented athletes can be even more difficult in some environments.

In Australia it is complicated by the fact that in this sports mad country almost every talented youngster has already been recruited by other sports long before we begin to look at them between the ages of twelve and fifteen. In addition, neither track and field nor pole vaulting have a high profile. They are certainly not seen as sports with professional career prospects. As a result vault coaches must work hard to sell the event, not to the children who only have to try it once to be sold, but to parents who have never seen the pole vault but who have a feeling that it must be dangerous!

This issue is dealt with in greater detail in Chapter Twenty which deals with Field testing.

Integration of new athletes into a squad

Every squad has a pecking order based on performance and time in the squad. New recruits have to fit into this situation – it can be done easily or with great difficulty. There is little doubt that a new potential superstar can cause immense problems, without even trying!

CHAPTER FOUR

Risk management in the pole vault

"The most important thing coaches can do to help their athletes jump safely is to teach them how to jump properly"

Alan Launder

The focus of this book is on how to teach young athletes to jump properly. However as we suggest in Chapter Ten, it will take a novice coach some time to build the experience necessary to become a truly effective instructor. On the other hand, anyone with common sense who is prepared to follow some simple principles can make a valuable contribution to ensuring a safe environment for pole vaulting.

Safety is important because a major problem for the pole vault is the perception that it is a dangerous activity. While even a cursory glance at accident statistics will confirm that skiing, skateboarding and even driving a motor vehicle are far more dangerous than pole vaulting, the perception is what matters. However accidents do occur in the vault and it is clearly important to understand why they can happen and to do everything possible to prevent them. A serious accident has the potential to destroy a young life, traumatise a family forever and cause the elimination of the pole vault from a school program.

Even a minor accident can have a major impact. It may delay an athlete's development, cause them to miss a meet they have trained for for months, and even induce psychological problems which will impact on their performance for a long time. Equally significant, because of the general perception that the pole vault is "dangerous", any rumour of injuries associated with the event may negatively impact on recruiting. Parents prefer their children to remain unhurt!

Risk management therefore becomes a critical aspect of a pole vault coach's role. Much of this is common sense, but to help novice coaches speed up their understanding of this important area we have provided a detailed outline of the key issues below. This begins by ensuring that the facilities, and especially the landing pad, meet or even exceed the designated specifications. This is an ongoing process because of the inevitable wear and tear from hard use. Old pads are particularly risky simply because the foam in them will gradually deteriorate over time, especially if they are not looked after.

Simple routine procedures will help maintain the quality of the foam. Make sure the pad does not touch the ground. Although it is possible to buy custom made bases, we have found that good quality wooden pallets are ideal for this task. If a pad does get soaked because the weather cover has blown off or the ground sprinkler system has been left on too long, it is important to turn the pad units upside down to get the water out otherwise the foam will deteriorate much more quickly.

Simple things like checking that the straps which tie the individual units of the pad together are in good condition and buckled properly, are important, especially after a pad has been moved from one position to another. The wear pad should be inspected regularly because it is critical to safety as it ties the whole pad together and ensures that vaulters cannot drop through a gap between individual units to hit the ground.

It is important to check that the front of the pad is the correct distance from the back of the box, especially after a pad has been moved OR when athletes are competing at an unfamiliar venue. This is important because if a flexing pole hits the pad it is forced to recoil prematurely and this may prevent the vaulter from penetrating onto the pad.

The pole vault standards must be securely fixed to prevent them falling onto the pad especially if a bungy cord is being used. Even a strong wind has been known to blow standards over. A sand bag or even the rubber box plug can be used to keep them stable.

The base protectors which are usually supplied with the pole vault standards are an out and out nuisance! Despite this they must be kept in place because they have been constructed to protect the ankles of the unwary or unlucky from the potential danger of the base runners for the standards. It may also be worthwhile wrapping the standards with protective foam up to a height of six feet, if only to protect poles from damage.

After a pad has been moved or when athletes are competing at a different venue it is worthwhile checking that the standards are correctly positioned and calibrated. Occasionally they are misaligned. The problem is that if an athlete jumps with the bar not positioned where they think it is, it is possible that they may become disoriented during the jump and land off balance or in the wrong spot.

The pole vault box should be checked even though it causes few problems. Care must be taken when competing at a facility which has been neglected. Occasionally the front lip of the box may not be absolutely flush with the ground and it is possible for a jumper who lowers the pole too soon to catch the lip standing proud. The result can be quite horrific.

To reduce distractions in the pole vault area it is worthwhile setting up an exclusion zone around the pad AND the run up. It may even be worthwhile roping the area off, especially during a major competition such as a relay meet where youngsters are likely to be running around everywhere and may cross the vault runway without thinking. It is also important to ban play with balls of any kind near the vault area. Finally, no one should be allowed to sit on the sides or end of a pad, both popular spectator positions, when anyone is jumping in competition or training.

Routines

The practice of establishing set procedures or "routines" to minimise danger is accepted practice in many activities where accidents are possible. The pilots of aircraft from the smallest glider to the largest jet, meticulously follow specific routines to ensure safety, as do stunt men and trapeze artists in the circus. While young people never really appreciate the fact, they are not immortal!

They must first learn to respect their poles.
- Keep them in their tubes whenever they are not being used.
- Never allow them to lie around on the ground unprotected.
- Check them for scratches before they use them.
- Check pole tips regularly and replace when necessary
- Make sure the cap is in place. This may seem unimportant but without it the unprotected fibreglass at the end of the pole could cause serious injuries – we recommend that you use a pole tip to replace the cap.
- In training and wherever possible in competition, make sure someone is in position to stop poles falling to the ground or hitting the stands. In our squad this was mandatory; if

either incident occurs vaulter and/or the catcher are 'punished' by being timed out from training for fifteen minutes or more.

Gradually the vaulter must be taught to
- Select the correct pole for the conditions
- Select the correct grip height for that pole
- Ensure that their run up is correctly measured
- Prepare mentally for each jump
- Avoid all distractions when preparing to jump – especially from well meaning friends!

Attitude - the key to safety

There is little doubt that a macho attitude is one of the major causes of accidents in pole vaulting. So while everything possible must be done to create a safe environment, safety really begins with the right attitude. Athletes must understand that the pole vault is one of the DISCIPLINES of track and field, it is not an 'extreme' sport. Vaulters must learn to respect the challenge of this event and then follow specific routines which will enable them to jump high with safety.

One of the first things a coach must do is to build a culture of safety and to back it up with rules and routines which are rigorously enforced. This is no easy task when dealing with adolescent youths, but it is critical to both safety AND improved performance. Occasionally it may be necessary to remove an athlete from the group, at least until they have developed the necessary self discipline.

Good technique – the foundation of safety

The most important thing coaches can do to help their athletes jump safely, is to teach them how to jump properly. There is little doubt that bad technique is a major cause of injury and even death in this event. It is therefore vital to ensure that, from the very beginning, youngsters develop those elements of technique which will lead to safe pole vaulting.

Coaches should remember that performance and safety in the pole vault both stem from a technical model -
- Which is completely integrated.
- Which has a sound basis in biomechanics.
- Which is comprehensible by novice coaches and athletes.
- Which can be used by any athlete.
- Which evolves from the 'Working model' used by beginners.

CHAPTER FIVE

'Style', 'Technical Models' and Biomechanics

An athlete's style – overlays their 'Technical model' – which should be based on the Principles of biomechanics!

In 1983, as an unknown young athlete from the Ukraine, Sergey Bubka won the men's pole vault at the first ever World Championships in Track and Field, held in Helsinki, Finland. He went on to win five more World Titles, gain an Olympic Gold medal and to set 27 World records. His best performance of 6.14 metres (20'1") has remained the World Record for men since 1994.

> Figure 5.1 shows Bubka over the bar in his winning jump of 6.01 metres (19'7") at the Athens World Championships in 1997. Japanese sports scientists have since calculated that on this jump he would have cleared 6.40m or 20' 10". This would make it arguably the highest jump in the history of pole vaulting.

We believe that Bubka introduced a completely new "Technical model' to the pole vault.

A 'Technical model' in track and field is simply a specific method of solving the biomechanical problems posed by the event. The most obvious example of the introduction of a new 'technical model' in track and field is the 'Flop technique' of high jumping, which was developed by American Dick Fosbury in the late 1960s and which he employed to win the Olympic Title in 1972. While it is now used by every high jumper in the world, the 'Flop' was completely revolutionary when it was first introduced. However it quickly became clear that it was biomechanically superior to the 'straddle technique' used by every high jumper before Fosbury developed his new model. Figures 5.2 and 5.3 illustrate the great differences between these two 'Technical models' of high jumping.

Figure 5.1

Figure 5.2

Figure 5.3

However while the Flop has now superseded the straddle in the high jump, we have an interesting situation in the Shot Put where two completely different technical models are presently being used successfully by world class athletes. Athletes using the older technique, 'The Shift' – originally developed by Parry O'Brien in the 1950's – are holding their own against throwers using the more modern 'Spin' technique.

While the differences between these 'Technical models' for high jumping and shot putting are blindingly obvious, the differences between the Petrov/Bubka 'Technical model' and that used by many other pole vaulters are much more subtle. As a result, although the innovations they introduced to the pole vault were as significant and revolutionary as the flop technique of high jumping, his Technical model is still not completely understood nor accepted by many athletes and coaches.

This is unfortunate because any objective analysis of Bubka's technique will confirm what he himself believed – that his superior technique gave him a definite advantage over his rivals. Ambitious athletes must work to master this model and any ambitious coach of the pole vault should try to understand it.

'Style' in the pole vault

While a 'Technical model' is based on the principles of biomechanics and the constraints imposed by the rules of the event, each athlete's 'Style' is based on their unique personal characteristics.

In fact some coaches still believe that the technique of each athlete should be determined by their unique physical qualities. This particular misunderstanding is dangerous for two reasons – first it contains a grain of truth and secondly it is sometimes promoted by experienced coaches.

The fact is that vaulters must possess certain physical qualities just to participate in this event. To succeed at international level, vaulters must be superb all round athletes who can run fast, jump and throw well and execute complex gymnastic movements as they interact with a flexing and recoiling pole. The key relationship is captured by the phrase we have coined

"What is technically desirable must be physically possible".

However we believe that the athlete's individual characteristics determine their 'Style', **not their 'Technical model'.** This may seem like splitting hairs but it is necessary to make this distinction if coaches are to fully understand modern technique.

An athlete's 'Style' OVERLAYS their 'Technical model'. This is well illustrated by considering two athletes employing the same technical model, Dimitri Markov and Giusseppi Gibilisco, both World Champions. Illustrations in Chapter Seven will clearly show that while there are great similarities between them throughout the jump, there are also differences which can be readily identified. **The critical point here is that while the SIMILARITIES are determined by biomechanical imperatives, the DIFFERENCES are determined by their unique characteristics.** So an athlete's 'Style' overlays their 'Technical model'; a tall rangy athlete may look completely different from a shorter stocky athlete even when both are using the same technical model. So

- An athlete's **Style**
- overlays their **Technical model**
- which should be based on the **Principles of biomechanics!**

The problem here is that sports scientists have yet to provide a coherent and rational bio mechanical analysis of vaulting with a flexible pole. They have provided a great deal of information, some knowledge, but very little wisdom in the form of a clear statement of the fundamental principles which should be used to develop the most practical and efficient technique of pole vaulting. In effect they have simply observed the performance of many successful vaulters and presented this as evidence to support their opinions about modern technique. To our knowledge no sports scientist has, so far, gone back to the first principles of the physics of human motion and used these principles to develop an ideal model of pole vaulting – or even to explain the amazing success of Bubka. While it may be useful to know what many athletes do, it would be far more valuable to know what they should be trying to do to optimise their performance!

Here it must be said that this is not an unusual state of affairs in track and field. If we consider the two events previously mentioned, the high jump and the shot put, we find that the evolution of technique in those events has been driven by individual athletes, not sports scientists, even though both depend almost entirely on the ability of the athlete to develop and apply forces efficiently. In the high jump the most effective technical model, the 'Flop', was developed by Dick Fosbury through the almost classic mode of playing at jumping high and seeing what worked! In the same way the 'Shift' technique of shot putting was developed by Parry O'Brien through his own analysis of the event, while the 'Spin' seems to have evolved through experimentation by many athletes.

However in the pole vault we have the strange situation where sports scientists appear to be unwilling or unable to accept the rational basis for the Petrov/Bubka technical model. This despite the fact that both coach and athlete have detailed the bases for their methods. Not only that, but the biomechanists appear to have joined many coaches in ascribing Bubka's amazing performances to his unique physical and mental qualities and not his technique.

While this was understandable when he first appeared, it is inexcusable now. A few weeks after Bubka became the first athlete to clear 6.00 metres (19'7") in Paris in July 1985 his coach, Vitaly Petrov, presented the technical model Bubka had employed, at the European Coaches Congress in Birmingham, England.

There it became clear that, for the first time, a critical analytical methodology had been employed to develop a technical model for the pole vault. Prior to Petrov, technical development in the pole vault was largely intuitive, as individual athletes attempted to solve the problems posed by the event in the same way that Fosbury developed his famous 'Flop'. At the same time the methods of world record holders or Olympic Champions in the vault were often subjected to little rigorous analysis and blindly copied. As a result there were many individual 'Styles' but no clearly defined and accepted 'Technical model'.

'Our' take on the biomechanics of the Petrov/Bubka model

As we studied the Petrov/Bubka model of vaulting it became clear to us that it had a rational basis and that it matched the theoretical principles of the event. These are
- From start to finish the pole vault is a continuous movement where every element interrelates with every other to produce the end result.
- The vaulter should arrive at the take off point at optimum (greatest controlled) speed.

- The initial pole bend should be the result of a take off which maximises both the vaulter's impulse and the pole/ground angle.
- The vaulter should attempt to put energy into the pole continuously throughout the vault but especially while moving into a position to best exploit that energy as the pole recoils.
- With these points in mind the vaulter will try to
  - Grip as high as possible, bearing in mind the need for safety
  - Use the stiffest possible pole so as to maximise the vertical speed of the recoil and thus the vertical distance they are projected.

Clearly this is only an outline but it at least provides a template against which any technical model, or even an individual athlete's style can be compared.

'Stiff pole' vaulters

Early on in our study it became clear that many of Petrov's ideas were based, in part, on an analysis of the vaulters of the stiff pole era, in particular the techniques of the great Cornelius 'Dutch' Warmerdam of Fresno State and dual Olympic Champion, Bob Richards. As a result we reviewed some of the literature on the pole vault during that period. The summary of our findings is presented in Chapter Twenty One in Part Two of this book.

A study of the stiff pole technique of 'Dutch' Warmerdam is very revealing.

Figure 5.4 shows Warmerdam solving the problem as he vaults to yet another world record in the 1940s. He –

- Accelerated in,
- Planted the pole,
- Jumped up in a dynamic toe tip take off to drive the pole forward,
- Executed a long pendulum swing of the whole body around his hands
- Before tucking his legs as they passed the pole
- Then rolling back to get the hips above the shoulders,
- Before flying away over the bar.

The biomechanics of Warmerdam's technique were relatively straightforward as he fully exploited what the coaches at the time called 'the double pendulum'. As the pole – the first pendulum - rotates towards the vertical, the vaulter – the second pendulum - swings their body on

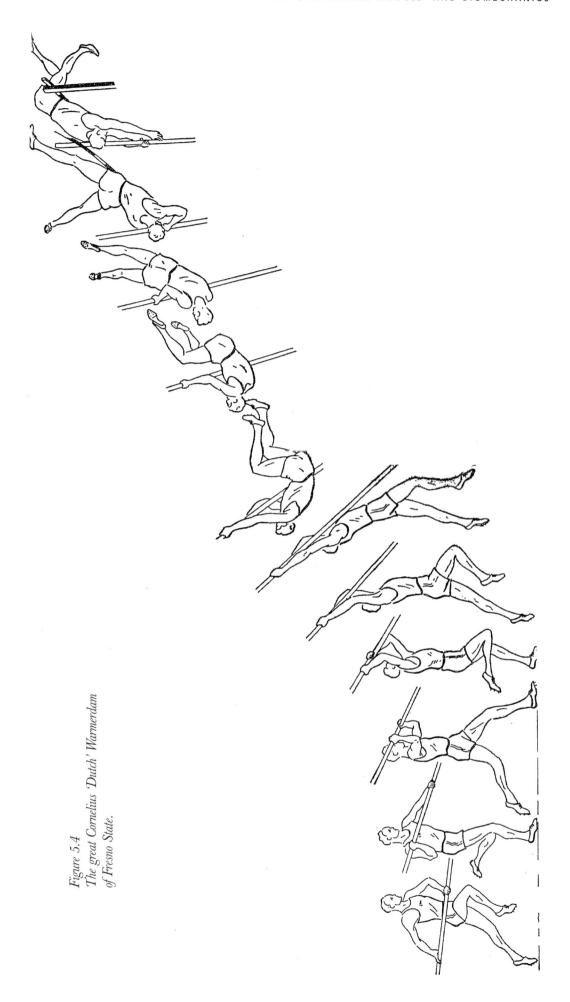

Figure 5.4
The great Cornelius 'Dutch' Warmerdam
of Fresno State.

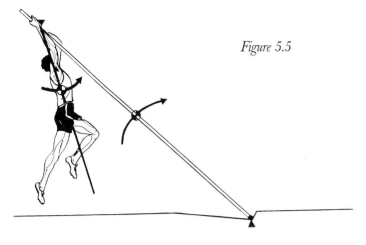

Figure 5.5

the pole. Figure 5.5. The run up and take off drove the pole forward after take off. Then, the long pendular swing of the whole body around the hands put energy into the system in the same way that children can drive a swing to the horizontal and beyond.

This long extended swing also served to keep the centre of mass of the system low – so that it would continue to move forward quickly. This whole process was relatively straightforward because no energy could be stored in the pole and the keys to success were a strong take off and the long swing into inversion.

Warmerdam's technique met the biomechanical requirements of vaulting on a stiff pole at least as well as that of any other athlete of the period and, as with Bubka, this may have been the reason for his great success.

The flexible pole

The advent of the flexible pole seemed to change everything. Coaches and athletes alike appeared to become obsessed with the magic of the flexible pole – they wanted to see it bend a long way and then to 'catapult' the athlete above the bar! So the emphasis switched almost immediately from driving the pole up and forwards at take off, to bending the pole. One result of this switch in emphasis was that the basic principles of efficient pole vaulting were forgotten.

It is interesting that Bubka himself made this point very strongly at the UCS Spirit clinic, held in conjunction with the 2003 World Junior Championships in Jamaica. There he said

> *"Before the fibre glass pole, pole vaulters put their focus on moving the pole, then, when the flexible pole appeared many people put their focus on bending the pole. The pole (should) bend as a result of the speed and mass of the jumper, therefore, it is more important to concentrate more on moving the pole towards the plane of the bar, rather than being aware of bending it."*

However the problem did not stop there. The mistaken emphasis on trying to bend the pole at take off, blinded coaches and athletes alike to the other important innovations in the Petrov/Bubka technical model.

The Biomechanics of pole vaulting

Obviously one of the major advantages of the flexible pole is that it can store much of the energy which has caused it to bend, as 'strain energy' and it can then return some of this energy to the vaulter as it recoils. Clearly the more energy the vaulter can put into the pole in the first place, the more effective energy there is to recover and the faster the pole will straighten as it recoils.

However what is usually neglected is that as the real pole bends, the biomechanical pole shortens! As Bubka left the ground the real pole was straight and 5.20 metres long. When he released it to fly over the bar, it is again straight and 5.20 metres long. Between these two points, the length of the real pole was virtually irrelevant! From a biomechanical perspective what really mattered was the distance between the vaulter's top hand and the tip of the pole in the box. This distance, which is shown in Figure 5.6 is called the CHORD of the pole. **From a biomechanical perspective the CHORD of the flexing pole IS THE REAL POLE!**

This has two important but rarely understood advantages.

First the shortening pole – the chord of the real pole - rotates faster towards the vertical. This is the metronome effect. This is one of the reasons why athletes using flexible poles can grip so much higher than those who used stiff poles.

Understanding the notion of a series of straight poles can help to clarify the advantages of the Petrov/Bubka technical model and also provide a clear rationale for our approach to teaching the pole vault.

First think of a pole vault pole as a lever which has to be driven to the vertical to take the athlete up and over the bar. In the era of stiff pole vaulting this was basically all the pole vaulter had to do. The major limitation was how high an athlete could grip on this lever and still be able to drive it to the vertical. If they gripped too low they reduced the potential height they could jump, too high and they would land back on the runway.

This idea is best illustrated by considering the Metronome, a device used in music to establish a set rhythm in music. When the weight is set low the metronome ticks quickly but as it is raised it moves slower and slower. The lesson for the vaulter is obvious, keep the weight down in the early phases of the movement and swing up late and fast.

So the key is to stop thinking of a single - flexible - pole!

Instead, think of it as an infinite series of straight poles of varying lengths!

Again Figure 5.6 should help to explain what at first sight, may seem to be an extraordinary idea!

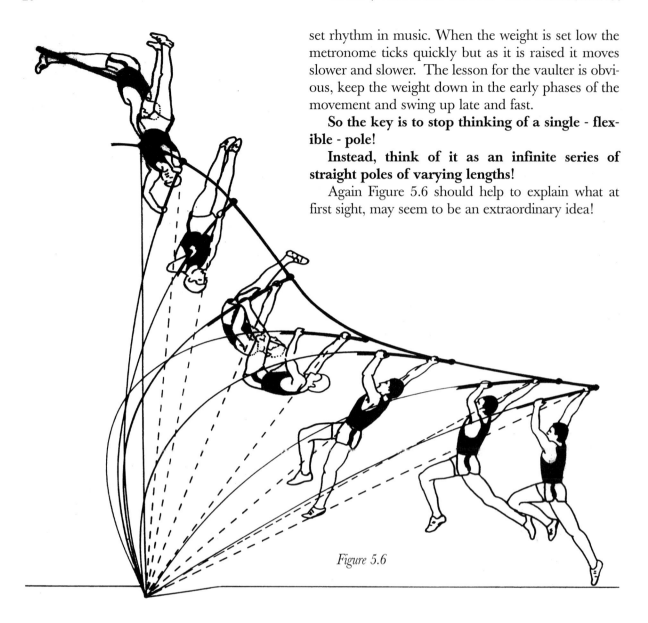

Figure 5.6

In other words, in biomechanical terms the athlete is vaulting on a series of straight poles, each infinitely shorter than the last until the pole reaches maximum bend and then, as the real pole recoils, they become an infinite series of lengthening straight poles.

The second advantage of the shortening pole is more subtle. Because the shortening pole is moving forward rapidly it allowed Bubka to increase the amplitude (Distance and Time) of the pendular swing of his take off leg from the instant of take off until he began his inversion, or rock back. Not only did this put more energy into the pole but it further shortened the chord and allowed it to roll forwards even more rapidly. Not all coaches understand the importance of optimising this phase of the vault although it is readily apparent in the techniques of the athletes shown in Chapter Seven, who have also used this advanced model of vaulting.

Bubka's biomechanics

We believe that Bubka exploited the advantages of the flexible pole more effectively than any other athlete. His secret was simple. He maximised the energy he put into the pole and then ensured that he was in the best possible position to exploit that energy when the pole returned it to him. He did this by introducing two revolutionary principles and fully exploiting three others, which although employed previously by other athletes had never been fully understood. This ensured that he maximised the energy he put into the pole but also enabled him to move into good positions to exploit the recoil energy of the pole.

The Petrov/Bubka technical model -

1. **Exploited the potential of an active pole drop to increase both his speed and his cadence over the final six steps of the runway.** In this way he turned the potential negative of the high

angle pole carry, which was essential if he was to control a long pole with a relatively narrow grip, into a positive aspect of technique.

2. **Attempted to put all of the kinetic energy of his take off into the pole AFTER he left the ground!** This was a revolutionary idea which meant that there were no speed losses before take off. **Figure 5.7, possibly the most significant photograph ever taken of a vaulter, clearly shows his revolutionary approach to the take off in the pole vault.**

3. **Used the long swing of his body to drive the pole forwards.** While other athletes, especially stiff pole vaulters like Warmerdam had done this, Bubka exploited the shortening of the pole to increase the amplitude, that is the length of the swing, better than any other athlete.

4. **Redirected some of the energy of the whip of the take off leg to initiate the 'inversion' or 'rock back'.** This enabled him to position his centre of mass closer to or even above the pole before it reached maximum bend and to thus exploit the recoil more effectively than other vaulters.

5. **Uniquely, Bubka put energy into the pole even as he swung into inversion.** Just before the pole began to recoil he executed a shoulder drop/hip drive movement in which he drove his shoulders down towards the pad while simultaneously punching his hips up. This shoulder - hip drive kept the pole flexed for a fraction longer as it rolled forward and enabled him to stay tight alongside the pole as it straightened.

Figure 5.7

Why is this Chapter included in a book written primarily for the benefit of novice coaches?

The first and most important reason is that our whole approach to coaching the pole vault is based on using the Petrov/Bubka model as our target technique. Coaches who wish to follow our methods need to study his technique as carefully as possible.

The second is that all coaches begin their careers as novices, but many of them want to increase their understanding of this great athletic challenge as quickly as possible, because they know that they will then be better able to help the young athletes they work with.

However we believe that readers may also discover that -

• Much of the misunderstanding which surrounds the pole vault will be eliminated.

• The relationship between stiff pole and flexible pole vaulting is obvious.

• The rationale for our approach to developing the vault becomes clear.

• The specific advantages of the Bubka technical model become apparent.

Chapter Six will illustrate and describe Bubka's technical model.

CHAPTER SIX

The Petrov/Bubka 'technical model'

As we suggested in the preface, the advantage of a book is that it gives the reader the opportunity to interact with the information, knowledge and wisdom it contains. There is time for reflection and serious study of both the text and the accompanying illustrations. However although we have carefully chosen the illustrations, it is impossible to capture the effort, timing and rhythmic qualities of a movement, especially one as dynamic as the pole vault. Readers should be aware that from take off to bar clearance takes approximately 1.24 seconds! They should also remember that the pole vault is about creating, controlling and exploiting the **energy of movement**.

It is also important to note that although we have broken Bubka's technique down into its' component parts, his model of pole vaulting must always be seen as sequential and interactive, with every phase depending on and melding with the previous phase. This is well illustrated by Figures 6.1.et al which show Bubka's first ever 6.00 vault. More than any other model of pole vaulting the Petrov/Bubka model must be viewed as a WHOLE, from the moment the athlete steps onto the runway until they shoot almost vertically from the top of the pole, over the bar and onto the pad.

For example, Bubka used a relatively narrow spacing between his hands as he gripped the pole at the start of the run up. He did this because the narrow grip enabled him to drive both hands very high at take off and then allowed him to swing more easily on the pole, into what is traditionally called the 'rock back'. However to control a long pole using a narrow grip, he had to use a high angle pole carry at the start of his run and then to employ a carefully structured pole drop in order to control the falling lever. This confirms the tight link between major elements of his technique.

The Petrov/Bubka Technical model

We use the term 'Technical model' because the movement patterns involved can be replicated from one vault to the next and more importantly from one athlete to the next. However even with Bubka, every attempt was unique, a one off, as

all the varied elements came together at that instant in time. Inevitably there were small variations from one jump to the next which are clear to anyone who watches much of Bubka's vaulting. Two jumps in particular stand out.

The first is a jump he took at the 1988 Olympic Games in Seoul. As he waited to be called for his third attempt at 5.90 metres, a clearance would give him the Gold, a failure would leave him in fourth place. For the first time that day there was a slight tail wind so when he was called, he immediately stepped on the runway and began his approach run to try to take advantage of it.

With a small tail wind blowing and the adrenaline pumping, he was faster down the runway on this jump and so took off 'under', not in his preferred spot beneath the top hand. From then on he was responding intuitively to save the jump; film shows him desperately attempting to keep his body away from the bar as he begins to drop towards the pad. The rest is history as they say!

The second example has already been presented in Chapter Five. Bubka's 6.01 metre clearance to win his final World Championship in 1997 was probably the highest jump in history. What is interesting about this jump is that despite its obvious success Bubka was clearly out of control as he came off the pole and this shows in his off balance position over the bar.

So while Bubka had a clear idea of what he was attempting to do on every jump – his technical model – he could not always achieve his goal! In fact it is clear that in some of the later phases of a jump the intuitive – feeling - reaction of the athlete becomes vitally important. We believe that this is especially the case with the movement into inversion which is so dependent on every element which precedes it.

Remember that what we are presenting here is the Petrov technical model as performed by Sergey Bubka. This means that the images shown represent the Petrov model overlaid by Sergey's 'style', for like every athlete, he brought his unique personal characteristics to the challenge of pole vaulting.

Figure 6.1

Bubka's Technical model was characterised by

- **A relatively narrow grip.**
This was important for driving his hands high and so maximising the angle of the pole to the ground at take off.
Many vaulters use a wide grip in order to better control the pole during the run. However this creates problems for them at take off. It means a lower pole ground angle at the plant and often encourages them to run 'under'.

Figure 6.2

- **The pole carried at a high angle at the beginning of his run up.**
This allowed him to minimise the problems of accelerating to sprint speed while carrying a long pole with a relatively narrow grip. Figure 6.2. The key is that the pole must be supported by the skeletal structure of the body and not kept in place with muscle power. This is achiev-ed by letting the pole rest in the V of the left hand which is positioned level with the centre of the chest, with the elbow of the left hand tucked close to the left side.
A horizontal pole carry will create enormous torque forces which would destroy the vaulters running posture. However any coach can try the simple experiment of picking up a 5.20 metre pole with a narrow grip and try to keep it horizontal They will find that controlling a pole with muscular power alone creates enormous tension in the system; the effort involved will force changes in their posture.
This problem is seen especially with vaulters who place their left hand over the top of the pole instead of underneath it and so do not support it with the skeletal structure.

- **A structured run up**
In a work of this kind it is impossible to illustrate every step of Bubka's run up. This is unfortunate because each step in the twenty step run up, including the first, was important. While the great majority of vaulters decelerate over the last five metres before take off because of a bad planting action and/or because of a poorly structured run up.

Bubka continued to accelerate from his first step until the instant of take off.

In an attempt to convey the importance of the run up to success in the pole vault, we have used photographs instead of drawings to illustrate this aspect of good technique.

With his twenty step run up Bubka used a 14 – 6 pattern. This meant 14 steps of smooth acceleration with gradually lengthening strides and then six steps of increasing cadence. This structure enabled him to run fast but with great accuracy and control in the approach and take off.
Many young athletes simply set off down the runway with no idea how many strides they are going to take!

- **A powerful accelerating run** with high knees and a 'clawing' foot strike where the foot is raked down and back to hit the ground on every step, from the very first step. Figures 6.3, 6.4, 6.5 and 6.6, show Bubka running tall and 'in front of himself'. This allowed him to more easily control the pole.
Athletes who lean forward and 'run behind themselves' often have to fight the pole all the way down the runway.

- **An increase in leg speed or 'cadence' six steps from take off**, to keep the hips and trunk high and to prepare for an upspringing take off. This also prevents the athlete from overstriding in this critical period before the take off while continuing to accelerate.
Many athletes overstride in this phase of the run up. Not only do they slow down but their hips drop and it becomes difficult for them to make an up springing take off.

Figure 6.3

Figure 6.4

Figure 6.5

- **A precisely timed lowering of the pole tip beginning approximately six steps from take off.** This ensured a moment free or 'weightless' pole drop. This is important because although a pole only weighs 3 to 4 kgs when held vertically, the apparent weight increases enormously when the pole is carried horizontally because of what are termed torque forces. Anyone can prove this to themselves by picking up a 5.20 metres pole at the end and trying to hold it horizontal.

  If athletes are forced to counter the torque forces which are caused by the long lever in front of the vaulter, their run up posture is affected and this makes a perfect take off impossible.

- **An early, controlled plant** in which he attempted to keep the left hand high as a fulcrum around which the pole rotated as the right hand drives the pole up. Figure 6.7. This action finishes with both hands being driven as high as possible through the take off. Figure 6.8

  The first element is important because it meant that the left hand and the pole do not have to move a great distance to be in the correct position. The second element – both hands driven high - is important because it maximises the angle of the pole relative to the ground at the instant of take off. Maximising

Figure 6.6

Figure 6.7

the pole/ ground angle is important because it allows the pole to be driven towards the vertical more quickly.

Many vaulters destroy any chance of even a reasonable performance by beginning the planting action too late. This leads to many problems including a low plant and a low pole ground angle, which hinders pole bend and prevents an effective take off. There is also a common tendency to let the left hand drop to the level of the hips in the last two steps. This means that the pole has to be moved through a greater distance if it is to be correctly positioned for take off.

Linked to

* **A further increase in cadence in the final three strides before take off** to ensure the athlete drives into the take off tall and ready to spring upwards. It is vital that these final strides are clawing strides with the foot actively striking the ground.

It is very common to see athletes backing off and employing passive poking strides which cause them to decelerate at a point when they should be reaching maximum speed.

* **The take off foot raked back and down in an active 'claw strike'.** This ensured that the take off leg remained virtually straight throughout its contact with the ground. This meant that the foot was in contact with the ground for a minimal time.

Many vaulters push or poke the take off foot forward defensively at this point. This not only means that they slow down but that the take off leg is forced to flex. The athlete stays in contact with the ground for too long and energy bleeds away.

* **A take off below, or even 'outside', the top hand. FIGURE 6.9** This is another critical element of Bubka's technique which is often neglected, misunderstood or even disputed despite the evidence provided not only by Bubka but by athletes like Dimitri Markov.

The vast majority of vaulters around the world still take off 'Under', that is the take off foot positioned ahead of the top hand at take off. Figure 6.10 This means that they can never fully exploit the advantages of the flexible pole and, in extreme cases, may put themselves in danger.

* **A powerful upspringing take off in which he tried to ensure that he left the ground before the pole tip touched the back of the box**

This meant that he treated the pole like a stiff pole at take off and concentrated on moving it up and forward, not on bending it.

Many vaulters plant the pole in the box and then try to bend it before they leave the

Figure 6.8

Figure 6.9

Figure 6.10

Figure 6.11

ground. *The energy to do this must come from somewhere; since their body mass remains constant, it must come from their velocity. They therefore lose speed before they take off.*

• What Petrov called a 'free take off' and what we have termed a 'pre jump' is one of the most controversial but important innovations in the history of pole vaulting. We have therefore decided to provide a more detailed statement of this, the most important phase of any vault. As Figure 5.7 in the previous chapter confirms, Bubka did indeed manage to leave the ground before the tip of his pole touched the box and he himself was in no doubt that this was an important element of his technique. He stated in Jamaica

"In pole vaulting the crucial factor is how to transfer energy to the pole, through the complete body of the vaulter: the arms, shoulders, hip, back and legs. But if the pole begins to bend while the vaulter is yet on the ground, it is impossible to transfer the energy; all the energy is lost and goes to the box. The point is. How to achieve this? **The free take off is a very short period of time, we can say no more than hundredths of a second, going from the end of the take off and the moment in which the tip of the pole reaches the end of the box.** *But this short time makes a big difference that allows the competitor to greatly improve their results."*

The critical advantage of the 'Free take off' is that no kinetic energy is wasted in bending the pole before the vaulter leaves the ground. If the athlete can 'prejump' they gain the additional benefit of increasing the pole ground angle. Again Bubka states

"Additionally we can increase the angle between the pole and the ground in the moment of taking off. **This angle is a very important technical factor, because the bigger this angle, the better the result."**

This issue is dealt with in greater detail in Chapter Twenty Two.

• **The pole 'hit' with a solid body. Figure 6.11** To achieve this he tensed his body to make it a solid unit from the top hand to the take off foot. This ensured that the kinetic energy of his body was efficiently transferred into the pole. One simple but important element in ensuring a solid body was that Bubka drove the heel of the right foot up to the buttocks and punched the knee thigh up. This not only helped create a solid body but the upward punch and 'block' of the knee/thigh added a vertical impulse to the take off.

When vaulters take off 'under' their hips are usually pulled forward and the power position of the body is destroyed . As a result energy bleeds away into their body and the box as they are pulled off the ground – energy that could have been used to used to drive the pole forward. In addition, many athletes allow the right foot to drift forward to a position under the knee before or immediately after take off and so lose the benefit of the upward punch of the right knee/thigh.

• **The take off finished with a complete extension of the take off leg and ankle. Figure 6.12.** This not only helped to ensure that maximum energy was driven into the pole but also put the take off leg into the perfect position to make a long forward whipping swing which put even more energy into the pole.

Figure 6.12

This seems so obvious that one would think that every aspiring vaulter would make it a priority in their technique – but they do not! Observation of hundreds of vaulters up to international level suggests that many do not finish the take off strongly. For many it is impossible simply because they take off too far 'under' on every jump.

A simple cue for coaches is to carefully observe where the left toe is pointing immediately after take off. It is pointing vertically down or towards the rear it indicates a completed take off, if it is pointing towards the box, or even worse towards the pad it suggests that the athlete has not jumped at all but been pulled off the ground by the pole!

- The bottom arm allowed to flex immediately after take off so that the bottom hand moved back above the head. Note that this was not a passive flexing of the left arm but rather a dynamic controlled flexion. To emphasise the importance of not driving the left arm into the pole at take off we have provided two Figures 6.12 and 6.13, taken from film of Bubka's jumps, to illustrate this concept of controlled flexion.

This approach had many advantages. It let Bubka drive the chest/trunk 'through' the shoulders to 'chase' the rapidly shortening pole. However the more important effect was that it allowed him to swing around the top hand just like a stiff pole vaulter.

Large numbers of vaulters emphasise a strong and straight bottom arm at take off. This shortens the axis of rotation and reduces the length and speed of the pendular swing. This in turn reduces the energy the vaulter can put into the pole during this phase.

This is where a subtle element of technique can make a big difference. When Bubka planted the pole he could 'look through the gap' between his bottom arm and his top arm. This is also clearly shown in Figure 6.13. This was possible because the bottom arm was rotated slightly

Figure 6.14

outwards at that instant, so instead of the left elbow being directly under the pole it is slightly off to the left side. This simple element allows the arm to dynamically flex at the elbow as the shoulders are driven forward.

Even more subtle is the fact that as the chest is 'driven through the shoulders' and the left hand moved back above Bubka's head, the left shoulder is positioned to provide a firm base for the left hand and arm. The left hand can now press upwards as it chases the flexing pole.

- **Executed a very long pendulum forward whip of the take off leg.**

More than any other vaulter, Bubka exploited this opportunity to put energy into the pole by increasing the amplitude of the swing around the axis of the top hand. He was able to achieve this because of the two elements above which

– Created a pre stretch of all of the muscles from the top hand to the knee of the trailing leg Figure 6.14. Pre stretched muscles have an elastic quality which means that they will contract more rapidly than muscles in a state of rest. This also allowed him to maximise the distance between his top hand and his take off foot. Finally this enabled him to whip the take off leg through in an action which added energy to the vaulter/pole system. **Figures 6.15a and b show Bubka in positon for a powerful long whip of the left leg.** The speed of the leg whip is evident by the fact that, on film, the foot is often seen as a blur.

Few vaulters exploit the potential of this phase effectively. Either because they do not finish the

Figure 6.13

Figure 6.15a

Figure 6.15b

take off, because they try to punch a straight bottom arm into the pole at take off, because they pull a flexed – not fully extended - take off leg forward - or simply because they do not understand how important this element of technique is.

Note that some vaulters believe that simply attaining a 'C position' is enough. They must realise that this apparent C is simply the result of the vaulter correctly executing all of the technical elements which precede this phase. It is not something a vaulter should specifically set out to achieve.

The next element of Bubka's technique is the initiation of the inversion. This is both difficult to explain and even more difficult to describe. This is because although there are clearly biomechanical factors involved, the movements and timing of the body parts are so subtle and complex that they appear to be performed intuitively rather than deliberately learned and trained. They seem to be dependent on what the athlete's internal kinaesthetic – body feel – at that instant 'tells them' to do.

There appear to be two interacting components

- **A change in the axis of rotation from the top hand to the shoulders which starts as the body swings level with the chord of the pole. Figure 6.16 a and b.**
  This shortening of the axis of rotation has the effect of speeding up the swing of the body. This important

element of technique is poorly understood, mainly because it depends on the athlete's body feel.

Some athletes swing all the way into a vertical position with their body still fully extended. The problem is that their swing is so slow that even though they attain a vertical position the pole has recoiled before they get there!

This was combined with -

- **A change in body shape from an 'I' to an 'L' using an upward roll of the pelvis as the body flexes at the hips. Figure 6.17 a and b.**
  This also has the effect of speeding up the rotation of the body so that it can swing to cover the pole faster.

- **This was achieved through the use of muscle tension to 'connect' the legs to the hips and trunk once the initial flexion had occurred.**
  This is another aspect of advanced technique which is rarely discussed but this action

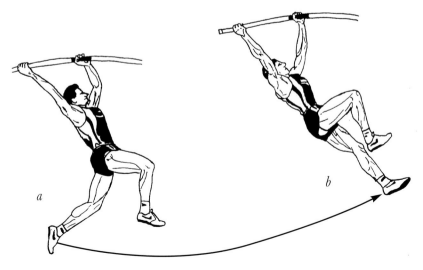

a

b

Figure 6.16

Figure 6.17a and b

enabled Bubka to transfer the energy of the whip into the hips and pelvis and so speed up the roll back of the body to 'cover' the pole. *Many athletes swing the legs up but they do not 'connect' them to the hips which remain low and under the pole. Again this leaves them poorly positioned to exploit the straightening of the pole.*

• **Continued the fast swing of the flexed body to 'cover' the pole. Figures 6.18 a,b,c and d.**
Note that Figure 1.3 in Chapter One – a photograph of Bubka preparing for Atlanta - illustrates this position infinitely better than any drawing can.

This put him alongside or even slightly above the pole in the best possible position and with the time needed, to fully exploit the recoil. In the first place he is closer to his target – the space above the bar. Secondly because he is

on top of the pole the recoil 'hits' him more efficiently. Thirdly by matching the pole with his body before it recoils, he was able to stay close to it all the way through that recoil. This meant that the pole punched him vertically.

Many vaulters swing into a rock back but finish underneath the pole, not alongside it or above it. This places them in a poor position to exploit the recoil and they can be 30 centimetres or more lower than Bubka when the pole begins to recoil.

• **Drove his shoulders towards the pad and punched his hips vertically upwards. Figures 6.19 a, b, c and d.**
This movement accomplished TWO important things. In the first place it put energy into the pole and kept it flexed fractionally longer. Secondly it ensured that his entire body was positioned close to the pole so that he could exploit the energy of the recoil efficiently. While this may appear to be a very complex movement, anyone who has ever driven a child's swing above the horizontal has mastered it!

Figure 6.18

Figure 6.19

Figure 6.20

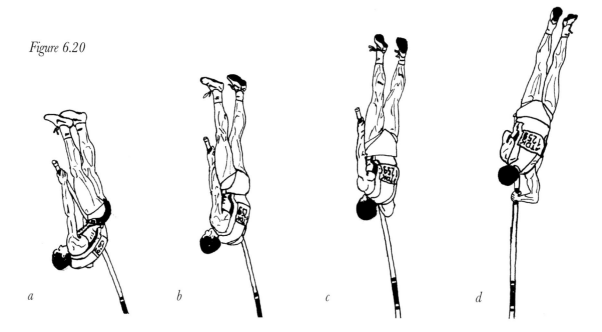

a   b   c   d

Most vaulters keep their trunk parallel with the ground, pull the knees of their completely flexed legs in towards their nose in a classic 'rock back', before shooting their feet towards the bar. They can put little energy into the pole during this phase and they find it difficult to keep their bodies aligned tightly with the pole. They therefore get kicked forwards and upwards towards the bar instead of vertically above it. They therefore waste much of the energy of the recoil.

- **Stayed close to the pole as it straightened. Figures 6.20 a,b,c and d.** The body was kept 'tight' and close to the pole and in a vertical position well before the pole finishes its recoil. Nothing confirms the advantages of Bubka's technical model more than the amazing photograph on the front of this book. Here Bubka is absolutely vertical on the pole which is still recoiling to punch him above the bar with a velocity significantly above that of any other athlete in history. His vertical alignment with the pole also meant that that his turn on the pole was a smooth upward spiral as the tip rotated easily in the box.

The vast majority of athletes never attain the extreme vertical position characteristic of many of Bubka's jumps. Instead they lose contact with the pole early and are projected out towards the bar. Remember that this is caused by problems earlier in the vault.

- **Finally Figures 6.21 a, b and c show Bubka being projected approximately 1.3 metres (4 feet) above his hand grip and over the bar.**

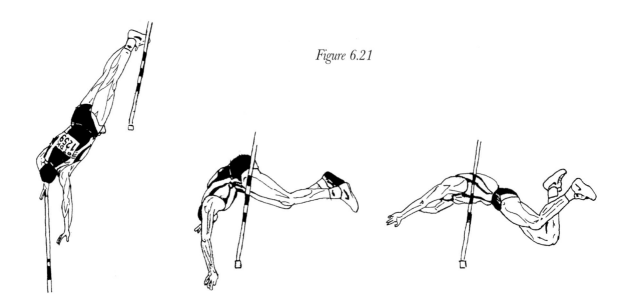

Figure 6.21

Summary

We realise that the information in this section may appear to be superfluous to coaches who are just beginning their career but we believe that it is important for them to begin to study the advantages of the Bubka model if they want to teach the event effectively. They need to know where they are heading from the very start.

Understanding the Petrov/Bubka model will make it easier to see the link between the three stages of technical development. It should also confirm that the technical elements mastered when learning to vault with a stiff pole can rapidly and efficiently be transferred to vaulting on a flexible pole.

Finally it is important to realise that despite his almost complete dominance of the event, Bubka never fulfilled his potential. This may seem an outrageous claim but the evidence is provided by calculations which showed that his winning jump in the 1997 World Championships would have cleared 6.40 metres, had a bar been set at that height. Unfortunately the pressure to accumulate wealth, an important issue for a young man in the disintegrating Soviet Union, meant that his improvements were slowed down. Then, when he WAS financially secure, a serious achilles tendon injury prematurely ended his career.

Ironically it was Bubka's dominance which created this situation. Had there been another vaulter pushing him, as Svetlana Feofanova and Yelena Isinbyeva have pushed each other, the world record might well be close to 6.40 metres (20'10"). Then those coaches who still do not believe in his methods would have found it even more difficult to justify their position.

CHAPTER SEVEN

Elite athletes using the principles of Petrov/Bubka model

"My technique was responsible for my success".

Sergey Bubka 2002

Many coaches still believe that Bubka was unique, a one off, whose amazing performances stemmed from his unique physical and mental qualities. The aim of this chapter is to show that, while Bubka was indeed an extraordinary athlete, many other pole vaulters have adopted the technical model he employed, with great success.

However it is important to understand that although these athletes employ the same technical model as Bubka, they are not identical to him. The reason is simple. Although they aim to jump LIKE Bubka, they are not Bubka! As we indicated in Chapter Five every athlete has unique physical and mental qualities which impact on their technique and so help to create their unique 'style'. This is why it is important for coaches to understand the difference between a 'technical model' and an athletes 'style'.

Bubka's view of the importance of his technical model to his success, was summed up for Alan at the 2002 European Championships in Munich, Germany. There, while watching the men's vault final with Vitaly Petrov, the father of modern vault technique on one side and Sergey on the other, the latter made it clear that it was his technique and not any unique personal qualities that was the primary reason for his success. He could not understand why anyone doubted this.

Equally significant, Bubka went on to say that there were many athletes with superior physical abilities to his who were not jumping high because of their poor technique. The implica-

tion being that they should adopt the Petrov/Bubka model.

His opinion is supported by the success of those athletes who have adopted this model of pole vaulting. They include -

Rodion Gataullin, Russia: Silver Medal, 1988 Olympic Games. Personal Best 6.02 m.

Maxim Tarasov, Russia: World Champion 1999. Personal best 6.05 m.
Lawrence Johnson, USA: Indoor World Champion 2001. Personal best 5.98 m.
Igor Potapovitch, Kazakhstan: Indoor World Champion 1999. Personal best 5.90 m.
Dimitri Markov, Australia: World Champion 2001. Personal best 6.05 m.
Giusseppe Gibilisco, Italy: World Champion 2003. Personal best 5.90 m.
Svetlana Feofanova, Russia: World Champion 2003. Personal best 4.88 m.
Yelena Isinbyeva, Russia: Olympic Champion 2004, World record holder at 4.92m.

Readers should appreciate that it is not easy to ensure that all of the sequences we use are exactly to scale, or even that they show athletes moving in the same direction in the figures we have included. This is one of the limitations of producing a book for a very limited market with even more limited resources! However we believe that the drawings which John Gormley has produced will enable readers to understand the critical points we are making. They illustrate the common technical model these athletes employed and suggest that the differences between them are differences in style, not substance.

That said, at least some of these figures and photographs do appear to expose technical weaknesses in the athlete concerned. We have commented on this but it is important to remember that we are analysing only one of hundreds of jumps they would have taken in their career. The athletes themselves would have been well aware, even at the instant they made the error, that they had a problem and would have intuitively made adjustments to improve or save the jump.

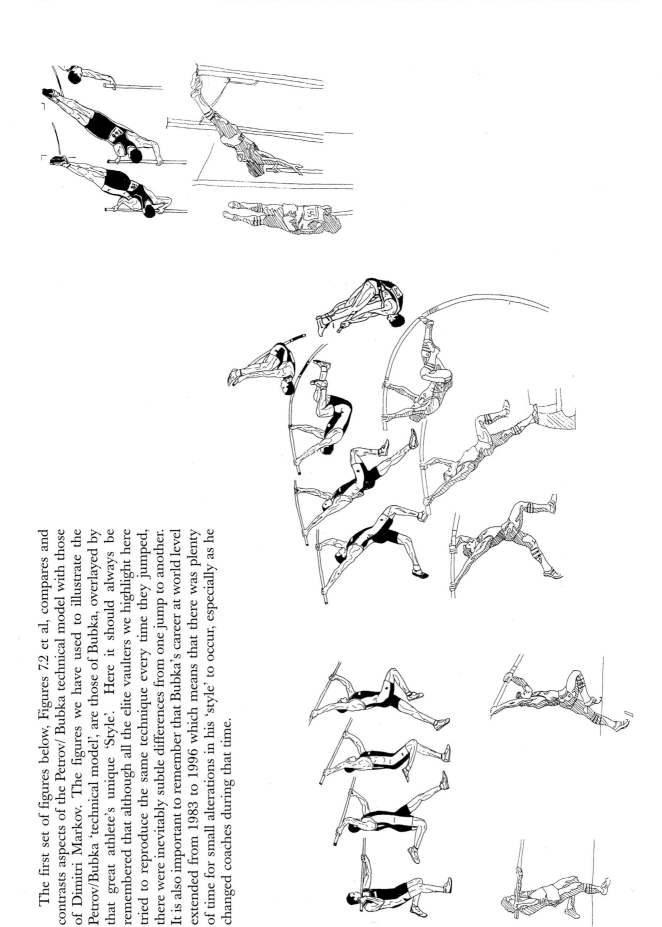

The first set of figures below, Figures 7.2 et al, compares and contrasts aspects of the Petrov/Bubka technical model with those of Dimitri Markov. The figures we have used to illustrate the Petrov/Bubka 'technical model', are those of Bubka, overlayed by that great athlete's unique 'Style'. Here it should always be remembered that although all the elite vaulters we highlight here tried to reproduce the same technique every time they jumped, there were inevitably subtle differences from one jump to another. It is also important to remember that Bubka's career at world level extended from 1983 to 1996 which means that there was plenty of time for small alterations in his 'style' to occur, especially as he changed coaches during that time.

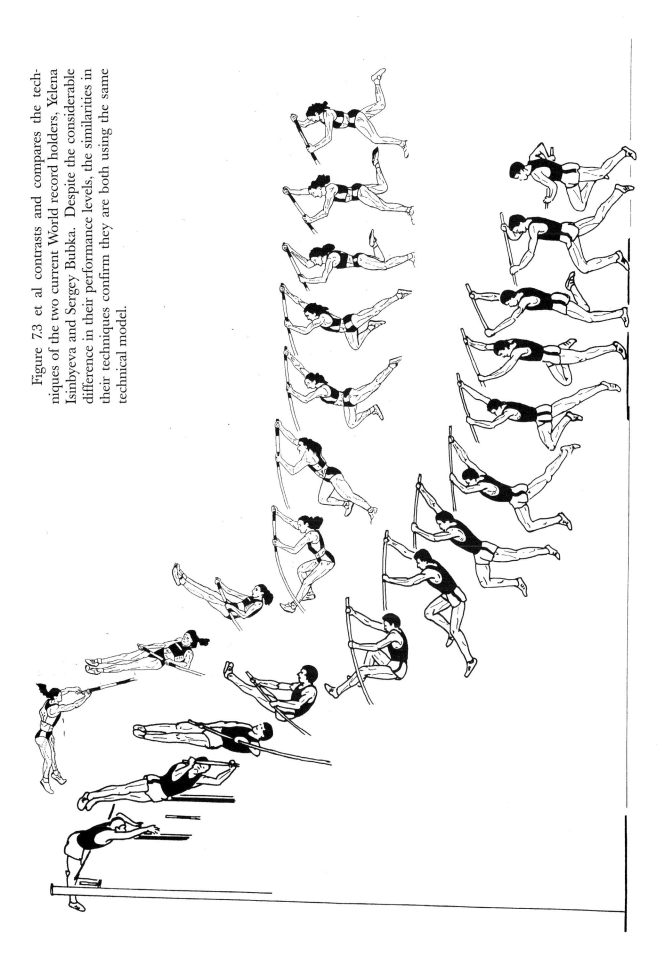

Figure 7.3 et al contrasts and compares the techniques of the two current World record holders, Yelena Isinbyeva and Sergey Bubka. Despite the considerable difference in their performance levels, the similarities in their techniques confirm they are both using the same technical model.

Figures 7.4 et al compare the take off positions of Dimitri Markov, Sergey Bubka and Giuseppe Gibilisco, all World Champions.

Figure 7.5

Figure 7.6

We have included photographs taken of Tarasov competing in the 1995 World Championships in Gothenburg. They are interesting because, despite the superb take off shown in Figure 7.5. we believe that the following photograph shows a technical problem which may have prevented this great athlete from fulfilling his full potential. Figure 7.6 shows that he has begun his inversion but although his legs are swinging up, he has not 'connected' them to the

Figure 7.7

pelvis through muscle tension. So while the legs swing up, the hips stay down in this critical phase at the beginning of the inversion. We believe that this lead to problems later in the vault because he could never reach the perfect position to exploit the full recoil of the pole. This problem is hidden because Tarasov still manages to get into a good vertical position after inversion, but, like many vaulters past and present, he gets there too late!

This kind of critical analysis becomes possible when there is a 'template' such as that provided by the Petrov/Bubka technical model. A comparison with Bubka at the same point in the vault makes it clear that Tarasov had a problem with this phase. It cannot simply be written off because of his 'ideo synchratic style'.

Figure 7.7 is interesting because it shows Lawrence Johnson of the USA in what is often called the 'hang drive' phase of the vault. However we believe there is never a 'hang' in a good vault. He has been captured immediately prior to beginning a vicious whip of the left leg, which will lead him into the inversion. Note the slight flexion in the left leg – this apparently small element of technique is very important to accelerating the lower leg and so initiating the whip. Compare this position with that of Bubka and Markov at the same point.

Finally, Figures 7.8 et al illustrate what all great athletes are aiming for – technical stability. They show Svetlana Feofanova completing two jumps at different venues. Although one jump was a clearance at 4.65 and the other at 4.60 metres, the similarity between the two jumps is very high.

Figure 7.8

CHAPTER EIGHT

Young Athletes and the Petrov/Bubka Technical model

"Even beginners can begin to master some elements of this model of pole vaulting".

The previous chapter confirmed that other elite pole vaulters use the Petrov/Bubka model of pole vaulting. However the examples we provided are all professional athletes with unlimited time to train; they also have great talent! However the reality is that the vast majority of pole vault coaches will never work with athletes approaching their talent so what does the advanced technical model have to offer them?

While it is true that to jump like Bubka you have be a Bubka, our experience suggests that athletes of average ability CAN master at least some elements of the Petrov/Bubka model. For example as Alan has often said, with tongue in cheek, there is no excuse for not getting the first step right! However the images and information presented below should confirm that many athletes can go well beyond this.

The 'history'

The World Cup competition held in Canberra, Australia in 1985 gave one of the authors the opportunity to meet and question the great Soviet coach, Vitaly Petrov, about his theories of pole vaulting and then to watch his protégé Sergei Bubka apply those innovative theories in the competition.

The combination of Petrov's logic and Bubka's performance convinced us that we should adopt their methods. Given their revolutionary nature, some concepts took some time to digest. However **we eventually discovered that even beginners could begin to master some elements of this model of pole vaulting**. So while it is true that to jump exactly like Bubka you have to be a 'Bubka', the illustrations below should confirm that it IS possible for 'ordinary' young athletes to dramatically improve their performance by applying their methods.

It should be noted that a major bonus of all of this was the personal friendship which developed with Vitaly as we met at major championships, at his training base in Formia and even in Adelaide, over the past twenty years. Novice coaches should understand that this is not unique, for virtually all elite coaches in this event are both professionally competent and personally approachable. Go and talk to them!

Figure 8.1
Carolyn
Broadseal
executing a drill
in her eaight
training session.

The comparisons

The illustrations below show the techniques of a range of young Adelaide athletes compared with the world class vaulters highlighted previously. It is important to remember that while these youngsters were encouraged to become pole vaulters, they were not specially selected. They are amateurs in the truest sense of the word. They even have to contribute to the cost of the poles they use and to pay for their own travel to competition. None of them has made a full time commitment to the event and several of them had trained for less than two years at the time they were filmed.

Note that many of the illustrations were taken from amateur videos. In some cases the filming was carried out at some distance from the action, while in others it was impossible to ensure the best possible camera angle. At times this made the process of producing the necessary drawings very difficult; despite this we trust that they are still good enough to confirm the close relationship between elements of the techniques of our young athletes and those of the world class performers we have chosen.

Figure 8.2

Jamie Scroop came to the pole vault in November 2000. She was a tall lanky thirteen year old who had previously been involved in track and field in the long jump and high jump. In her first National Under 16 Championships in April 2001 she finished 9th with a personal best of 2.40metres. The following year she jumped 3.40 to finish third and after winning the National Under 18 title in 2003 with 3.70m she went to the World Youth (Under 18) Championships in Sherbrooke, Canada in July. There she finished seventh with a personal best of 3.80m (12'5").

The sequence of Jamie (centre) then aged 15, which is shown in Figures 8.1 et al was taken from the film of the Sudbury jump. The initial phases of her technique are contrasted with approximately the same phases as those of Olympic Champion Yelena Isinbyeva (below) and Svetlana Feofanova (above). Unfortunately the drawings had to be made from a film taken in Sudbury and it was difficult to do her technique justice. However we still believe that there is evidence to confirm that she was attempting to use the advanced technical model we are aiming for.

Jamie had been vaulting for two years and had completed approximately 80 training sessions at that point in her vaulting career. At no point has Jamie made a professional commitment to the pole vault and her training load varied from one to three sessions a week.

Figures 8.3 et al below compare and contrast 17 year old Lauren Eley in the inversion phase of the vault with the great Sergei Bubka at the same point in the vault. Lauren is shown winning the Australian Under 18 Schools Championship with a personal best jump of 3.85m (12'8"), a World Junior qualifier.

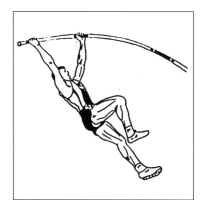

Figures 8.4 et al were taken from film of Patrick Jesser clearing a personal best of 5.40 metres (17'9") in the Australian Olympic trials in August 2000. Sadly Patrick, aged18, injured himself on this jump. This injury may have cost him a chance to win the 2000 World Junior Championships held Santiago, Chile, where the pole vault was won with 5.35 metres.

It is easy to see the similarities between Patrick's technique and the technical model we are aiming for.

The next series of Figures are interesting because they show twin brothers Tom and Chris Lovell aged 18 both jumping 5.00m/16'5" in a World Junior trial in Adelaide in July 2000. Tom is a right hander while Chris is left handed. Figures 8.5 et al contrast Tom's technique with that of Bubka.

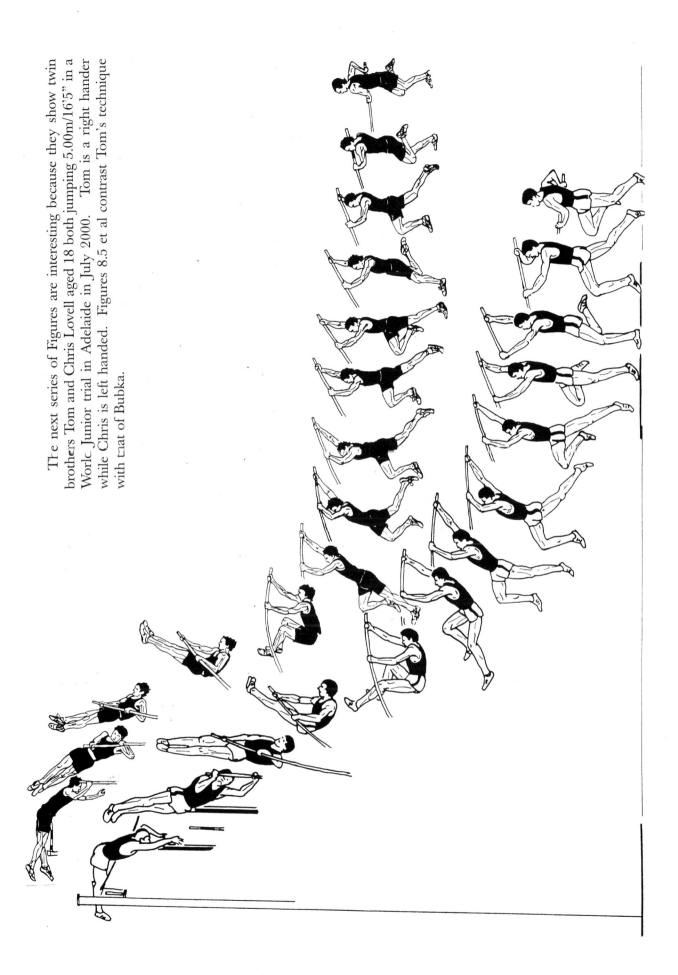

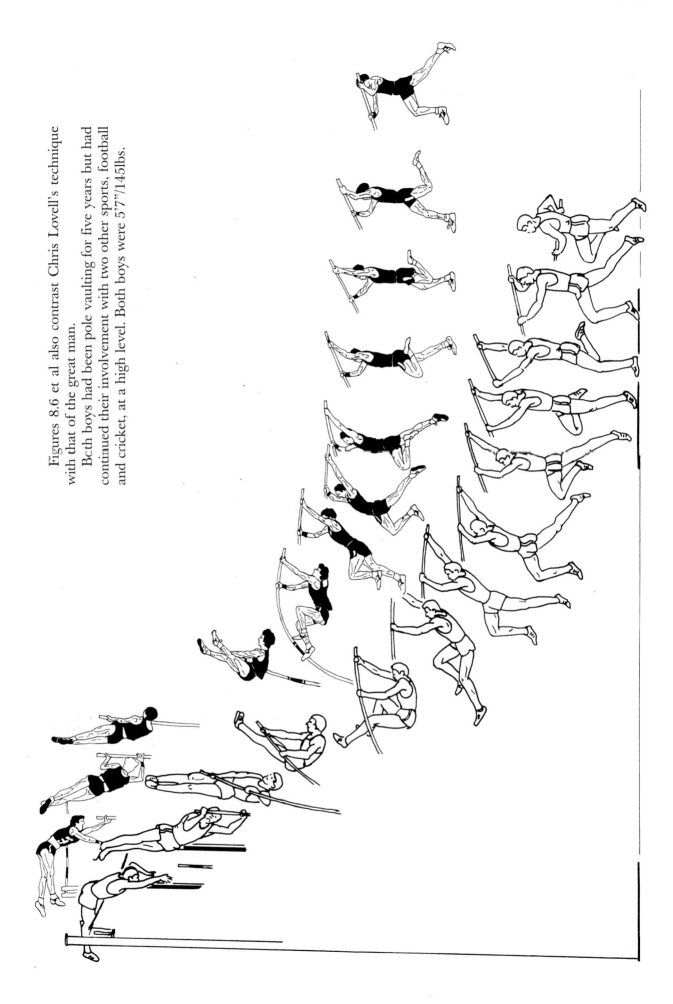

Figures 8.6 et al also contrast Chris Lovell's technique with that of the great man.

Both boys had been pole vaulting for five years but had continued their involvement with two other sports, football and cricket, at a high level. Both boys were 5'7"/145lbs.

Figure 8.7

Figures 8.7 shows Jana Tancosic, then aged 15, in the final phases of the inversion on her winning jump of 3.85m (12'8") at the Australian Under 18 Championships in Adelaide in 2002. This was a personal best and a World Junior Qualifier. Because of her lack of experience, Jana's technique is clearly not perfect; however some of the key elements of the advanced technical model can be clearly seen.

Jana had been vaulting for only eighteen months. She improved from 2.40 metres at the Australian Under 16 Championships in 2001 to 3.85 metres (12'8") in April 2002. Before taking up the vault Jana had been a discus thrower and 400 metre runner with PBs of 32.00 metres and 62 seconds respectively.

The photographs of 15 year old Jenny Lovell, Figure 8.8 shown competing in the Sydney Olympic Stadium and World Champion Dimitri Markov Figure 8.9, training in Adelaide, show distinct similarities, despite marked differences in size and experience. Jenny was the Australian Under 16 Champion with a personal best of 3.70 metres (12'1"). She finished 9th in the 1999 World Youth Championships held in Bydgorsk, Poland.

Figure 8.8

Figure 8.9

Figure 8.10

Figures 8.10 show nineteen year old Wendy Young in the early phases of her 4.40 metres (14'4) jump in Adelaide in March 2004. **Note the very limited bend in the pole even after she has left the ground.** Wendy is another Adelaide athlete who made it to the World Youth Championships where she finished 6th in 2001. It was here incidentally that she lent Julene Bailey of the USA, the poles which enabled her to finish 8th. This in turn established a firm friendship between Alan and the Bailey family from Nampa, Idaho.

In 2002, Wendy then aged 17, cleared 4.10 metres (13'6") at the Adelaide Grand Prix. Wendy came to the vault at 14 after experience in track and field as a horizontal jumper; she had also had a gymnastic background. She continued with her other events as she gradually moved to specialise in the pole vault.

Missing Images

Unfortunately because of the change in video formats we have few images of many of our athletes. Figure 8.11 shows Adam Steinhardt jumping in the 1990 Commonwealth Games. Adam jumped 5.15metres (16'9") at the 1988 World Junior Championships in Sudbury, Canada, where he finished seventh. This is the only image we have of Adam whose personal best as a World Junior was 5.26 metres.

Figure 8.11

Figure 8.12

Figure 8.12 is the only image we have of Christie Elwin, who pioneered the development of the pole vault for junior women in Australia. Christie won seventeen consecutive National School and Junior Age titles, competed in a World Junior Championships as a seventeen year old and had a personal best of 3.99 metres, before taking up a scholarship at the University of Tennessee.

Matt Filsell was another unfortunate athlete. All of his video and photographic material was borrowed by a friends and never returned. In 1995 Matt jumped 5.30 metres at age seventeen to win the Australian Junior Championship but injury prevented him from competing effectively at the World Junior Championships in Sydney the following year. The vault was won by another Australian, Paul Burgess then coached by Steve Rippon, with a jump of 5.35 metres.

Figure 8.13, shows one of the first elite athletes to emerge from our group, Simon Arkell. Simon cleared 4.90 metres as a junior in Adelaide. He competed in the 1986 Commonwealth Games and then had the good sense to accept a scholarship at the University of New Mexico. There he continued his development and here he is shown clear-

ing 5.80 metres at the 1996 Adelaide Grand Prix.

The performances of Adelaide's better young pole vaulters are shown below.

Boys 1986 – 2000

	Age	PB	
Patrick Jesser	18	5.40m	17'8"
Matt Filsell	17	5.30m	17'4"
Adam Steinhardt	18	5.26m	17'3"
Steve Wilson	17	5.25m	17'2"
Aaron Grey	18	5.10m	16'7
Greg Halliday	18	5.00m	16'5"
Chris Lovell	18	5.00m	16'5
Tom Lovell	18	5.00m	16'5
Sam Christie	18	5.00m	16'5"
David Cardone	18	4.95m	16'4"
Adrian Barei	18	4.90m	16'3

Prior to 1986

| Simon Arkell | 18 | 4.90m | 16'3" |

Girls 1996 - 2003

	Age	PB	
Wendy Young	17	4.10m	13'6"
Christie Elwin	16	3.99m	13'1"
Lauren Eley	17	3.85m	12'7"
Jana Tancosic	15	3.85m	12'7"
Jamie Scroop	15	3.80m	12'5"
Tracey Young	18	3.75m	12'3"
Emma Draisey	18	3.70m	12'1"
Jenny Lovell	16	3.70m	12'1"

It is important to point out that, with the exception of times when they were actually trav-

Figure 8.13

elling and competing with an Australian junior team, none of these athletes were given special attention. They were always part of a large group of young athletes ranging from absolute beginner to world class juniors, and were given no more, and no less attention, than other athletes in the squad. In 2002 for example seven Adelaide girls competed at the National junior championships, having cleared the qualifying height for entrance of 3.20 metres, six of them cleared 3.40 metres or better. In 2000 Patrick, Tom and Chris had to share coaching time, not only with each other but with several other boys jumping 4.60 metres (15'0") or better,

Because we had to work hard to bring youngsters into the sport, coaches worked with beginners while older athletes completed their warm up and basic drills. In fact the latter were themselves often expected to help beginners during their own training sessions. This unfortunately meant that our better athletes probably did not receive the support they merited but the 'context' of coaching in Adelaide forced that situation upon us.

Figure 8.14 et al show Laurens clearing at 3.85m. At this time she had been vaulting for two years and had had less than one hundred training sessions.

CHAPTER NINE

The Adelaide approach to developing pole vaulters

"We are prepared to coach anyone who arrives at the track with the dream of becoming a pole vaulter."

The aim of this book is to help novice coaches learn how to teach one of the most challenging of all the disciplines of Track and Field, the pole vault. In fact we hope that the clarity of our presentation will enable parents with no formal training to begin to understand this event well enough to assist their own children learn to vault, if no other coach is available. However we believe that some of the unique insights may even help experienced vault coaches gain a better understanding of this apparently complex event.

The unique contribution of this book is that it will show how to bridge the vast technical gap between beginners and elite athletes. This is important because many young athletes are allowed, even encouraged, to develop their own pole vault technique with little or no clear direction. They then bypass many important drills and, even worse, are often introduced to vaulting with flexible poles before they are ready.

What is astonishing about this situation is that parents would never allow their children to take part in a gymnastics or skiing class unless they knew that the instruction would be safe, progressive and clearly focussed.

An 'anything goes' approach to teaching the pole vault can lead to major problems. Young athletes who develop their own technique may -
- Put themselves at risk every time they jump.
- Limit their ultimate performance level.
- Have to deal with conflicting advice as they progress.
- Be forced to make continual adjustments to their technique as they encounter new coaches.

We believe that all young athletes should be introduced to the most effective technique of pole vaulting as early as possible in their career. We are committed to this because every young boy and girl, no matter what their apparent potential, deserves the chance to jump in safety and to fulfil their potential, whatever that might be.

The title "From Beginner to Bubka" might seem to represent an incredible claim. However our experience indicates that **it is possible to teach beginners some of the important elements of Bubka's technique and then to help** talented youngsters progress towards mastery of Petrov 'Technical model'.

Developing the Petrov/Bubka Technical model

It is clear that beginners cannot immediately begin to jump like Sergey Bubka, so we have developed a three stage approach to developing the pole vault. The Bubka 'technical model' is the third and final stage of development; it is the advanced 'Target technique' we want our athletes to aim for from the very first session. This is why even though this book is aimed primarily at developing young athletes, we have provided an outline of the Petrov/Bubka technical model.

In the first stage we introduce beginners to a 'Working model' of pole vaulting technique. This 'Working model' strips the event to its bare bones and simplifies it to the point where beginners can begin to 'pole vault' on a stiff pole in their very first session. However, what is unique about our approach is that this working model incorporates important elements of the target technique. It is not a dead end technique which leaves young vaulters with numerous faults which must then be eradicated in the future.

Mastering the 'Working model' provides athletes with a safe and sound platform to progress to the 'Basic technical model', where they are taught how to vault with a flexible pole. There is a continued emphasis on the key elements of technique which have been developed on a stiff pole, but now young vaulters are taught how to begin to exploit the advantages of the flexible pole.

Finally, athletes who have the talent, commitment and opportunity can progress towards mastery of the 'Target' technique which Bubka exploited so successfully. Chapter Seven outlined the techniques of other world top class athletes who use Bubka's advanced technical model while Chapter Eight confirmed that young athletes in South Australia have also mastered elements of this model. This despite a sports culture in our State which emphasises ball games, where track and field has a very low priority and where only two schools have safe facilities for pole vaulting.

All three of these technical models are tied together by the notion of treating the flexible pole as an infinite series of stiff poles. Readers should note that this concept will be revisited later in the text.

So we present a unique approach to teaching the event in which learners are first introduced to the 'Working model' of pole vaulting through a progressive series of practices which move from the simple to the complex. **All of these initial practices are carried out with a stiff pole so that young athletes learn the fundamental elements of effective pole vaulting in safety.** Only after they demonstrate that they have mastered the 'Working model', should committed young athletes be introduced to the 'Basic model' of vaulting on a flexible pole.

Every progression is carefully described and a large number of figures, diagrams and photographs are used to illustrate the associated key points.

The rationale for our approach

There are literally hundreds of exercises which can be used to develop pole vaulters. If coaches and athletes have unlimited time for training, almost all of these exercises could be used at some time during an athlete's development.

However in our coaching environment in South Australia, time is a very precious commodity. The coaches are 'amateurs' with tight constraints on their availability, while our athletes can give only limited time to training because of pressures of study, work or just living!

This has meant that although we have studied the ideas and methods of many of the world's leading pole vault coaches, we have been forced to develop a very tight and rational approach to coaching this great event. As a result, every practice, every drill, every exercise and every element of gymnastics we use is carefully selected and taught to ensure the continual progression of our athletes.

Five important principles underpin our methods.

1. We have a clear understanding of where we are heading from the very first step. **From the very beginning we teach young athletes elements of the Petrov/Bubka 'Technical model' outlined in Chapter Six.** This means that all of the instructional drills and cues we employ emphasise important elements of that model.

2. **There is a close relationship between vaulting on a stiff pole and on a flexible pole.** In the rush to exploit the obvious advantages of the flexible pole, many coaches have forgotten this critical fact. As a result their athletes never master many fundamental elements of good technique. This limits their performance potential and may even put them at risk every time they try to vault high.

3. **There must be a balance between practice and 'play' when beginners are introduced to the pole vault.** Ensuring a 'play' element is important because in Australia, youngsters have many alternative sports to choose from. **We have to 'sell' pole vaulting.**
   As soon as the beginner is ready they are given the chance to jump over a soft bar which is progressively raised until they reach their maximum height. We try to do this within the first hour of practice and our goal is to have everyone clear their own height in the first session. This 'play' component is included in every session until it is clear that the young athlete is prepared to make a genuine commitment to becoming the very best pole vaulter they can possibly be. At that point the emphasis swings towards 'training'.

4. **There must be a close relationship between any practice and the real activity of pole vaulting.** This will assist the transfer of the training effect into the athlete's performance in the pole vault and also ensure that time is not being wasted on activities unrelated to the event.

5. The fifth principle is driven by the saying, **"Perfection is not achieved by doing extraordinary things, but by doing simple things extraordinarily well"**! This is a critical concept because it explains why it is possible for young athletes to reproduce some of the 'extraordinary things' that athletes like Sergey Bubka or Yelena Insinbyeva are capable of. In other words we have broken the 'extraordinary' performances of these athletes down into their 'simple' elements. These 'simple' elements can then be mastered by young athletes through well structured and thoughtful practice.

This approach has many advantages

- The balance between practice and play keeps beginners motivated, while the carefully graduated progression means that they are always doing SIMPLE things. They just have to commit themselves to doing those simple things extraordinarily well!

- It is time efficient. Because athletes are doing simple things, they learn quickly. In addition, since they learn to do those simple things correctly from the beginning, they do not have to continually unlearn bad habits. This is important because as any experienced teacher or coach will confirm, it is far easier to learn a new activity than to eradicate a fault.
- It is logical and progressive. Each element is clearly linked to the next in the sequence so it is easy for youngsters to understand how the simple elements fit into the total technical model. This speeds up the learning process and also allows intelligent youngsters to begin to visualise both the perfect execution of the drills and the whole vault, and so make even more rapid progress.
- We continually emphasise why the simple elements of technique are important and show how they are based on the principles of biomechanics. A good example involves asking beginners what they have to do to drive a child's swing above the horizontal. This easily leads into an understanding of how the energy needed to do this is generated and applied. This in turn transfers into an understanding of the importance of the powerful forward whip of the trail leg after take off. This approach provides another avenue of learning for those athletes with the interest and ability to understand why they are doing what they are doing and as a result can lead to more rapid progression.
- Many of the drills used for teaching the event can be used again and again to refine elements of technique throughout an athlete's career. This can save a great deal of time over a fifteen year period!
- It tends to develop thinking athletes who are well prepared for coaching roles at an early age. In fact we often use our more experienced athletes, sometimes as young as fifteen years of age, to introduce beginners to warm up exercises and simple drills. We continually use them as 'models' to demonstrate or to emphasise specific elements of technique.

- It provides a sound platform for any athlete to learn to vault safely and effectively and to progress as far as their talent and commitment will take them.
  Here it should be remembered that all athletes undergo enormous physical and psychological changes between the ages of thirteen and twenty. This is why no youngster should ever be turned away and why coaches must be patient. They must understand that they are on a journey of discovery with a young athlete, a journey which may contribute mightily to the overall development of both parties!
- It provides a solid base for athletes with the ability, dedication and opportunity, to go to the highest levels of our sport, even to become world record holders. It is often forgotten that athletes like Sergey Bubka and Yelena Isinbyeva began their careers with no notion of setting world records or becoming Olympic Champions, yet it happened.
- Because of all these factors, the athlete continually grows in confidence. As any coach knows, confidence is a vital factor in performance at every level but it is especially important with beginners who may still be uncertain of their potential or their commitment.
- **This approach is easy for novice coaches to employ.** Most importantly, none of the drills we recommend involves 'spotting' which is an important component of many other approaches to teaching the vault. The problem with drills which require spotting is that the instructor must physically support an athlete through a movement. This demands specific skills, skills a novice coach may not possess so that there is always the potential for accidents.
- Finally it is important to remember that many young athletes have the natural ability to master a physical challenge. They just need to have the task clarified. Their minds and bodies can do the rest, even after little formal instruction. When they choose to become pole vaulters, they can make coaches into 'good coaches'! It has certainly happened to us.

CHAPTER TEN

The Instructional Process

"The barber learns his trade on the orphan's chin."

Arabic proverb

The Arab proverb above sums up the process of becoming an instructor in many fields of endeavour, we suspect even in Neurosurgery! Along with the need for many positive personality traits, the challenging role of 'Instructor' requires wide ranging knowledge and skills which can only be honed through reflective experience. Novice instructors will inevitably make mistakes, so the key to improvement is reflective analysis of ones performance. In this way mistakes are less likely to be repeated.

The 'P's of Perfect Pedagogy' were developed by Alan over thirty years ago to help young student teachers better understand the fundamental principles of instruction. This 'Working model' of instruction has been taken up and applied by many Australian coach education programs because it reduces the complexity of the global task of teaching and makes it accessible to novice instructors. It is presented here because 'Instruction' is an important component of effective coaching in an event seemingly as complex as the pole vault.

The key factors in a good learning situation in the pole vault are –
- The desire of the learner to improve.
- The amount of practice.
- The quality of that practice.
- The relationship of that practice to the pole vault.
- The enthusiasm, knowledge and skill of the instructor.

While all of these are clearly important, the one that pole vault coaches must always bear in mind is the relationship between practice and the actual event. This is important because for some reason pole vault seems to attract more weird and wonderful training exercises than any other discipline of track and field. An understanding of the long established principles of "The transfer of training" is valuable.

For the training effect of a particular exercise or drill to have any effect on improving performance in the vault the following principles should be followed;
1. There have to be many common elements or similarities, between the drill and the vault.
2. These similarities, along with any major differences, must be pointed out to the learner.
3. Practice of the drill should be followed, as soon as is possible, by an attempt to apply the elements which have been learned, to the real vault.

By understanding and applying these principles, coaches will be able to effectively use drills which highlight or even exaggerate specific elements of technique, as with the running drills outlined in Chapter Fourteen. They will also be able to integrate the simple high bar exercises outlined in Chapter Sixteen with the learning exercises detailed in Chapter Eleven and to better understand the characteristics of good drills for developing pole vaulters.

Because this book is aimed at helping beginning coaches, this Chapter outlines 'The P's of Perfect Pedagogy'. In this 'Working model', each of the 'P's' represents an important element in the instructional process. Each can then be studied and gradually mastered through reflective experience. As with many aspects of the coach's role, complete mastery will take several years.

The essential components of the 'P's model of instruction' are

PLAN the experience

Sound planning will ensure that best use is made of the time available. While experienced instructors can do this almost subconsciously, novices may have to write down a list of the activities they intend to use and how much time they will allocate to each activity.

Here the importance of routines must be emphasised. A set warm up routine will free the coach to deal with the inevitable problems at the start of any practice session. In the same way a specific routine of basic drills, such as 6 x 2, 6 x 4 or 6 x 6 step stiff pole 'take offs' into a sand pit will ensure a high volume of purposeful activity early in a session. This approach will reduce the amount of time the coach spends in presenting the task and will allow them to concentrate on interacting with athletes and providing the feedback essential to improvement.

PREPARE the learning environment

Safety is always an issue in the pole vault, so coaches should check the facilities and poles on a regular basis. This issue is dealt with in greater detail in Chapter Four. Gymnastics equipment such as high bars, ropes and parallel bars should also be checked periodically. Preparing the learning environment before a session starts is also important to ensure that no time is wasted during the session.

PREPARE the learner

There is ample evidence to confirm that the desire and determination of the athlete to improve is a critical factor in their im-provement. While this is an individual characteristic there is little doubt that, especially with beginners, the interpersonal skills of the coach can have a positive impact; a smile, a joke, almost any pleasant interaction can have a big effect on the way an athlete prepares for a session. Two other factors can have a major impact.

The first is the culture of the training group. If young athletes join a squad where the more senior athletes set an example of dedicated, thoughtful practice it is almost certain that novices will follow this model.

The second factor and the key to motivating athletes of every level is that they feel that practice tasks are enjoyable, challenging and achievable.

PRESENT THE PRACTICE TASK clearly and quickly

The instructor should demonstrate and explain
- The specific technical objective of the practice or drill
- The cues that will help the athlete achieve the objective
- The way the practice itself is to be structured – eg How many steps/what grip height/How many repetitions?

More time is wasted by instructors 'Presenting the task' than in any other phase of instruction. Novice instructors in particular tend to talk too much! If a coach is in any doubt about this they should arrange to be timed with a stop watch to find out how much time they spend in a session giving instructions and how much time the athletes are practising. If they find that they spend a lot of time talking, they may need to practice key aspects of a presentation beforehand. Early in their career some instructors may need to prepare and rehearse a script to ensure they get it right. This may seem extreme but the 'Instructional process' is critical to successful coaching and 'Presenting the task' is a vital part of that process.

Never forget that a picture is worth a thousand words. One of the advantages of a squad approach is that young athletes can learn a lot from the visual images of senior athletes, assuming of course that they are good models! The process by which this learning occurs, involving what are termed 'Mirror Neurones', is only just being recognised and is still not fully understood. Coaches would be well advised to have their inexperienced athletes watch older vaulters execute their drills. While some coaches may be able to demonstrate themselves, novice athletes may gain confidence from watching fellow squad members execute a practice well.

Ideally, practice sessions should be supplemented by video analysis of the technique the instructor is aiming for, so that learners can understand how the various drills and practices they are doing relate to the whole activity. While there will always be some athletes who simply want to be told what to do at all times, **our goal is to ensure that when an athlete retires, their understanding and knowledge of the vault is such that they could immediately take on a coaching role.**

PROVIDE PLENTY OF PRACTICE

If there is one single indicator of effective instruction, it is a simple analysis of how much time athletes actually spend practicing. In the end only "Plenty of Perfect Practice", not listening to the coach, will ensure improvement.

This means that coaches, especially those with large squads, must look carefully at how they structure a practice session. Athletes will not learn to jump standing on a runway waiting for their turn. One solution of course is to use multiple pads and runways; if this is not possible the coach may have to use a group approach with athletes rotating through a group of related activities, one of which is actual vaulting onto a pad. This is also where a large sandpit is very valuable because it is possible to have three athletes doing drills into the pit at the same time. Another possibility is to stagger training times or to have a system where groups do their vaulting on different days.

However it is done, it must be done. **Learning can only be done by the learner; the best way to learn to pole vault is to pole vault!**

PRACTICE which is PERTINENT

There are thousands of exercise and drills for a coach to choose from. Full time athletes working with full time coaches probably have the time to use them all at some time in their career. However for those of us who have limited time to work with athletes, the key is to choose only those drills which will have the most direct impact on performance. In other words those which are the most pertinent or appropriate. **This is what we have tried to do in this book.** It is worth remembering that it takes an athlete time to learn every new drill, time which might be better spent refining one that they have already learned.

PRACTICE which is PURPOSEFUL

There is practice and there is practice! Motivated groups or individuals will almost invariably practice purposefully, that is they will remain focussed on carrying out the practice to the best of their ability and not allow themselves to be distracted. However this is not the norm for many ordinary youngsters who are the products of the "keep me entertained" modern culture.

So instructors should try to rapidly change this culture. One way to ensure purposeful practice is to ensure that training tasks are varied, challenging and attainable. If training tasks are too difficult for them, many youngsters may give up trying to achieve them, if they are too easy they will become bored and uncommitted. However there is little doubt that good coaches, like good teachers, have high expectations. They communicate those expectations to their students and expect them to be met. The statement by J. Yahl, **"Perfection is our goal, excellence will be tolerated"**, sums this up perfectly; it could well be the motto of all ambitious pole vaulters and their coaches.

PRACTICE which is PROGRESSIVE

It is very easy for a coach working with a large group to allow the routines outlined above to drift along into pointless repetition. Practice should always be progressive to match the continued development of the athlete.

This is an art because the instructor must decide when an athlete is ready to move to the next practice or drill. As we have suggested previously, progression which is too slow leads to stagnation and boredom on the part of the learner, while if it is too fast you may be taking the athlete into danger. The instructor must balance the introduction of new challenges with the need to revisit previously acquired elements of technique. This is especially important if too rapid progress has caused a youngster to lose confidence.

Taking them back to drills which they have previously mastered can give them a chance to catch their breath and rebuild their confidence prior to trying the new challenge again. As with many aspects of coaching, experience will be the best teacher.

PROVIDE "PHEEDBACK" on the athlete's performance.

This is vital because practice does not make perfect, it makes permanent. If you practice the wrong thing you will become better at doing the wrong thing! The problem here is that it is far more difficult to eradicate a fault than it is to learn it in the first place. The sooner the athlete is put on the correct path the better. No matter how efficiently an instructor presents the task an athlete's early attempts are not likely to be perfect. The instructor must therefore watch every attempt and then provide the FEEDBACK needed to help the vaulter bring their performance more into line with the required model.

The notion of 'feedback' is often confused with 'positive reinforcement' or praise. While positive reinforcement is important and is usually linked with feedback, it is not the same thing. To make the distinction clear it may be worthwhile using the term "Technical feedback". This is feedback which contains specific information about the athlete's performance and makes it crystal clear what has been done well and what needs to be improved or changed.

This feedback can be in the form of specific verbal cues, by the instructor demonstrating the movement again or by athletes watching a videotape of their performance. Feedback can even be provided by 'Manual manipulation', where the instructor puts the athlete into position and then manually corrects what they are doing. This can be especially valuable during the plant phase and at the point of take off. Here the 'Good way' – 'Bad way' method can be used. The instructor allows the athlete to take up the position they feel is correct and then the instructor moves them into the correct position. This is repeated several times. Strange as it may seem the research evidence suggests that it works!

Because feedback often implies that the athlete is 'wrong' it is important to precede any critical comment with an empathetic statement. So a coach might say "That was a pretty good effort – but WE need to improve this part of the drill/vault so I would like you to focus on …… ", "This is what I would like you to do….." . Naturally this must be followed by very precise and pertinent advice as to what the athlete should/could do.

Here it must be emphasised that there is little point in telling athletes what they have just done! They need to know what they must focus on in the next attempt.

PACING

It is important to ensure that practices and drills do not drag on to the point where athletes lose interest. There must be a balance between 'getting it right' and maintaining the level of motivation necessary to ensure purposeful practice. There is a law of diminishing returns. So the instructor must always be aware of the need for variety and new challenges. Every experienced coach knows that even the most jaded old campaigner will perk up when a new idea or drill is introduced into the training regime.

PRAISED performance

Praise, or positive reinforcement as it is more formally termed, is important in improving performance, especially with beginners. Remember that while elite performers are goal oriented and are prepared to accept extreme levels of constructive criticism if it will help them attain their goals, beginners are already nervous simply because they are trying something new. They need constant positive reinforcement if they are to persist, far less improve.

Positive reinforcement can take many forms, from the simple 'well done' or 'good job', to small tokens such as the jelly beans given out by the great Indiana University swim coach 'Doc' Counsilman. He believed that personal bests should always be recognised in training as well as in competition. We took this idea and award candy 'pythons' every time an athlete achieves a personal best.

We have found that an annual Awards night is a very effective form of praise because it recognises a whole years effort. We have a range of awards from the very serious which recognise performances up to Olympic level, to the quite frivolous which remind everyone of the quirky things people did or the strange situations which arose. Every athlete, and often each of the coaches, gets an award of some kind.

One of the most interesting is "The soft as melted butter award", which no one wants to receive because it is awarded to the athlete who managed the biggest failure during the year! Naturally this has to be handled with some sensitivity but we can put the award into perspective

when we point out that the first recipient, Simon Arkell, who received it for no heighting at his first two national titles, went on to win a Commonwealth Gold Medal and set both Commonwealth and National records! Equally significant he gained a Track scholarship to the University of New Mexico and in his senior year finished third in the NCAA Championships.

POSITIONING and PROXIMITY

One of the important practical skills of instruction is Positioning. Not only is it important for an instructor to be able to SEE what is happening at all times but they must also be seen to be 'with it'. They must know what is going on at all times in order to prevent the small negative interactions which are inevitable when adolescent boys are trying to outdo each other from escalating into showdowns and stupidity.

Part of this skill is what we have termed the skill of **Proximity**. The instructor makes sure that they move around a group in such a way that they are close enough for one on one interaction to occur. This can have a major impact on the performance of every individual.

PROVIDE EMPATHY

The struggle towards excellence in the pole vault is long and hard. There will be many failures along the way, both large and small. The instructor must always try to understand the problem from the athlete's perspective and support them when the going is tough.

PRACTICE IN THE BRAIN!

While it is impossible to learn a complex physical skill without actually practicing it, there is considerable evidence to suggest that when a physical skill such as pole vaulting has been learned, it can be reaffirmed and reinforced through a process called mental rehearsal. Given that all learning is done in the brain, this is not as strange a concept as it may seem at first sight. In fact there is evidence to suggest that mental imagery can produce the same nerve impulses as are produced when the vaulter actually performs the event. Mental rehearsal can both speed up and reinforce any aspect of the learning process. This has many benefits; it allows the athlete to 'practice' whenever they have free time away from the track, while mental practice is far less physically draining than the 'real' thing. It also allows the athlete to practice when they are injured.

The vaulter should therefore include visualisation of the event in their training. They can focus on a specific element of technique or they can run the entire performance through their mind. Of course the better an athlete knows their event and the better they can image and feel it, the more benefit they will gain from mental rehearsal.

THE NEVERS

Never use exercise such as running laps or doing press ups as a punishment; remember that as coaches we are trying to sell a 'culture of the physical'.

Never be sarcastic

Never publicly embarrass an athlete

Never tell an athlete to do something they are not capable of doing

Never lose your desire to help young people improve

Remember that this is only an outline of a very complex process. However our experience suggests that even this outline can provide a useful base on which to build a more comprehensive understanding of the instructional process. Remember also that it takes plenty of perfect practice to become a perfect instructor! Certainly the authors looks back ruefully at long careers riddled with mistakes; the only consolation being that they learned a lot from them.

CHAPTER ELEVEN

Teaching the pole vault

"...perfection comes from doing simple things extraordinarily well."
Anonymous

The aim of this book is to present an approach to teaching the pole vault which can be used by instructors with limited knowledge of the event and who may have access to the most basic facilities and equipment. However we have assumed that readers are ready to become serious students of the event and prepared to try to put our recommendations into practice.

The minimum requirement for teaching the pole vault is a well dug sand pit and a pole of some kind! Ideally the sand pit should be 3 metres/10' wide and 8 metres/ 26' long and filled with clean sand. It is possible to use a narrower pit but then the concrete edges must be protected with sand bags at the very least. Even if a good pad is available, it is still advisable to use a sand pit. This is because it is easier for beginners to plant the pole in sand and, more importantly, jumping into sand emphasises that this is a 'discipline', not an extreme sport!

In our system, both boys and girls are introduced to the simple elements of our target technique as early possible. As soon as beginners feel comfortable with riding the pole they are encouraged to

- Punch the free knee/thigh UP with the heel under the buttocks.
- Maintain a strong body and keep the shoulders high.
- Punch the pole up and forwards with a strong right arm.
- Drive off the ground with a full extension of the take off ankle and leg.
- Keep the leg extended behind the athlete as they ride the pole to land in the sand on the right foot. The objective here is to encourage them to keep the take off leg back and extended and not to let it **drift** forward to land in the sand.
- Whip the extended leg from take off, up and over the head when trying to clear a bar.

All of these elements replicate the movement patterns of Bubka in these phases of the vault.

However it is clear that beginners will not master every one of these elements immediately! The process will take several sessions and

progress will depend on the a range of factors, some of which may be outside the instructors control. Among the more important factors are the quality of the facilities, the availability of poles and the potential of the athlete. However the most critical factor is the instructor, which is why every coach should do everything possible to improve their knowledge of the event.

Note here that although we have recommended a certain number of repetitions, typically six to eight, for each exercise, we are very conscious of the fact that young athletes learn at different rates so ultimately each coach must decide when athletes are ready to move on to the next progression.

The process of teaching the pole vault

Remember Plenty of Perfect Practice makes Perfect!

The emphasis in the first session is to

- Build the confidence of the young athletes and convince them that they CAN pole vault.
- Introduce the idea that pole vaulting is not an extreme sport.
- Teach them to take off strongly, gripping at the correct height on the pole.
- Give them the feel of the whole movement by jumping over a soft bar as soon as possible.

We try to combine teaching the simple but important elements of technique, with opportunities for beginners to jump over a bar. It is clear that while beginners cannot 'jump like Bubka', they can begin to master a 'working model' of pole vaulting which contains elements of his technique. Both the simple drills we use AND the indirect competition provided by jumping over a bar can contribute to this if they are correctly structured. While the drills enable athletes to focus on specific elements, the competition gives them a chance to get a feel for the whole movement pattern. This is important both as a means of motivation and because learners in any activity will make faster progress if they understand the whole picture.

With these points in mind we recommend the following teaching progression – detailed as always for right handed vaulters!

Important safety notes

1. It is important to teach young vaulters to 'stay with the pole' and not simply drop off it, if they feel off balance or out of control. If they stay with the pole they are far less likely to get into serious difficulty.
2. While it is important for vaulters to learn to rock back early and fast, beginners should not be encouraged, or even allowed, to try to rock back in any drill until they have demonstrated their ability to move the pole forward through a strong take off and a long whip of the take off leg.

Holding the pole

- Place the pole almost vertically in front of the body. Figure 11.1
- Grip it with both thumbs uppermost and with the dominant hand reaching as high as possible; the lower hand should be level with the elbow of the upper arm. Figure 11.2. This simultaneously establishes both the width of the grip and the way the hands should grip the pole so that if the athlete brings the pole down to a horizontal position the hands will be correctly positioned. If this is not done youngsters often become confused about which way the hands should face when gripping the pole; typically, confused beginners will hold the pole with the right hand facing inwards instead of outwards.

It is important to note that from six steps or less the width of the grip should be kept to the distance between wrist and the elbow of the athlete. From eight steps the grip width can be increased by 10cm/4".

- Place the tip of the pole in the sand six inches from the edge of the pit and approximately twelve inches in front of the left foot.
- Ensure that the grip is high enough to just take the athlete off the ground when they ride the pole into the pit.

SESSION ONE
The first exercise

- The 'vaulter' carries out a standing JUMP to ride the pole into the sand pit. SOME children may need to be helped with a gentle

Figure 11.1

Figure 11.2

Figure 11.3

push in the back – the only time when a 'tap' is allowed in our system! Figure 11.3.

- Do not allow athletes to pull on the pole with their arms. Encourage them to swing with long arms.
- Encourage them to jump and to drive the take off leg back.

Most beginners should repeat this practice 4 – 6 times. However each coach must assess the situation and decide if some youngsters should have more practice before progressing.

As they gain in confidence, youngsters should be encouraged to grip up higher with both hands. This forces them to take off more powerfully on each jump in order to drive the pole past the vertical. **In fact a powerful springing take off is one of the simple but essential elements of good technique at every level of performance - it must be continually emphasised.**

It is important to help youngsters keep track of where they are gripping the pole in this, and every other progression. It is advisable to mark teaching poles at 10 centimetre/ 4" distances or to simply give the athletes a strong rubber band which they roll up the pole as they improve their grip height.

One of the first problems a coach will meet is a right handed athlete who wants to jump off the right leg. Some authorities suggest that in this case the athlete should be encouraged to jump off their preferred leg and thus become left handed vaulters. We disagree with this strongly. What is termed 'mixed laterality' causes confusion and increases learning difficulties for the young athlete. It is far better to have the athlete jump as a right hander and then do everything possible to improve their jumping ability off the left leg! It is important to note that youngsters should never be allowed to jump right handed AND off the right leg, as this will cause immense problems later in their career.

The second exercise

The next progression introduces a two step approach.

The vaulter grips the pole at the same height as on their last standing jump; this ensures that they will have no problems getting safely into the sand pit. At this point the athlete should never be encouraged or allowed to 'overgrip' the pole; at some point they will make a mistake in the take off and overgripping puts them at risk.

Now they position the pole with the right hand on the right shoulder and point the tip towards the planting hole in the sand, this should be approximately 30 centimetres (12") from the edge of the pit. Positioning the pole over the shoulder in this way reduces the complexity of the movement. The athlete does not have to concern themselves with the action of planting the pole and can concentrate of jumping.

Here the young vaulter is replicating the position that Bubka arrives at two steps from take off. Figure 11.4. This is the first

Figure 11.4

Figure 11.5

hand is moved up to a position just above the head and then both hands are punched up for an early plant as they move onto the left foot to execute a springing takeoff. It is important that both hands are driven as high as possible as the pole tip hits the sand. Figure 11.5.

On every take off the young athlete must be encouraged to 'finish the take off', that is, complete the driving extension of the take off leg and ankle which characterises a jump! One simple way of checking this is to watch the take off foot. If the athlete has **jumped**, the sole of the foot should face back down the run way. Figure 11.7 shows a series of drawings of Patrick Jesser executing the stiff pole take off the way we want this exercise carried out from 2, 4, 6 and even eight steps, into the sand pit or onto the pad. **If they have not jumped**, the toe may still be pointing at the box or even at the pad after take off – there has been no extension of the ankle. This means that they have missed the chance to drive the pole forward!

Finishing the take off with a powerful extension of the take off foot also ensures that the take off leg is momentarily straight as shown above.

Figures 11.1, 11.5 and 11.6 show a beginner, 13 year old Scarlett Koehne who had completed eight practice sessions of approximately forty minutes each.

of the modifications we make to simplify the task of vaulting for beginners.

The athlete sets up in this position, two steps out from take off with their weight on the left foot and with the right foot back. As they step forward onto the right foot the top

Figure 11.6

Figure 11.7

Figure 11.8

The natural thing for beginners to do is to bring the take off leg through flexed, not extended Figure 11.8, This 'pick up' of the take off knee must be discouraged or else it will lead to many problems later in the vault. While it may not seem important at this stage, it becomes a vital factor in positioning the leg for its powerful forward whipping sweep immediately after take off. Therefore it is very important to stress this apparently minor element of technique. **This is another of the simple elements which can, and must, be mastered if young athletes are to become effective pole vaulters.**

Each beginner should have four to six attempts, emphasising a long jumping take off to ride as far as possible into the pit. As they gain in confidence, they should be encouraged to move their grip up by one finger, two fingers or even a hand width at a time. The coach simply watches to see how quickly they rotate the pole forward to land in the sand and moves the grip up accordingly. At this point, marking the teaching poles as suggested earlier, becomes invaluable.

If youngsters can keep their left leg extended after take off they can now be allowed to swing it forward to complete a two footed landing in the sand.

The third exercise

The above practice is repeated with a 'four step' approach. The grip should be moved up by a hand width immediately and then adjusted upwards by one, two or three fingers after each jump. Maintain the start position with the right hand positioned on the shoulder at this point. Every simple element of technique which has already been introduced must continually be re-emphasised. The drill should be repeated six – eight times.

The fourth exercise

Move to a 'six step' approach and repeat the drill six - eight times. The grip should be raised by one handgrip immediately and then by 'fingers' as before. Again start with the right hand over the shoulder and re – emphasise the same technical elements.

Platform jumping

Note that at any point in the sequence it is possible to introduce jumping from a platform into the sand. The height of the platform will depend on the age, confidence and strength of the athlete but it will give them the chance to experience a longer ride on the pole. It will also give them more time to take up a good position on the pole as shown in Figure 11.9. This practice is valuable in its own right but also leads to an important progression later on.

Figure 11.9

Figure 11.10

The fifth exercise

Now move to the pad. It will help if the runway is marked at 30cm (12") intervals. This makes it easier for beginners to work out where to begin their run as they gradually increase the number of steps.

Note that it is important to teach beginners exactly where the pole should be planted in the box. This apparently simple element is often for-gotten. To make the transition to the plant box easier, it may be worthwhile emptying a bucket-ful of sand into the box. This not only cushions the shock of the pole hitting the box, but can also provide a clear target for athletes to aim for.

Begin with the same grip height as used in the last jump in the sand pit. Use a six step approach to take off AND hold the hips behind the pole. Remember that this is a critical aspect of technique because it sets the body up for the vital long pendular swing around the top hand after take off. Figures 11.10.

Note that Figure 8.2 in Chapter Eight shows this phase of the event performed by Lauren Eley.

This element of technique is important in stiff pole vaulting but becomes even more significant when the athletes move to flexible poles.

Again use 6 - 8 repetitions

The sixth exercise

The platform is invaluable for the next practice. The athlete drives off as before but then whips the delayed trail leg through alongside the lead leg to land in a long sitting position on the pad. The use of the platform in this way means that the athlete only needs to concentrate on the take off and whip – they do not have to worry about planting the pole.

If a platform is not available, simply use a six step approach to plant into the box and swing onto the pad to land on the backside. Figure 11.11. This practice is best done with the athlete concen-

Figure 11.11

trating on 'finishing the take off' in the first two or three attempts and then focussing on a long swing in subsequent attempts. Eight repetitions.

The seventh exercise

Repeat this exercise with an eight step approach; Eight repetitions. Now the athlete will be moving quite fast so it is important to make sure their run up is accurate. Remember that no matter how carefully an athlete measures their run up they will also need to develop their ability to 'steer' over the last six steps into take off.

The eighth exercise

Repeat the above exercise but get the athlete to jump over a low (one metre) soft 'Bungee' bar. Continue to jump off eight steps with the bar being raised with every successful jump. The aim is to get youngsters to clear their own height in the very first session. The 'working model of technique is shown in Figures 11.12 a, b and c.

As athletes grow in confidence encourage them to whip the extended take off leg up above the bar. At the same time try to discourage them from pulling the leg though bent at the knee. Although this is a very natural mistake, it will cause problems in the athlete's development if it is not dealt with promptly.

If a youngster needs to build confidence, let them make three clearances at the same height before moving on. Depending on the progress of individual athletes introduce them to the concept of swinging and turning over the bar.

At every stage it is important to get beginners to gradually raise their grip height to ensure that the pole rotates forward at a controllable speed. If it is too low the vaulter will rotate forward too quickly, if the grip is too high it becomes difficult to move the pole towards the safety of the pit. As suggested earlier, use a simple system of 'Move up one Hand grip' or 'Three fingers', 'Two fingers' or even 'One finger'.

A talented youngster can complete this sequence in a single session of around 60-80 minutes – **IF the instructor provides very clear instructions and ensures that the athlete is practising, not listening, most of the time.** However this will obviously depend on the number of athletes involved in the session and how much time the coach has with each athlete. The fewer the athletes involved in a session the faster they will progress.

SESSION TWO

The second session will often be a repetition of the first, although we usually cut back the number of repetitions in the early practices. Again the coach has to make an assessment of how many attempts they need in each practice.

In the second session we continue to stress
• Drive the pole up and forward.

Figure 11.12a

Figure 11.12b

Figure 11.12c

- Drive the free heel up to the buttocks and punch the knee/thigh up.
- Finish the take off with a driving extension of the takeoff leg and ankle.
- Drive the take off leg back to maintain the split between the legs
- Roll the pole forward to land on the lead leg – then sweep the trail forward to join the free leg.

FOLLOWING SESSIONS

Subsequent sessions follow the same pattern until we believe the athlete is 'Hooked'. In other words they have decided that they want to become a pole vaulter. This can take from two to fifteen sessions, by which time youngsters should be able to take part in a 'real' competition using a stiff pole and an eight to twelve step run up.

As athletes grow in confidence and technical ability it is important for coaches to begin to plan for the move towards vaulting with a flexible pole. All of the technical elements already developed will make that transition an evolutionary process. However one small additional element needs to be emphasised to make the transition even easier. Now, in all of their short run jumps, the athlete must try to keep their chest away from the pole as they swing on it. They do this by bracing their left arm instead of allowing it to collapse!

Figure 11.13

Figure 11.13 shows a talented young Adelaide vaulter David Cardone, performing this drill.

This small adjustment is just enough to keep pressure on the pole and to slightly delay the forward swing of the lower body. Combined with the extension of the take off leg which comes with 'finishing the take off' these elements help to keep the centre of mass of the vaulter behind the pole in the early stages of the jump.

> **The notion of putting upward pressure on the pole with the left arm assumes greater importance as the young vaulter begins to bend the pole and then moves to higher grips and stiffer poles.**

Again it must be emphasised that all of the technical elements we introduce in these early stages are the same elements which are important to elite vaulters. **Many of these basic practices can and should be used throughout a vaulters career.** In the Petrov system for example, even experienced vaulters are required to take multiple 2, 4 and 6 step jumps during the preparation period of their training year. This issue is developed in Chapter Sixteen which clarifies the use of drills in coaching the pole vault.

It should be noted that even after setting multiple world records using a flexible pole, Sergey Bubka continually returned to jumping with a stiff pole from six steps. The reason is simple. A long run up allows the athlete to cheat at take off because they can use the momentum from their run to move the pole forwards; with only six steps they are forced to JUMP at the take off if they wish to 'move the pole'. This important element of good technique must continually be revisited, even by the great athletes.

The Plant

Once youngsters are 'hooked' – we introduce the correct planting action. This is important because the quality of the plant will determine the effectiveness of the take off. It will only be mastered by constant repetition along with continual feedback to ensure that the athlete IS executing the precise movement pattern correctly.

To simplify this process we teach a 'Three - Three Plant'. With the pole correctly gripped, and positioned at a relatively low angle – but with the left hand **under** the pole as shown in Figures 11.14 a and b. Figure 11.14c shows the common mistake many athletes make.

• A right handed vaulter stands with their weight on the left foot
• The right foot positioned to the rear.

a   *b*   *c*

Figure 11.14

- They walk forward three steps, which are counted One –Two –Three,
- Then as they take the next step onto the left foot they begin to move the right hand up, keeping it close to the side of the body.

As they continue walking forward, the right hand moves the pole to the shoulder and then the left hand joins in to drive the pole as high as possible as the athlete moves onto the take off foot. The overall rhythm becomes One –Two – Three – PLANT-Two-Three. When the athletes begin to trot, then to run, the pattern becomes

PLANT-two-Jump!

We have found that progress will often be speeded up if the coach walks with the athlete and manipulates the pole into the correct positions and with the correct timing. However this critical phase of the vault will only be mastered through hundreds of repetitions and it is here that the youngster with a great determination to succeed can move past less dedicated individuals.

The run up

Because most young athletes will want to compete as soon as possible we introduce them to run up which can vary from eight to twelve steps depending on their ability. Although twelve steps is a little too long for many youngsters it does connect easily to the Three/Three planting action detailed above. The right handed athlete stands with their weight on the left foot, right foot back as before with the pole correctly positioned. They first walk six steps, counting only lefts so the structure of the whole twelve step run up becomes One – Two – Three – then – One-two-three plant two three! This is done first by numbers and very slowly to ensure that the athlete masters the structure of the run up. They then walk it, jog it, run it and then sprint, all the time under control.

Many young athletes should begin competing from a run up of eight steps. They will tend to lose control if they run further than this early in their career. We have also found that twelve steps is long enough for talented girls to vault at international youth and junior level while boys can certainly go to State level on the same run up. Once athletes are introduced to a twelve step run up they can continue using it for several years. Equally important, as an athlete progresses it is easy to increase the length of the run by two steps at a time.

The issue of developing the run up is dealt with in greater detail in Chapter Fourteen

Figure 11.15

Supplementary Training for 'beginners'.

Once we believe the athlete is 'hooked' we introduce them to the notion of 'training' to improve their performance through supplementary work in gymnastics and running.

While these activities are detailed in Chapter Sixteen, one exercise is so closely related to the vault that we introduce it as soon as possible. The athlete simply hangs from a high bar or a rope and we manipulate them into the position they should attain immediately after take off Figure 11.15. This is a valuable exercise on its own because it allows the athlete to 'feel' the correct position without having to worry about any other aspect of technique.

However the next phase is even more valuable because it teaches the whipping action of the trail leg after take off. Having set up in the position outlined above, they now try to whip the take off leg through in a kicking action. Figures 11.16 a, b and c . When the relationship between this practice and the vault is pointed out, there is a strong possibility of transfer from one to the other.

Figure 11.16a

Figure 11.16b

Figure 11.16c

The basic technical model and beyond

In an ideal situation all of the youngsters who have shown promise in mastering the working model of technique will want to become "Pole vaulters". This will take between ten and fifteen sessions but after this they should be ready to move on to "The Basic technical model" detailed in the next Chapter.

It is at this point that many potential champions are lost, not because they lack ability but simply because the necessary infrastructure is not in place. If young vaulters are to jump above 10' in safety, foam landing pads which meet all safety requirements are needed.

Equally important, continued development will depend on access to a range of poles, because while it is possible to enjoy pole vaulting on stiff poles and to achieve relatively good performances, eventually athletes must move to flexible poles. The problem here is that they usually need more than one of these poles; indeed if they are very talented they may progress through ten different poles in their first year of training!

CHAPTER TWELVE

Learning to vault on a flexible pole

"The bending pole allows you to hide technical mistakes"

Sergey Bubka 2002

Many young athletes equate the ability to bend the pole with 'real pole vaulting' and are not interested in spending time learning to jump properly with a stiff pole. Sadly this may well be a short cut to failure and injury.

The mistaken emphasis on trying to actively bend the pole at take off began soon after flexible poles first appeared over fifty years ago. Unfortunately the euphoria which surrounded this technological breakthrough lead many coaches and athletes to neglect the fundamental elements of pole vaulting which had been successfully employed by great vaulters like Dutch Warmerdam for many years.

In an ideal scenario, young athletes should not try to compete on flexible poles until they can -

- Use a controlled and accurate run up of up to 12 steps.
- Control the pole as it is moved from a carry position into the beginning of the plant.
- From a 6 or 8 step approach run, carry out a three step plant in which the pole is brought smoothly into position for the take off.
- Take off with a strong body.
- Drive the pole up and forwards with high hands.
- Finish the take off with a full extension of the driving ankle and leg.
- Execute a long whipping swing to take the hips up in a vault over a bar set above body height and 80cm back.

On a stiff pole!!

We do recognise it is not always possible for young athletes to perfect all of these elements before they move to flexible poles. However they should be used as guidelines because we believe that if young athletes are not competent "vaulters" before they move to flexible poles they are likely to meet many problems which could have been avoided.

The problem is that it is easy to make a pole bend, even to bend excessively. All the athlete has to do is to use a pole well below their bodyweight, take a long run, take off under, push hard with the bottom arm and/or pull down with the top hand. **Any one of these ERRORS can ensure that even a beginner can bend a pole!** When two or more errors are combined, it is even possible for vaulters to bend poles well above their body weight.

However an emphasis on actively bending the pole at take off can lead to several problems. As long ago as 1985 Vitally Petrov stated

"Making or encouraging the vaulter to force bending the pole as much as possible in penetration means allowing them to commit a crude error. They bend the pole and may even pass through the vertical but their vault will not be dynamic, it will fade away in rhythm and they will be left hanging above the bar."

This is precisely what the authors have observed when watching many vaulters, especially in the United States, over the past five years; although in some cases the unfortunate athletes were left hanging over the box, not the bar!

The first problem is that any attempt by beginners to actively bend the pole will generate errors in technique which may be impossible to eradicate in the future. Bubka summed this up with his comment

"The bending pole allows you to hide technical mistakes".

He went on to say

"But if the pole begins to bend while the vaulter is still on the ground, it is impossible to transfer the energy (the kinetic energy of run and take off into the pole), all the energy is lost and goes to the box."

and

"The pole (should) bend as a result of the speed and mass of the jumper, therefore it is more important to concentrate on moving the pole towards the plane of the bar, rather than being aware of bending it. If the vaulter can put all of their speed into the pole, the bending of the pole will happen in a very natural way."

However the second, and even greater problem with a misplaced emphasis on trying to actively bend the pole at take off is that it may cause coaches and athletes to lose sight of the big picture – which is to vault high with safety! **It simply does not make sense for the athlete to put great energy into the pole at take off if -**

1. **They put themselves at risk every time they jump!**
2. **They are unable to get into a position to exploit that energy when the pole straightens**

The Basic Technical model

It is for this reason we believe that it is important for a young athlete to be proficient in the fundamental elements of technique on a stiff pole before they move to flexible poles. In fact once they have mastered the Working model with a stiff pole, **the progression to** the Basic model with **a flexible pole should simply be evolutionary.** A vaulter using a pole of body weight or even above, gripping at the correct height, will cause the pole to bend whether they want it to or not!

For example Figures 12.1 and 12.2 show two young athletes vaulting on poles up to thirty pounds above their body weight. Yet they have both generated a usable bend without doing anything extraordinary. They certainly have not driven the lower arm into the pole to cause the bend! Both were using a twelve step run up and neither was running faster that 7 m/s at take off. **What they have done is to stay behind the pole with the mass of their body!** All the left arm did was to ensure that the body did not swing past the pole early. This element of technique should transfer directly from the practices the athlete has done with stiff poles.

What is even more significant is that both of these very inexperienced athletes were able to drive the flexing pole forwards and swing into the inversion fast enough to be in position to exploit the recoil of the pole. On both jumps the athletes concerned cleared personal bests of 3.85 metres in a National Championship. Readers might like to revisit Chapter Eight to remind themselves of the latter stages of both of these jumps.

Figure 12.1

It is absolutely critical for coaches to understand there is little point in an athlete forcing the pole to bend at take off, if they are then unable to put themselves into a position to exploit the straightening pole when it recoils!

Helping young athletes to exploit ALL of the advantages of the flexible pole, progresses through a series of sequential stages in which the vaulter gradually learns

- How to get the pole to bend naturally after take off.
- To use the long pendular swing of the take off leg to add to the pole bend.
- To redirect some of the energy of that swing to initiate the inversion.

Figure 12.2

- To position themselves alongside or 'above' the pole before it begins to recoil.
- To drive the shoulders down and back and to punch the hips vertically.
- To stay close to the pole as it straightens.

It is important to remember that each of these elements depends on and melds with the preceding one.

Clearly the speed with which athletes master all of the above elements of pole vaulting will depend on a range of factors, not least their natural ability! So while the technique of 17 year old Lauren Eley shown in Figure 8.2 in Chapter Eight almost replicates some aspects of the Petrov/Bubka model in the inversion phase, 15 year old Jamie Scroop shown in Figure 8.1, had only mastered the take off and the swing to the chord of the pole. While there may be several reasons for the difference between them, the most likely is that Jamie had had forty less training sessions than Lauren at that point in their careers.

Again it is important to remember that mastering the 'off ground' elements will depend on
- A well structured run up,
- An early plant,
- A powerful upspringing take off, hands punched high through the pole after take off,
- The take off leg driven hard off the ground,
- A fully extended take off leg and ankle,
- A long swing of the whole body around the top hand, which begins immediately the toe of the take off foot has finished its driving extension,

From all of the above it becomes clear that there is little point in
- Teaching vaulters to bend the pole excessively before they leave the ground
- Attempting to teach athletes the Inversion phase until they have mastered the preceding elements.

Summary
If youngsters can repeat all they have learned on the stiff pole, the transition to bending the pole will simply be evolutionary.

The problem
As we suggested above, many athletes will find it easy to bend the pole when they have mastered the elements of vaulting with a stiff pole. However there may be youngsters who still cannot get a pole to flex. This typically occurs with small or light athletes who cannot grip high enough on a pole of the correct body weight to cause the 'natural' bend they should be aiming for. Here it is important that young athletes learn to work out which is the 'soft' face of the pole they are using, because the pole will flex more readily if that face is pointing towards the centre of the pad at the instant of take off.

With Spirit poles this is simple. All the vaulter has to do is stand with pole gripped correctly and ensure that the Spirit logo is uppermost; as the pole is planted the pole rotates so that this logo is now facing back towards the vaulter. With older poles where there is some uncertainty about the soft face the vaulter simply cups the pole in one hand with the tip on the ground and rolls the pole in their palm until it settles with a slight bend towards the ground – that tells you the soft face of the pole. If this test is performed with Spirit poles the logo should again be on the 'top' of the pole.

The problem is that unless the pole bends when the athlete does everything correctly - they do not get the feedback they need to tell them that - they have done everything correctly! The novice who is learning to bend the pole must be able to link the feeling of the pole bending to their actions as they hit it! If they are unable to feel this link they may try to bend the pole doing the wrong things – then if it bends they will 'feel' that they have done the right thing! So the dilemma which must be resolved is.
1. A pole needs to be gripped in the recommended range 15 – 45 cm (6"- 18" from the top) if it is to flex naturally.
2. In order to maintain control and avoid injury as they learn to bend the pole, beginners must use a short approach run.
3. **BUT** a short approach run means that they cannot grip very high on the pole.
4. This means the pole is likely to be too stiff for them to bend, doing the 'right' thing.
5. Which means that they will be tempted/ encouraged to make the pole bend by doing the 'wrong' things.

This implies that a vaulter must have access to a range of poles of different lengths as well as stiffness! It will them enable them to grip high enough on the pole for it to flex - if they take off properly - but low enough for them to vault successfully from no more than eight steps!

Unfortunately for many coaches and athletes this solution is no solution, because they are not in a position to obtain a great range of poles. We suggest the following approach, which we believe is used by all leading Australian coaches.

Under normal circumstances – that is when using a full run up – vaulters should never use poles rated below their body weight.

However a sensible coach would never think of introducing young athletes to bending the pole using their full run. In the first case a youngster is unlikely to be in full control, so increasing the risk of an accident. Secondly, the inevitable variation in the accuracy and speed of the run up means that the athlete would rarely get to the take off point ready to jump with confidence, so many attempts would be a wasted.

It is important to remember that one of the keys to bending the pole is **impulse**. This is a function of the vaulter's mass times their velocity. If you reduce the velocity you reduce the impulse – which means that the athlete can use a pole below their body weight IF they reduce their run up to six or eight steps. Naturally the aim is to move the athlete onto poles at their body weight, then to poles above their body weight as their technique improves and their confidence grows.

Using a lighter pole gives youngsters the chance to experience the kinaesthetic – body feeling - of the pole bending, as they jump. Conversely vaulters who have to learn to flex a pole which is too stiff, may well be able to muscle it into bending but may also be developing bad habits as they do so.

So we suggest two possible solutions to this dilemma. The first is to jump from six to eight steps with a pole which will give a limited flex. Beginners vary enormously from one jump to the next so the initial practices must be controlled to ensure that there is very little pole bend. Figure 12.3 shows a very small flex in the pole, which is what a vaulter should be aiming for initially. Athletes who have mastered vaulting on a stiff pole may be able to achieve this on a pole of body weight with a run up of 6 – 8 steps, because the major elements of good technique are easily transferred from stiff to flexible poles.

The athlete should simply run, plant and take off as they would on a stiff pole. The previous emphasis on 'finishing the take off' and bracing the left arm will now pay off. They help keep the vaulter's lower body and hips behind the pole. The athlete should concentrate either on keeping the pole in front of them – or for them to stay behind it, by bracing, but not pushing with the left arm. Figures 12.1 and 12.2 above confirm should confirm this.

Young vaulters would be well advised not to try to move into the inversion until they can complete the following exercises satisfactorily! For four to six jumps they take off and simply stay behind the pole and ride it through onto the pad. This is simply an extension of what they have already learned to do on the stiff pole.

Figure 12.3

Now they repeat this but add the long whip of the take off leg to land on the pad on their backside (butt)! This exercise confirms the importance of the pendular swing in adding to the pole bend and driving the pole forward and should be repeated until the athlete becomes consistent.

This whip will be accentuated if there is a slight flexion at the knee of the left leg immediately after take off Figure 12.4. This allows the athlete to initiate the whip by 'kicking' the foot forward as if they were striking a soccer ball.

Figure 12.4

Figure 12.5

This is a natural movement and helps to accelerate the take off leg; if this is not done and the leg remains perfectly straight after take off, the swing will be too slow and athlete will be unable to put much energy into the pole or to complete the inversion effectively.

We have found a third exercise to be of particular value in teaching this action. We have developed an exercise we call "Long swings". Here the athlete finds a pole which will flex easily and using an approach of six or eight steps, tries to complete a swing on the pole to land on their backs as far into the pad as possible. This is shown in Figure 12.5 a, b and c. Note the close relationship between the initial elements of this drill and the model we are working towards.

This practice allows the athlete to feel how the whip is extended because the pole is moving away from them as it shortens. This increase in the amplitude of the swing, which is made possible by the flexible pole, is another advantage technology has brought to the event.

Readers should note that this aspect of technique will be dealt with in greater detail in the following Chapter.

The second solution to this problem is to have the athlete take off from a raised platform as shown in Figure 12.6 a,b and c. They position the tip of the pole firmly in the box, grip as high as they can reach, drive off and ride the pole to land on the pad. Initially they will land on their feet but they can quickly move to landing on their backside/butt. This practice eliminates the need for a run up and plant and allows the athlete to grip higher on the pole even though they are only using a one or two step approach. A higher grip means that the pole will flex more readily even without a run up.

Figure 12.6

By eliminating the need for a run up, the vaulter can more readily focus on the key elements of technique. With a strong right side/top arm, a braced left arm and a strong 'upspringing' take off, the athlete will gradually find the pole flexing as they swing on it. If they then begin to add a whipping swing of the take off leg they will begin to feel and to understand the contribution that specific movement can make to moving and flexing the pole. Through this experience, a beginner may also begin to understand that finishing the take off by driving the foot back hard and extending the ankle has three benefits. It

1. Enables them to easily drive the pole towards the pad; this is the key to safe penetration.
2. Puts the take off leg into position to initiate its forward whip.
3. Ensures that the hips are kept well away from the pole in the early part of the swing

It is possible to use a converted gymnastic box for this exercise, but we have found that the higher platform is better, so we have made one which solves the problem. Another solution, which some top class athletes use when they need to move their grip up onto bigger poles in practice, is to use a deeper box, but this is not as practicable as using a platform with beginners.

The Basic Model

At any time a coach believes the athlete is ready, they can let them jump from no more than eight steps over a soft bar set back at least 80 centimetres. The first task is to work out which pole will initially give about a twenty percent bend. As youngsters improve it is important to move them to stiffer poles, but this should be a gradual progression!

The action of jumping over a bar, especially as it is gradually raised, will automatically lead the athlete into the early phases of the inversion, especially if they 'finish the take off' to move the pole forward and then instantly whip the take off leg through to try to 'cover the pole' to be in position to exploit the recoil. This has been clearly shown in Figure 8.2. This can be repeated 6/8times.

This is a gradual process as the young athlete learns how to convert the energy of the take off and swing into the inversion phase. The critical point here is that the pole will flex simply because the vaulter has hit it hard with high strong hands and arms and a tensed body and not because they do anything specific to make the pole bend. Certainly they should not try to bend the pole by pushing with the bottom hand and pulling down with the top hand!

Learning to bend the pole properly is just the beginning. However even this enables young athletes to grip up and so jump higher. Using the notion of an infinite series of stiff poles, it is easy to see that the pole will roll forward i.e. rotate around the poles tip, more quickly, as it shortens and will then give the athlete their grip height back when it straightens. This means that if an athlete only clears their grip height they will go higher than they would on a stiff pole – even if they go over the bar sideways or upside down. Therein lies the trap.

Pushing up the grip seems to be the easiest and quickest way to jump higher and there will

be occasions when it is justified in a one off situation. However this approach will limit a vaulter's long term development and may take athletes into danger. **We believe that this should be avoided.** Here it might be worth remembering that although Bubka used a high grip, he was also able to project himself 1.30 metres/four feet and more above that grip! It is far better for young athletes to grip low and work hard to improve the inversion phase of their jump than to significantly raise their grip in an attempt to achieve short term results. Not only will this be safer but it will give the athlete a better chance of realising their full potential.

Talented youngsters can develop a "Basic" technique in thirty sessions or less with a competent coach. South Australian girls like 14 year old Christie Elwin cleared 3.50 metres/11'5"and more within six months of first trying the event and one 15 year old boy, Matt Filsell, jumped 4.82 metres/15'8" within one year of taking up the pole vault. Christie went on to clear 3.99 metres/13'1" as a seventeen year old before she took a track scholarship at the University of Tennessee, while Matt jumped 5.30 metres/ 17'4"at the age of seventeen.

CHAPTER THIRTEEN

Teaching the inversion

Because of the significant differences between the method and the old notion of a 'rock back' we believe that it is important to give this action a different name – hence the term 'Inversion'.

We have deliberately separated this detailed discussion of the inversion from the previous chapter because we suspect that almost every reader wants to know how to 'teach the rock back' before they deal with any other aspect of the pole vault! There seems to be a common belief that the rock back is the most important phase of the vault. There also seems to be a belief that it can be separated from all the elements that preceded it and so can be developed in isolation from them. As a result there are numaerous methods used to 'teach the rock back', some involving complex pulley systems and drills.

This is a comment and not a criticism, because until Alan met Vitaly Petrov at the World Cup competition in Canberra, Australia in 1985, **he too was obsessed with the 'rock back'.** It was a big surprise when Vitaly dismissed his repeated questions about this aspect of technique as being irrelevant. Vitaly insisted that the only thing that really mattered was the run up and the take off. Since the discussion took place through an interpreter Alan began to wonder if Vitaly simply did not understand the question. Perhaps the wires were crossed somewhere!

Over the next two days, it gradually emerged that he did understand the question but was not going to answer it! He continued to affirm that only the run up and take off were important! If the vaulter got that right, everything else, including the 'rock back' occurred naturally. The discussion of the take off also included his notion of a 'free take off' which challenged everything Alan had believed about vaulting with a flexible pole.

Gradually Petrov's revolutionary ideas began to make sense and we tried to apply them with our athletes. This chapter is an attempt to explain the 'Inversion phase' of the vault and to suggest an approach to helping young athletes improve this element of their technique.

It is worth explaining why we use the term "Inversion" and not the traditional term 'the rock back'. In the first place the Petrov/Bubka technical model introduced a completely new approach to this phase of the pole vault. Whereas traditional approaches encouraged athletes to simply swing into a tight tuck in readiness to ride the recoil of the pole, the Petrov approach was based on the notion of continuing to put energy into the pole throughout the entire vault. As we indicated in Chapter Six, Bubka whipped his body up to cover the pole and almost instantaneously drove his shoulders down and towards the pad while at the same time punching his hips vertically upwards. He was therefore able to keep the pole flexed for fractionally longer, while at the same time positioning himself perfectly to exploit the recoil of the pole, as shown on the front cover of this book.

Because of the significant differences between this method and the old notion of a 'rock back' we believe that it is important to give this action a different name - hence the term 'Inversion'.

As we suggested in the previous chapter, the process of helping young athletes to exploit ALL of the advantages of the flexible pole progresses through a series of sequential stages in which the vaulter gradually learns;

- How to get the pole to bend naturally after take off.
- To use the long pendular swing of the take off leg to add to the pole bend.
- To redirect some of the energy of that swing to initiate the inversion.
- To position themselves alongside or 'above' the pole before it begins to recoil.
- To drive the shoulders down and back and to punch the hips vertically.
- To stay close to the pole as it straightens.

It is important to remember that each of these elements depends on and melds with the preceding one. It is also important to recall that ideally, young athletes should not try to compete on flexible poles until they can demonstrate their ability to;

- Execute a controlled and accurate run up of up to 12 strides.
- Control the pole as it is moved from a carry position into the beginning of the plant.
- Carry out a three step plant in which the pole is brought smoothly into position for the take off.
- Take off with a tensed body, which firmly links the top hand with the take off foot.

- Drive the pole up and forwards with high hands.
- Finish the take off with a full extension of the driving leg and ankle.
- Execute a long whipping swing to take the hips up in a vault over a bar set above body height and 80cm back.

We have deliberately chosen to repeat the above points which were outlined in the previous Chapter, to re-emphasise that the inversion is dependent on all of the preceding elements. There is no point in a vaulter trying to graft an "inversion" or even a 'great rock back' onto a technique which is not based on sound fundamentals.

The Inversion

First it is important to understand that the Inversion is not achieved through some semi magical process or even through superb abdominal strength, but by the application of the basic principles of human movement. This is not to say that muscle power is not important but that it is not employed in the way many people think. The critical issue is the ability of the athlete to use muscles to 'fix and hold' key positions in a correctly timed sequence of movements. This is where dynamic core strength is important.

Our discussion of the nature of an effective inversion begins once the athlete can execute a long fast swing of the whole body from top hand to the foot of the trail leg. Once vaulters have mastered this they can then work at speeding up the rotation of their whole body by changing the point of that rotation from the top hand to the shoulders. These elements are all shown in our target technique which is described and illustrated by Sergey Bubka in Chapter Six.

Since the shoulders are solidly connected to the trunk and hips the actual and obvious change takes place in the next lower area which is free to move - from the hips down. So as the body swings to the chord of the pole, the athlete stops the forward movement of the shoulders by bracing OR CHASING– not necessarily pushing - the left arm up though, not forwards into, the pole.

Readers can carry out two simple experiments to clarify what seems to be a very complex issue. All they have to do is attach a small weight, a bunch of keys will do, to a piece of rope 60cms or 2' long. In the first 'experiment' they swing the weight in a circle noting the speed of the rotation; they then allow the rope to rotate around their arm. On each rotation the length of the moving

rope shortens and the weight will clearly be seen to speed up. In other words the shorter the axis of rotation the faster the speed of rotation.

The second 'experiment' is even simpler. Swing the weight in an arc and at a convenient moment stop the swing by placing the other hand in the way of the swinging rope. Immediately the point of rotation will change from the hand holding the end of the rope to the point where the other hand stopped the forward movement; again the rotation will be speeded up. This experiment can be carried out even more dramatically for the benefit of athletes by swinging a running shoe held by its laces and stopping the swing as suggested above. The shoe will instantly loop back over the top in an 'inversion'.

The athlete must learn how to change the axis of rotation from their top hand to their shoulders at precisely the right moment in order to speed up the rotation of the body. This is important because **if the whole stretched body** continues to swing around the top hand after it passes the chord of the pole, **it cannot rotate fast enough** for the athlete to reach a vertical position before the pole has completed its recoil.

Our experience suggests that many talented youngsters can execute the correct movement almost intuitively.

As suggested earlier the old fashioned solution was to flex both legs and pull the knees in towards the nose in a tight tuck. However this often leaves the athlete still under the bend of the pole and in a poor position to exploit the energy of the pole as it recoils.

In the Bubka model the vaulter does not do this! Here as the vaulter swings level with the chord of the pole they break at the hips; this shortens the axis of rotation and causes an increase in the speed of rotation of the swing. However they do not pull the knees into the nose. Because they have greater energy in the system as the result of the efficiency of their take off and swing they try to keep the trail leg especially, as long as possible – for as long as possible!

Very talented youngsters will learn to 'connect' the whipping legs via the hips to the pelvis and lower trunk. In this way some of the energy of that swing is transferred into the athlete's hip – pelvic region and so speeds up their movement so that they can positon themselves alongside or even above the pole. This is what Petrov terms 'Covering the pole'. While some athletes can do this naturally, others may find specific high bar exercises of value.

Having swung up to cover the pole, the vaulter now drives their shoulders forcefully towards the pad while simultaneously punching the hips upwards to match the straightening pole. **Athletes who can manage this are evolving towards the advanced technical model.** Clearly this takes time to master and many youngsters will not get this far because of insufficient training time or, unfortunately, lack of physical ability. However Chapter Eight showed that ordinary young athletes can begin to get very close to the methods of the great vaulters who use the Petrov/Bubka model.

We have found that the best way to help athletes to develop this phase of the vault is to use an evolutionary approach. If a suitable range of poles is available we begin with "Long swings" from eight steps where the athlete tries to swing to to land on their backs towards the rear of the pad. Then as they gain in confidence and efficiency we gradually move them to stiffer poles and stiffer poles until they are swinging into an almost vertical position Figure 13.1 on a flexible pole.

The next stage is simply to put up a soft bar and let them jump over it off eight steps, completing the inversion and turn over the bar. The shorter run enables them to take many more attempts in a session and cuts down the problems with the inaccuracy a full run up might engender.

It is important to remember to use a narrow grip, from wrist to elbow is a good guide, for all short approach jumps. This is because from a short run up, the athlete cannot grip very high on the pole - which in turn means a steep pole/ground angle - which will lead the left arm to an almost horizontal position - which will tend to encourage them to push forwards through the pole with the arm, instead of up through the pole.

Now, with a narrow grip to ensure the left arm is not horizontal when the pole is planted, the athlete progresses through a series of exercises which emphasise the following technical elements in sequence;
- A tall high cadence approach run
- then progressing to
- Run tall and Plant high
- Drive the hands high and take off with a strong body
- Finish the take off with a driving extension of the left leg
- Ensure a slight flexion at the knee – which should occur naturally as the result of a powerful take off – but which may still need special attention.
- Stay behind the pole early
- Kick/Whip the take off foot forward
- Connect the lower leg kick to the upper leg and continue the whip
- Slow the movement of the upper body/

Figure 13.1

trunk with the left hand while simultaneously rolling the pelvis.

- Dynamically fix the flexed body – into what is sometimes referred to as the L position, and roll the pelvis back to cover the pole.
- Drive the shoulders towards the pad while simultaneously punching the hips high.
- Stay alongside the pole as the vaulters body spirals upwards around it.

Focussing on these elements in sequence is likely to be far more effective than trying to deal with every element every time the vaulter jumps. For one thing if the coach tries to see everything in a single jump, they are likely to see nothing useful. With the athlete's efforts focussed for each jump, it is easier for the coach to see what is happening at each stage and to give constructive feedback. Novice coaches in particular find that this approach will help them to develop the 'Coaches eye' so essential to success. **Both coach and athlete then know what the specific objective of that particular attempt is!**

It is in these final phases of the pole vault that it becomes a 'gymnastic event'. Body feel becomes very important as does the athlete's awareness of their orientation to the bar. Complex as this process may seem, some young athletes can master many elements quickly, simply by relying on their own motor skill to feel their way through the vault. If it is possible, serious young vaulters should try to work with a good gymnastics coach who is prepared to give time to an athlete. The problem is that few gymnastics coaches have time left over from their primary role, but persistence and a little pestering may help. However if it is not possible to get help in this way, there is little doubt that mimicking the movement with exercises on the high bar or a hanging rope can have a major impact.

This of course means that every ambitious coach and athlete must ensure they have ready access to at least a high bar. In the USA a good example of what is needed has been developed by Bob Fraley at Fresno State University in California. The outdoor gym in Adelaide which was developed by one of our coaching team, John Hamann is shown in Chapter Sixteen.

Figures 13.2a, b, c and d show our favourite high bar exercise extended until the vaulter is virtually 'inverting' on the high bar. Because of the close relationship between this exercise and the actual vault there is considerable transfer of the skill acquired on the bar.

We recognise that every athlete brings their unique personal qualities to the event. Since we

Figure 13.2

never turn any youngster away and encourage everyone to fulfil their potential they inevitably develop a "Style" which reflects those qualities to a greater or lesser degree. The most obvious problem occurs when athletes are not good 'springers' because it is virtually impossible for them to take off "out" and to forcefully drive the pole forwards and up in the take off. Inevitably they tend to be pulled off the ground no matter what instruction they are given; we come back again to the notion that "What is technically desirable must be physically possible."

CHAPTER FOURTEEN

Young athletes and the run up

"Many young athletes are more interested in learning to 'rock back' than improving their run up"

By now readers should be aware that the run up is a critical factor to success in the pole vault, as in all of the jumping events. Despite this, it seems that the vast majority of young athletes are far more interested in learning to 'rock back' than in improving their run up.

The coach must rapidly change this attitude for two reasons. The first, repeatedly emphasised in this book, is that every aspect of the vault after the athlete leaves the ground, depends on the effectiveness of their run, plant and take off. Unless those three elements are well developed a vaulter is unlikely to be able complete the inversion effectively and safely, no matter how hard they try.

The second is that it is much easier for an athlete to improve their run up than it is to master the inversion phase of the vault. In fact if they execute the important drills correctly, they can make major improvements to their run up on their own, without even a coach present.

The first thing to understand about the run up is that it is not a matter of how far or how fast, but HOW WELL IT IS EXECUTED! For while it is true that Bubka approached take off at speeds of just under 10m/sec, the vast majority of athletes will achieve better results by focussing on a controlled, balanced and strong position at take off, not on speed.

The keys to developing an effective run up with young athletes are
1. Controlling both the length of the run and the speed. The key word is optimum! In the context of pole vaulting, this means the shortest run up distance necessary to produce the highest possible speed which the athlete can actually control.
2. Ensuring that the run up has the correct structure. The importance of this aspect of the run up has been widely neglected.

With these points in mind we strongly recommend that coaches restrict the approach run of their young athletes. Absolute beginners can compete from eight steps while it is possible for girls to reach World Youth and World Junior qualifying heights around 3.90 metres (12'8") from twelve steps while young men can attain the

World Junior qualifier of 5.10 metres (16'8") from sixteen steps. Of course many young athletes use longer run ups but it would be interesting to study them to find out if they do indeed accelerate all the way into take off. It is the athlete's speed at take off that matters, not speed ten or even five metres out.

Because most young athletes will want to compete as soon as possible, we initially introduce a run up of eight steps. Thirteen year old girls can clear 2.20 metres (7'3") or more in their first competition from a run up off eight steps while boys are able to jump 3.00 metres (9'8").

Although twelve steps is a little too long for many youngsters to cope with, it does connect easily to the Three/Three planting action detailed in Chapter Ten. So as soon as they are ready we try to move young vaulters back to twelve steps. We use a very formal approach to developing the run up structure. This not only emphasises the importance we attach to it but also ensures that the whole exercise is carried out in a systematic progression.

The right handed athlete stands with their weight naturally balanced with both feet together and positioned comfortably apart. At this time the grip, the position of both hands and the pole angle are all checked and adjusted if necessary using the 'good way/bad way' strategy of instruction. Now the right foot is taken back as shown in the photograph of Bubka Figure 6.2. The athlete next walks six steps, counting only lefts. They then continue counting each step with an increasing cadence. The structure of the whole twelve step run up becomes -

1	2	3	1 2 3	plant23
Left	Left	Left	RLR	LRL

With plant beginning as the athlete moves into the penultimate left step.

This is the only time in our system we use the 'counting lefts' method. Apart from the fact that it has the potential to confuse left handers, it does not encourage the cadence change we believe is so important in the vault run up.

This practice is done first by numbers and very slowly to ensure that the athlete establishes the rhythm of the run up. They then progressively walk it, jog it, run it and then sprint it, all the time under control.

This approach introduces a specific structure and rhythm to the run up, which will have important benefits as the athlete develops. It encourages them to stay tall throughout the entire run and also emphasises the importance of cadence from six steps out. This encourages the athlete to attack the take off and also helps them to better control and then exploit the pole drop, when they begin to use the high carry necessary to control bigger poles.

Note also that this formal approach of **'Feet together/body and pole balanced/ take right foot back/focus/begin run up'.** has other advantages which should be emphasised from the very beginning. It eliminates the 'hop and skip' that many young athletes want to include at the start of their run up. Even more importantly, with beginners it makes the movement pattern automatic so that they are unlikely to begin their run up with the wrong foot - a not uncommon error when young athletes meet the pressure of competition for the first time!

There are many drills to improve running technique and athletes can be introduced to them gradually as they increase their training commitment. This may take up to twelve months as athletes gradually increase their training loads. These drills can be found in any text on sprinting or by watching a single training session with a good sprint coach. While young athletes may benefit from many of these drills, we emphasise three in particular because they are specifically focussed on important aspects of the run up.

It is worth noting that these drills are all 'exaggeration drills' in which the youngsters movements become almost a caricature of what they will eventually do on the vault runway. This is necessary because by the time athletes come to the vault they have been running a long time – usually ten years or more – but without a pole in their hands. Even the best natural runners must quickly learn how to run fast under control carrying the pole. Those youngsters who have never really learned to run 'properly' even without a pole will have a lot of work to do if they are to have much success in the vault – no matter what their 100 metre times say! The drills we recommend are designed to deal with the basic technical problems even some fast sprinters have and to redirect their running patterns to the needs of pole vaulting.

The first drill we use is termed 'Straight leg claws'. This is a common sprinting drill but one not valued or used nearly enough by vaulters. The critical point here is that with a long pole in front of the body the centre of mass of the vaulter/pole system moves further forward. Unless the athlete counters this shift in some way they will inevitably run nose down and off balance.

This drill, where the athlete runs with perfectly straight legs, emphasises a claw strike of the foot slightly ahead of the centre of mass. The backward 'raking pull' of the leg projects the athlete forward using the hamstring and gluteal muscles, while ensuring an exaggerated tall running posture.

The second drill, 'Ostrich runs' is an extension of the first drill. Now the athlete punches the knee/ thigh high, extends the lower leg until the whole leg is straight as in the straight leg claw drill and executes the same clawing action outlined above. This particular drill is an exaggeration of the running action of a vaulter in the initial acceleration phase of the run up.

With both of the above drills the athlete should run 30 – 50 metres. This gives them time to build up the movement pattern and running speed in the early steps and to focus on correct execution in the middle phase before easing down gradually.

The third drill we use is one of the simplest and most effective drills ever devised to improve performance in the pole vault. In fact we recommend that on the first day an athlete makes a commitment to the vault they begin to run 20/20s! In other words they must run 20 steps within 20 metres – as fast as they can! This running drill is the simplest and most effective way to improve the pole vault run up and the take off, and should be included in every training program, every week, until an athlete retires!

The twenty metre (65'6") distance should be permanently marked somewhere on the track, placed so it does not impede other athletes in training.

The right handed vaulter, with their biggest competition pole held correctly, stands with the left foot on the start line and the right foot back. Whenever they are ready they set off to complete twenty steps before they reach the twenty metre mark, running as fast as they can. They do not need to try to plant the pole. It sounds simple, and it is, once you can do it! However very few athletes will complete more than fifteen steps the first time they try this exercise, because most do not know how to control their stride length as they accelerate. Once they can execute twenty steps in twenty metres on a regular basis, time

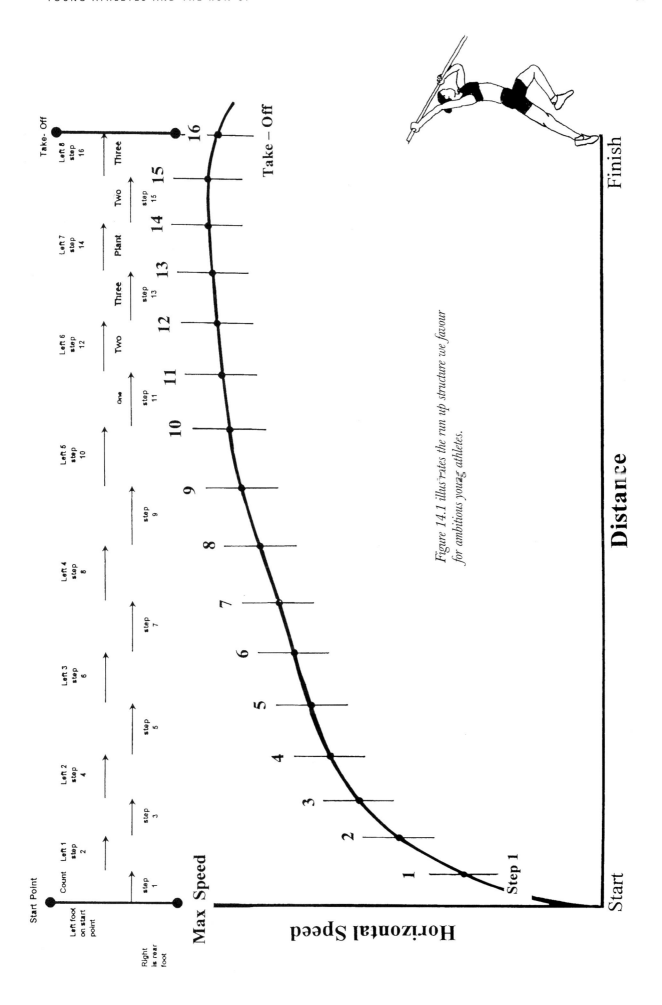

Figure 14.1 illustrates the run up structure we favour for ambitious young athletes.

them from the first movement of the right leg to ensure they are running at maximum speed and are not 'cheating' by shuffling to get the twenty steps in.

This simple running drill forces athletes to run with high knees and a controlled stride length. It is of course an exaggeration and does not represent how athletes should run at any point in their actual run up. However serious practice of this drill will cure many evils. It is especially effective in dealing with the problem of overstriding, a problem which affects many vaulters at all levels of performance. Most importantly, it forces athletes to run tall with high hips and knees and puts the vaulter into a position where they can more easily counter the forces of the dropping pole over the last six steps. Most importantly it positions them for a springing take off.

As athletes progress, it is possible to turn this into a 20/25 or even a 20/30. Many athletes will claim the 20/20 is impossible but we have had Victor Chystiakov completing it successfully and he is 6'7" tall and had previously run a flying 10.3 100 metres.

If there is time in a training program for only one running drill, vaulters should do 20/20s!

The critical elements of the 'Ostrich drill' and the '20/20 drill' are brought together in the following way. An athlete using a 16 step approach for example, stands in the correct position, steps back with the right foot and runs 10 Ostrich steps down the track. The coach positions themselves close to the point where these 10 steps will be completed. As, or even just before, the athlete completes their initial ten steps the coach shouts 'CHANGE' and the athlete must immediately change gear into the 20/20 pattern. Once these distances are established, the coach can use markers, such as hurdles, to provide a cue for the athlete to change gear. So the pattern becomes 10 powerful clawing steps and then six fast cadence steps with exaggerated high knees.

Obviously this process will take time but this practice has the great benefit of emphasising the importance of ;
• Staying tall throughout the run up.
• Running 'in front' of the body.
• Changing gear to increase cadence six steps out.
• Controlling the pole throughout the entire run

up, and especially the pole drop in the final six steps.

Gradually the exaggeration drops away until the athlete is running fast and freely – but with these important elements still clearly evident in their run up – as they are clearly shown in film of Bubka's approach run.

Coaches must drag their athletes away from the pole vault pad to do running drills, both with and without the pole to improve the run up. If they meet determined resistance to this idea, coaches may find the following approach useful.
• Have the athlete do a standing plant in the box. Use this to establish exactly where they should take off.
• Move away from the vault runway, put down a marker to indicate the start point and then ask the athlete to run and plant wherever they feel comfortable but with the aim of hitting the same spot each time. There should be no target to plant into.
• The coach stands at the take off point and discreetly marks the take off point with chalk on every attempt. Over six attempts there will almost always be considerable variation. Note the variations.
• Go back to the box and ask the athlete to position themselves in line with the variations. Then ask them what they believe the effect of those variations will be on each jump.

This will take a little time but it should convince all but the most blockheaded athletes that they need to improve their run up.

Once they are committed to the vault, athletes should do at least one set of eight to ten full pole runs every week throughout the year. Early in the preparation period this involves planting into a rolled up towel but gradually we move to a wooden triangle which simulates the plant box. We do this because **we believe that a run up has a specific rhythm.** The rhythm of a twelve step run is different from a sixteen step run. We realise that this is at variance with the approach used by many coaches from the former Soviet Union, who believe in a gradual increase in the run up throughout the training period, but it works for us.

The issue of the run up is dealt with again in Part Two.

CHAPTER FIFTEEN

The process of Technical Coaching

"Perfection is our goal, excellence will be tolerated"

J. Yahl

"Technical coaching" is the term which defines the process a coach uses to help an athlete improve their technique. It is useful to distinguish this aspect of the coach's task from 'Psychological coaching', which may also become an important part of their role as the athlete progresses.

No single element of the coach's role is as complex and difficult as the process of technical coaching. It is usually only mastered through years of reflective coaching experience with a range of athletes. However the aim of this Chapter is to provide an insight into the process of technical coaching to help inexperienced coaches fast track their understanding of this important aspect of the track and field coach's role.

Figure 15.1 shows the great guru, Vitaly Petrov, in Formia doing what he both excels at and loves.

The first point to be made is that **coaching is a 'people business'**. Every interaction between a coach and an athlete is unique and is influenced by a vast range of factors. One of the most important of these is the specific 'context' in which the coach is working. For example, while a coach working with beginners should always be supportive and encouraging, one working with an ambitious, goal directed athlete might well be

very demanding - even mere excellence is not acceptable! So while Vitaly Petrov certainly subscribes to the latter philosophy, in Adelaide we have to walk a fine line between striving for excellence and encouraging our young athletes to stay in the sport.

The second point is that **an observer usually only sees what they are expecting to see!** In addition, because it is difficult if not impossible, to really SEE every small detail of an athlete's performance when the latter is moving at full speed, **the coach must focus their observation on one or two elements.** This means that it is possible for two coaches to SEE different things in the same jump simply because they are focussing on different aspects of that performance.

The final point is that **you can only SEE when you know what to look for!** This means that you must have a firm understanding of what is really important in the vault. As a wise person once said "If everything is important, nothing is important!" The coach therefore needs a clear understanding of the event. They need an accurate 'conceptual model' or 'mind picture' of it. Next they need a 'visual model' so they that can see the event in their mind's eye. This visual model provides a template against which they can compare what they are watching. A 'verbal

Figure 15.1

model' is also important because it enables the coach to transmit their knowledge to their athletes accurately and succinctly. Finally there is an additional benefit from having a 'kinaesthetic' or 'feeling model' of the event because this enables the coach to better understand the spatial and rhythmic characteristics of pole vaulting.

The Conceptual model

The coach should have a clear 'conceptual model' of the event. This means that they should understand the biomechanical principles involved and appreciate how these principles determine effective technique. We trust that the information, knowledge and even wisdom in the preceding chapters will have helped readers to build a better conceptual model of the event. Armed with this knowledge, a coach can

- Stand above the debate which continually swirls around technique in the pole vault.
- Understand the differences between varying 'technical models'.
- Understand the difference between a 'technical' model and an athlete's unique 'style'.
- Ensure that drills are closely aligned with the technical model.
- Ensure transfer between a gymnastics program and vaulting technique.
- Understand the relative importance of various elements of conditioning.
- Be better able to objectively analyse the vast range of audio - visual materials that are available.

A Visual picture

In addition to this conceptual model, a coach needs a 'visual picture' of ideal technique in their 'minds eye'. This ideal 'picture' may be a composite of the visual images of a vast number of individual athletes or it may be of a single athlete. Fortunately the wide availability of video tapes, CDs and DVDs showing the best vaulters in the world can reduce the time necessary for coaches to build a clear visual picture of the event – after they have studied this book! However it should be emphasised again that unless they have a clear conceptual model, a coach will only 'see' a series of interesting but essentially meaningless images!

This picture of 'ideal' technique provides 'the template' against which all vaulters can be compared. It also provides the target technique of the future for every ambitious athlete and coach. **However a coach must also have a clear 'picture' of the technique of the athletes they are working with. These are the performances they must actually deal with.**

As they watch any athlete, a coach can instantly compare what they 'See' with the twin templates they carry in their mind. Again it is important to note the difference between a 'Technical model' and an athlete's personal 'Style'.

Here it is once more worth emphasising the value of working towards a single technical model. It provides a fixed template against which the performance of every athlete can be compared. Without it a coach is left trying to decide whether the variations they are seeing in an athlete's technique are having a positive or a negative impact on their performance.

As an exercise, begin to compare the figures and photographs of the athletes shown in this text with each other. Then use a stop frame system on your video player to identify the same positions; next look at the videos in slow motion and finally at normal speed. The next step is to film your own athletes and repeat the sequence.

A Verbal picture

The coach also must be able to describe the event accurately and analytically. They need a fund of cue words and phrases they can use to capture and communicate the key aspects of performance to their athletes. The best verbal cues convey an effort or rhythmic quality as well as defining the spatial elements of a specific movement pattern. Most experienced coaches have a fund of such cues and novice coaches would be well advised to borrow them at every opportunity. However there is no point in using these cues if the athlete does not know what they mean. So a coach working with a new athlete must teach them what each cue means. Examples that we have found to be effective include -

- "Run TALL"
- "Claw strike"
- "CADENCE,CADENCE, CADENCE"
- "HIT the pole with a STRONG body
- "FINISH the take off"
- "WHIP the trail leg through"
- "Drop the shoulders and DRIVE the hips"

It should be noted that this is another area where athletes who move between coaches who believe in different technical models, may become confused. In addition, different coaches often use different phrases to describe the same technical emphasis. **For the athlete it is almost like learning a new language when they work with another coach.**

Kinaesthetic awareness

There is little doubt that kinaesthetic awareness - a 'feeling picture' - of the event, is valuable to a coach. This is one of the advantages of having been a vaulter before taking up coaching. On the other hand there is always a danger that former elite athletes may become 'locked in' by their own experience, the 'what worked for me' syndrome and so rely on their own experience too much and consequently are unable to take up new ideas.

Although at a disadvantage in this area, a coach who was not a vaulter can compensate by developing their verbal skills to a high level and by learning to demonstrate as many of the key drills as possible.

The Process of technical coaching

- The coach must be able to SEE what an athlete is doing. SEEING in this sense implies that a coach first knows what to look for, as suggested above. Then they must develop and continually refine their 'COACHES EYE'. Despite the benefits that video cameras bring, what we term 'Eye Balling' is still an important element of coaching. In fact it is one of the most underestimated elements of the coaching craft. It can best be developed through reflective practice.

The coach must first get themselves into the best possible position to 'see' what they need to 'see'! The first priority is to establish the best distance and the best angles to watch from. With a right handed athlete a position 15 metres/50 feet at right angles to a point midway between take off and the bar, is usually the best. However at times it may be worthwhile watching the athlete from a position at the back of the pad or even stepping onto the runway to watch from behind. This is valuable if you suspect that the athlete is off line or off balance at take off.

These same principles apply to the video taping of training or competition. While eye balling is an important coaching skill, it has major limitations. The human brain cannot take in all the information provided in a blur of movement, even at the instant of take off. What the brain CAN assimilate is the overall rhythm and movement pattern of the athlete and up to two individual elements. Coaches must focus their observation on the specific strengths and weaknesses of the athlete they are watching. They can rely on videotape replay of the performance to confirm their original impressions and to help them 'see' elements they missed. Here a slow motion replay facility is invaluable and it is impossible to coach the pole vault effectively without using this technology.

The coach must be prepared to watch many attempts by the vaulter to identify the overall pattern of performance. This is relatively easy with a top class athlete with a stable technique, but more difficult with beginners who may vary considerably from one jump to the next.

The best time to observe an athlete analytically is during competition. This is because higher levels of arousal invariably mean an increase in the effort qualities. This may lead to an outstanding performance but may also expose technical problems or even reveal psychological blocks which have been 'papered over' in training.

Coaches need to understand that all athletes make mistakes, even Bubka, who no heighted in what was for him the most important competition of his life. At the 1992 Barcelona Olympic Games there was a huge expectation that he would become the first Gold medallist for his country, Ukraine. In fact the President of Ukraine, which had just gained its freedom from the Soviet Union, went to the trackside to give Sergey a National flag just before the competition started. Whether this contributed to his failure is difficult to assess, but it is not easy for anyone to carry the weight of one's nation on their shoulders.

Mistakes are part and parcel of every sporting endeavour, the only way to avoid them is not to take part! The important thing is, how do the athlete and the coach react to those mistakes, do they learn from them and move on? Or do they allow them to become a load of baggage which prevent the athlete from ever progressing further.

It is important for coaches to understand that even with an international calibre athlete, virtually every attempt will be different, if only slightly different. Anyone who has worked with world class throwers will immediately understand this, because even when throwers are striving for perfection the implement will rarely if ever land on the same mark. This is true in all events, because when athletes are striving for maximum performance, even the smallest variation in the spatial or rhythmic qualities of the attempt will produce a slightly different result.

Following their careful observation of the athlete the coach must;
- **Compare** what they have just seen, with the 'model' of performance in their mind's eye.

They must rapidly decide what variations there are between these two pictures

- **Decide** whether the variations between the two pictures are significant or not. This is a complex business because the coach must not only consider the 'ideal' model of performance, they must consider where 'THEIR' athlete is technically, at that point in time. Was this attempt better than the previous one or not? In what way was it better? In what way was it not as good? Where did it diverge from the model most dramatically?
- **Determine** the cause of the problem. This is the critical phase of the process; many novice coaches tend to focus on the obvious symptoms they see, instead of dealing with the root cause of a problem. Here it is important to remember the sequential and interrelated nature of the pole vault; the 'fault' a coach 'sees' is often a reflection of errors made earlier in the attempt.

This means that understanding this issue of cause and effect is critical to effective technical coaching. The pole vault does indeed begin with the first step. A small mistake here can expand into problems which have a negative impact on the whole jump. In the same way problems with control and balance anywhere in the run can lead to an off balance take off.

A poor first step can lead to - uncontrolled off balance run up - leading to a poor plant - leading to a poor take off - leading to – etc. etc.

An important CAUSE of technical problems is that the athlete is not fast enough, strong enough, flexible enough or even skilful enough to produce the required movement pattern. However remember that this is often a temporary state of affairs because fourteen year old 'seven stone weaklings', both boys and girls, will often morph into tall powerful athletes at the age of twenty without any specialised training!

- The coach must therefore determine their **coaching priorities.** Generally they should have both a short term and long term focus, depending on the time available and ability and the objectives of both coach and athlete. It is at this point that the relationship between them becomes very important because at the elite level there must be complete agreement on any changes which need to made. With inexperienced athletes the coach must take responsibility for deciding what alterations are needed and how they can best be achieved. This is no easy task!
- Now the coach establishes a coaching plan

and **'prescribes' suitable treatment.** This may simply be in the form of verbal or manual feedback or it may require a program of progressive, carefully focussed drills. Here it must be remembered that while direct instruction with appropriate cues and appropriate drills is very effective, it is important to make sure that the athlete has a clear understanding of the big picture they are aiming for.

At the elite level it may also involve a long term conditioning program to improve basic physical parameters. Occasionally it may even require assistance from a sports psychologist to remove mental blocks which have crept in.

- Improvements must be made permanent. **This will only happen with tightly focussed technical training undertaken when the athlete is physically and mentally fresh and when feedback is plentiful and accurate.** However even then, this can be a difficult task because regression will often occur when an athlete moves from their usual autonomous – automatic - performance mode back to a cognitive mode where they have to think about every aspect of technique. The phrase "Paralysis through analysis" sums this common problem up perfectly.
- Finally the coach must try to ensure the **transfer** of the 'new improved' technique into the competition arena. Again this is not always easy because as we suggested earlier the cauldron of competition will often lead to meltdown! Here a competent sports psychologist can help!

Summary

This is only an outline of the process of technical coaching but it may help intuitive coaches better appreciate what they already do well and perhaps assist novice coaches to understand one of the critical skills of coaching. As in many areas of human expertise the key to improvement is reflective practice where the coach continually analyses their own performance and strives to improve it.

'Bench coaching'

The role of the coach during competition will vary with the experience of the athlete and the importance of the competition. **With beginners and young athletes in general, competitions should be seen as an extension of the developmental process.** This means that the coach may choose to provide technical feedback on the same basis as in a training session. However they must be careful to avoid overloading the athlete with information because this is only likely to add to the problem.

As the athlete gains in confidence and experience the technical feedback may fall away completely and the coach will confine themselves to 'foot catching' and advising on pole changes and the positioning of the bar. These are factors which can be dealt with instantaneously and require no major adjustments.

Gradually athletes should be expected to take even greater responsibility for their own performance. This process can be initiated by the coach simply asking – "What did you feel/think about the jump?" As they progress, the question becomes "Do you think you need to change your pole?" "How did the run up feel?" The process becomes a partnership with the athlete gradually assuming greater responsibility and the coach providing input only when absolutely necessary, or when they are asked for it.

The process of providing technical feedback in competition is an extension of the process of technical coaching. However there is extra pressure and less time to make crucial decisions. This process is yet another aspect of coaching the pole vault which has not been publicly articulated. It involves a complex, largely intuitive analysis of many variables as the coach decides what happened and what they are going to do about it! Here "Intuition" is defined as "The distilled essence of past experience."

As always it is useful to control as many variables as possible. So before the athlete gets on the runway the coach must know -
- The stiffness of the pole the athlete is using.
- The height of their grip.
- The position of the standards.
- The weather conditions, especially the strength and direction of the wind.
- The state of the athlete's mind as they prepare to jump.

Now, placing themselves in the best possible position to watch the competition the coach prepares to watch carefully. Have someone else video taping the action because it is impossible to do both effectively! Note that different coaches choose different vantage points. We have always found that a point approximately half way between the take off point and the bar is satisfactory but many coaches choose to be at right angles to the take off point.

The coach must now call up their two visual templates. The first is the ideal technical model they carry in their mind's eye, while the second is their visual image of the athlete who is preparing to jump. Clearly the observational focus will depend on the level of the athlete. An elite athlete will already have a well developed technical model and a distinctive style which the coach knows well. All they have to do is note the slight discrepancies between what they should be seeing and what they actually can see.

Coaches working with inexperienced athletes must focus on those elements of technique that the athlete is hoping to improve during the competition. They may watch -
- The whole run up from first step to take off?
- Pole carry, acceleration rhythm, balance?
- Plant, when does it start, how well is the pole controlled?
- Take off point. Out? Under?
- Body rigid?
- Hands driven high?

They will pay special attention to the key elements which will ensure a safe experience for the athlete. Was the athlete under control through the whole attempt? Where was the take off point? Was the pole suitable? Where was the high point of the vault? What knocked the bar off!? Clearly every individual athlete will present a unique set of pictures for a coach and there are no formulae available to make the process any easier. And watching is just the start!

The coach must now process all of these variables, feed in their assessment of the jumpers run up, pole carry, plant rhythm and effort qualities (especially at the instant of the take off), the pole bend, high point of the jump, what body part hit the bar? Clearly this is no easy task.

The following template, incomplete though it is, may help inexperienced coaches.
- Conditions favourable for jumping or not?
- Modify run up. Back for tail wind, forward for head wind or cross wind.
- How did warm up go? Run up and take off point established? Athlete happy with them??
- Correct opening height?
- Correct pole choice? If you have the luxury of choosing poles.
- Standards in the right place for that pole, the weather, the athlete's psyche? Note: always aim to have the bar as far back as possible to encourage the athlete to hit the take off. Only allow the bar to be moved forward if it gives them a better chance of making a third attempt.
- Run balanced and controlled? Pole carry ok?
- Did the athlete take off on the first jump?
- Take off point ok? What changes, if any?
- Result of the first jump? Changes?
- Plant too late, too low?

- If flexible pole. Pole too soft, too stiff?
- Take off strong – full driving upjump?
- Take off leg driven back? Take off finished?
- Athlete swinging long/fast on the pole?
- Is the pole rolling forward towards the pad fast?
- Has it been compressed too much – stopping forward movement?
- Body position before the pole begins to recoil?
- Body close to the pole as it recoils?
- Bar cleared; negative or positive grip height?
- How deep did the athlete land in the pad? If shallow??? Why??

The process now moves to the questions - Which was the most critical of these issues? What must be dealt with first?

Sometimes a coach working with very inexperienced athletes may have to withdraw them from the competition if they feel that they are at risk of injury in their early attempts jumps. This is clearly a very serious decision but one which may have to be made occasionally.

As in any sporting situation there are critical moments. In pole vaulting at every level, the coach will have to deal with the following two critical moments.

The first jump!!!!
Getting it right, or at the least 'getting off', with the first jump in a competition is really important in the pole vault. This is because even a failed attempt where the athlete actually takes off and completes the jump can be immensely valuable to the coach. They can analyse the attempt, decide what the problem was and suggest changes, ie adjust the run up, stiffer/softer pole etc. On the other hand if the vaulter is not really up for that first jump and runs through without taking off, the coach misses out on critical data. Although this data may be available after the second attempt there is now only one jump left – perhaps on a pole the athlete has never used before! Any experienced coach knows what that can mean!

The "Run through"!!!!
This is one of the most common and frustrating problems in vaulting. The cause can be as simple as major wind change a few steps out or it can be the result of deep seated problems in technique. While the latter will only be resolved through intensive work to improve the run up, pole carry and plant, many other problems can be dealt with through a simple process of refocussing.

One of the many challenges a coach will face is to teach athletes that they cannot expect miracles or magic from their coach – at least not immediately. One problem is that if youngsters fail in an attempt, they usually expect instant feedback about what happened and what they must do to clear the bar on the next jump. One of the tasks of the coach is to help them to understand that there is plenty of time to think things through, perhaps to talk back and forth, to compare notes, before a decision is made about what changes – if any - are needed as the athlete prepares for the next attempt.

This is where the coaching becomes a mix of science and art. Not only must the coach resolve complex technical issues, they must often reduce these to a single sentence which contains the essence of what the athlete should focus on for the next jump. With very experienced athletes this can become a brief interchange of ideas/feelings but with inexperienced athletes it may be a specific direction as to what they must now aim to do. Remember that here the coach is a teacher so that any comments should be positive and to the point. There is no point in berating the athlete or giving them a lecture on what they did wrong. Empathy and understanding should precede any advice, and especially any critical comments!

Summary

This aspect of the coaches role is one of the most difficult yet at the same time the most important of all the coaching processes. It is where science, in the form of a thorough knowledge of the event, and art, in the form of intuition, come together. The critical ability is that of being able to sift through the mass of data pouring into the brain and establish the critical facts about what the athlete is doing. The process of observation and analysis, along with a little guesswork must be executed rapidly so that the coach can quickly provide the athlete with the feedback – and the reassurance they are looking for.

This process of technical coaching has rarely been articulated despite its importance in effective coaching. As the Patrick O'Brian quote at the front of the book states *What a pity that an art so important .... should be so held by it's possessors that it cannot improve but must die with each individual*.

CHAPTER SIXTEEN

Training for developing young vaulters

"Reculer pour mieux sauter"

French proverb

The training program for any specific athlete will depend on a vast range of factors. This means that we can only provide the barest of guidelines for coaches to follow. For example we believe that absolute beginners should simply follow the pattern recommended in Chapter Ten. That should be their 'training', nothing else is required!

However we recognise that the combination of a determined and talented young athlete with an ambitious coach may well lead them down a path of almost professional training early on in the athlete's career. We would caution that developing bodies can only handle a limited amount of stress and that the repetitive drills needed to develop pole vaulters can place heavy demands on specific areas, especially the lower back, knees and ankles.

In Adelaide we ask beginners to make a commitment for only one training session a week for a minimum of six weeks. After this period both the coach and athlete have a good idea whether the youngster will continue. If they are going to persist we try to get them to continue to commit to one session a week until their first major competition but encourage them to increase it to two or even three sessions if they can manage it.

From that point, training depends on the commitment the athlete is prepared to make. In this way the number of training sessions, their volume and their intensity gradually evolves depending on what they want to do. Most of the youngsters who come to the pole vault in Adelaide are also involved in other sports so they usually have little time to commit. In fact those with the greatest potential are usually very talented in other sports and have often reached high standards. We simply point out their potential in the pole vault and try to support this 'sell', by highlighting their performances in standardised field tests. It is worth noting that the ideal candidates for the vault are either young long jumpers or high jumpers with a gymnastics background, or conversely, gymnasts who have grown too tall for their sport - but who are also reasonable sprinters.

One of the great things about the pole vault is that young athletes with average athletic talent but a great determination to succeed, can find their place in this event and indeed go on to achieve surprising success.

While we appreciate that in other coaching situations, coaches may place much higher demands on their athletes, we have found that giving youngsters this freedom and flexibility works well for us. It has clearly not prevented many of our group from attaining good levels of performance at National and International level.

Once they make a commitment to become pole vaulters the number of sessions gradually increases from two sessions a week at the age of fourteen, three a week at 15 and 16 and then up to six sessions a week for 17 and 18 year old athletes hoping to win a National Title or gain selection for a National junior team. In this approach the number of sessions an athlete can undertake will determine the priority given to various aspects of training.

With one session a week the emphasis is on pole vaulting, either with drills or jumping over a soft bar from a short run and using a 'working model' of technique.

With two sessions a week it is possible to add running training aimed specifically at improving the pole vault run up. This can be organised as one session of vaulting and one of running or as two sessions which include both elements which is what we prefer.

Three sessions a week gives even more flexibility. In the competition season the three sessions can be focussed as one on the vault, one on running drills and the run up and training in related events such as long jumping, high jumping, hurdling and sprinting. At the end of all three sessions the athlete will often complete power training or technical work in the outside gymnasium we have created.

In the off season, vault training should focus on the improvement of technique through carefully focussed drills. It is also possible to include gymnastics or weight training, depending on the facilities and expertise available. It should be noted that gymnastics is not critical to the development of young athletes. Indeed we regard it as a useful variation in a gradually escalating commitment to training and believe that the strength and power training which is a concomitant of gymnastics training can be more important than the gymnastic activities themselves. The problem is that regulation gymnastics activities are not closely related to pole vaulting so there is little direct transfer of training. However when athletes are ready to move to the inversion phase of the vault, specific gymnastic activities can help them develop the body awareness essential in this phase of the vault.

Given a choice we would prefer to work on a rope or a high bar because there it is possible to do exercises which are directly related to the whip phase of the pole vault. Parallel bars can be used to develop the shoulder drop/hip drive phase of the vault.

When an athlete is ready to make a 'full' commitment to the pole vault they are expected to train up to six sessions a week. This will include a minimum of two sessions dedicated to the vault, one session of gymnastics and three general sessions involving high bar work, rope work, running with and without a pole, specific hurdling drills, long jumping, and plyometrics. However the exact mix will depend on the strengths and weaknesses of the athlete and the time of the year. Since we train year round the weather can have a major impact on our priorities because we have no indoor training area. The only technical change we make at this point is to increase an athlete's run up to sixteen steps.

General training

Every youngster who makes a commitment to the sport should be encouraged to adopt a healthy lifestyle. Naturally this should include plenty of varied exercise. Prospective pole vaulters should be encouraged to begin a simple training regime of body resistance exercises. This can include sit ups and press ups, both of which can easily be 'loaded' to produce a greater training effect. For example the press up can be executed with the feet raised higher and higher until press ups in the hand stand position are employed, clap hands press ups can be used which can be done at home, along with chins and rope climbing if facilities are available. In fact we would recommend that any serious vaulter should have a high bar and a rope installed at home as soon as possible.

If, as in the United States, youngsters are only permitted to be formally involved in track and field for limited periods of the year, other sports such as Basketball and Volleyball can provide

excellent cross training effects for the pole vault. In fact our policy is to encourage our youngsters to have a broad based sporting experience, until the athlete is forced to specialise if they want to achieve specific goals in the sport.

Once athletes have committed to the vault at the age of seventeen or eighteen and are committed to training for six sessions a week, it is worthwhile planning three of four separate and distinct blocks of training in a year. The competition block is set by external factors which vary from country to country. So while the main outdoor competition period in the Northern Hemisphere is usually between April and September, in Australia and New Zealand it runs from November to March. This creates particular problems for athletes from those countries who are preparing to compete internationally, since most major competitions are usually held in the Northern Hemisphere.

The balance of training throughout the year is determined by the timing of the competition period. Once that is set, it is easy to see the need for a rest and recuperation block following the competition period. This period of between four and eight weeks, depending on the goals of the athlete, should be a period of active rest where the athlete stays away from the pole vault but continues with a broad based sports and recreational program. Naturally this is the best time to deal with the inevitable niggling injuries before serious training begins again.

The other two training blocks are also easy to understand. At the conclusion of the active rest block, the most important phase of training for young athletes should begin. This is the period when weaknesses in technique or physical preparation can be dealt with. Problems which had to be ignored during the competition block because of the need to prepare for the next meet, can now be analysed and rectified.

The emphasis should swing back to the development or reinforcement of the fundamental elements of technique through;
- Hundreds of short approach vaults from 2,4,6 and 8 steps.
- Bar and rope work.
- Weight training.
- Plyometrics.
- Running and sprinting over various distances and speeds.
- Continued practice of the approach run the athlete intends to use in the coming season.

The fourth training block bridges the gap between the heavy basic training of this rebuilding block and the competition period. Now the volume of training drops across the whole range of training while the quality and intensity goes up. Early in this block the majority of serious vaulting is done from eight and twelve steps, but as time passes this changes to vaulting from twelve steps and the full run up. Naturally the number of full vaults any athlete can take in one session is limited so this is where the year round emphasis on the run up will pay off.

This is a period when the athlete should be vaulting with a soft bar set thirty to forty centimetres above their best of the previous season – and always at the maximum distance back! Three to four weeks before the competition period begins the athlete can try a 'Three Jump competition'. Still using a soft bar, the athlete simply takes three jumps at a bar well below their personal best, the bar is moved up and three more jumps are taken. A fail is recorded if the athlete touches the bar - no matter how softly but they still take three jumps at every height. This continues until the athlete has completed up to eighteen jumps. This practice has many advantages. It builds confidence, develops consistency, provides athletes with a chance to assess their improvement, gives them a chance to work up through a range of poles and of course gives the coach an opportunity to suggest adjustments and to refine the training program as the first competition nears.

Finally there is a need for the athlete to get used to the regulation bar. The first try could use the 'Three jump' competition approach while the final training competition would be with both regulation bar and rules. Here it may be worth pointing out that in Adelaide we rarely use the regulation bar in training because with large numbers of athletes vaulting at the same time, continually putting the bar up after it has been knocked off wastes an immense amount of time. Even when working with only one athlete, if that athlete is jumping at a bar set at 6.00 metres, the effort and time wasted in replacing the bar is enormous.

Drills to develop the pole vault

In Chapter Eleven we detailed how the pole vault can be taught simply and easily using a sequence of progressive 'drills', which gradually lead the novice towards the real event. These drills reduce both the complexity and the potential danger of learning to pole vault and give learners the opportunity to build confidence as they develop a sound technique.

However, 'drills 'are an important component of training at every level of performance and one of the tasks novice coaches face is determining which drill to use from the hundreds employed by coaches around the world. **The French proverb above can be literally translated as "Go backwards so that you can jump further".** This captures the nature of training in the pole vault, because athletes must always be prepared to revisit the basic drills and re emphasise the fundamental elements of good technique if they wish to improve.

It is important to understand that there are no 'magic' drills which will solve every problem a vaulter may have. Nor are there very special drills that only elite athletes can or do use. In fact some very important drills are simply extensions of the practices used to teach the event. For example the two step, four step and six step stiff pole drills used in the very first session are included in the training program of many of the world's best vaulters.

Drills have many advantages. They can be used to isolate specific elements of technique and so allow the vaulter to concentrate fully on achieving perfection in that element or to eradicate a fault which has crept in during the season. Because they are, or should be, simpler than the real vault, they can be used to help the athlete build, or even rebuild, their confidence. If athletes are going to gain full value from the use of drills coaches should observe the following principles -

- Drills are a means to an end, not an end in themselves.
- There should be a close relationship between the drill and the technical model aimed for.
- Drills must always have a specific objective.
- The athlete must clearly understand this objective.
- The athlete must understand the relationship between the drill and entire vault.
- The athlete must strive for perfect execution.
- There is continual and logical progression.
- There must be a balance between drills and 'real' vaulting.
- Good drills are simple and easy for the athlete to learn.

Finally it is worth emphasising the KISS rule. The maxim "Keep it simple, stupid" is good advice here as in many other walks of life. There is no point in teaching athletes a complex training drill which takes a lot of time and effort to learn; it would be far more useful just letting them jump at a bar.

With these guidelines in mind it should be possible for coaches to pick from the vast range of drills used by other coaches or which they will find detailed in various books and articles. In Adelaide we have been very selective. With limited time at

Figure 16.1

our disposal and often with large numbers of young athletes training we have had to adopt a tight rational approach to drills and so keep the above points in mind when selecting them. We have found that the following, very limited, selection to be effective, especially when combined with specific high bar, rope and gymnastic exercises.

Because of the need to save time and the importance of continually reviewing basic elements of technique, we continue to emphasise the 2 step, 4 step and six step stiff pole drills we used to teach the event. Because of their importance in our program we are repeating the Figure which shows Patrick Jesser executing this drill and illustrating the important aspects of technique we focus on. Figure 16.1 Athletes work through these drills in the sand pit first because the ease of planting enables them to take off more 'freely'. As before it is important that the grip is continually pushed up to ensure greater control and to emphasise the importance of an upspringing take off. After six to eight attempts in the sand athletes repeat the same sequence on the pad.

We also repeat the six and eight step approach practices with a pole which can be made to flex. These were detailed in Chapter Eleven. They are carried out on the vault runway with the athlete landing on the pad.

In both sets of drills it is important to focus on each important element in sequence. Once this has been completed the coach can then concentrate on those elements which are really holding back an athlete's development.

Another simple drill we use has the athlete running from six steps to take off strongly in an attempt to brush their top hand against a soft bar stretched between an old set of high stands. This bar can be angled so that athletes of differing abilities can use it at the same time. The objective is to give coach and athlete a slightly more objective picture of the take off and planting action.

Coaches may find the 'Six' drill useful, especially if they have to deal with large numbers of athletes at the same time. We find it useful to have the athletes work in pairs with one performing and one observing to provide feedback. In this situation both youngsters gain.

The 'Six' Drill

With the correct grip and with the pole held at the correct angle the athlete positions themselves as if they were going to begin their approach run. They do not move until the correct position is established. They then walk six steps with the pole in the correct carry position.

Then six steps steadily lowering the pole keeping the left hand high.

Then six steps with the hands punched high with tip down

Then six steps with both hands driven high, pole parallel with the ground.

They then repeat this sequence while 'trotting' with a 'tall' body and high knees.

Repeat while running with high knees and an active claw/strike of each foot.

The advantage of this drill is that it gives young athletes a chance to hold a specific position for a period long enough for them to appreciate the difference between the right position and movement and the wrong one and to make necessary adjustments. It also gives the coach a chance to carefully observe and provide feedback. Remember that the good way/bad way method of providing feedback can be very productive.

We do not TEACH our young athletes the very popular rock back drill, although over time most of them mastered it. For example Figure 16.2 shows another talented young South Australian athlete David Cardone completing a swing to inversion. David, now an MD, specialising in anaesthetics, is typical of the young athletes of Australia who are forced to choose between their sport and their career.

Instead we encourage our young athletes to develop the inversion phase of the vault by jumping over a steadily raised bar. There are several reasons for this.

Figure 16.2

1. In the first place learning the rock back drill – as a drill - takes time which could be better spent on other practice.
2. It is very easy to learn to do this drill badly! Not only does this waste time, it encourages athletes to develop bad habits. They become so keen to show that they are 'real' pole vaulters, because real vaulters can 'rock back', that young vaulters
   - **often use a low grip which allows them to rotate back fast,**
   - **but which ensures they are 'pulled off the ground' instead of executing the driving take off essential for effective vaulting.**
   In the future this can lead to major problems because they never learn to take off properly and the early attempt at inversion usually means the pole will stall instead of rolling forward.
3. Jumping at a bar is much more enjoyable and productive and by using poles of gradually increasing stiffness athletes naturally learn to invert – as a natural consequence of doing everything right off the ground.

Gymnastics and the pole vault

If time is not an issue, vaulters can include many hours of gymnastics in their program. Even when there is no direct relationship between the gymnastics activities and the pole vault these exercises can contribute to the development of power and flexibility, especially with young athletes. There is little doubt that a broad based gymnastic program can

also contribute to the vaulters kinaesthetic awareness and body control. Bubka attributes his improvement in the final phases of the vault to the work he did with a specialist gymnastics coach. Our advice is to try to build a relationship with a gymnastics coach because this is a sport in its own right and few pole vault coaches can hope to master both sports. That said, the more a vault coach can be involved, even as a spectator in gymnastics sessions, the better they will see the relationships between the two.

As suggested in the introduction, both Isinbyeva, Feofanov and Balokonova also had strong gymnastic backgrounds and this showed in their ability to exploit the recoil of the pole. In Adelaide almost all of our young female vaulters came to the event after a time in gymnastics. On the other hand, none of our male vaulters came to vaulting with any experience in gymnastics and even when exposed to a program geared specifically to vaulting, most generally used the opportunity to be typical adolescent males!

The fact is that like many coaches around the world we do not have the luxury of time. So, as with all aspects of our program we had to make efficient use of this vital commodity. So first we build an outside 'gymnasium' next to the track to make it easy for young athletes to do some of the exercises of critical importance to good vaulting. This facility was developed almost single handedly by one of our dedicated coaches, John Hamman in his 'spare' time. Figure 16.3 shows John in front of the the outdoor gym he created.

Figure 16.3

Our second solution was to focus tightly on those exercises which had the highest correlation with the vault either in terms of technique or of power development. The list is a small one, but one which can make an immense contribution to the development of young athletes. This is especially the case when these exercises are integrated with the vault program and the relationships between them are continually pointed out to the athletes.

Readers may remember that we pointed out the place of some of these exercises in the learning program in Chapters Eleven and Twelve, they will be mentioned again in Chapter Twenty Four. In addition, these tech-nical exercises have a valuable specif-

Figure 16.5

ic conditioning effect. In the first exercise, from a long hang position on the high bar, the athlete swings up with flexed legs to touch their shins on the bar in a series of repetitions Figure 16.4; in the second they swing the body up with straight legs, Figure 16.5. This is clearly a difficult exer-cise and most vaulters will have to develop their abdominal strength through the first exercise before moving on to the second.

Peaking

One of the critical aspects of a good training pro-gram is sound planning to ensure that an athlete is ready to compete at their best in the most important competitions of the year. The athlete must be physically, technically and psychologi-

cally ready for a specific and limited period. This not an easy task but a vital one for athletes hop-ing to compete for medals at International or even National level. In fact the complexity is such that it may take experience over successive years to get it right – this is where keeping a training/competition diary is important.

Critical questions are
- What base has the athlete established?
- What kind of training should be undertaken in the four weeks before the first competition?
- How long is the competition program?
- How many competitions does the athlete need to reach absolute top form?
- How long can top form be maintained?
- How do you ensure that absolute top form is produced on **the** day?

Figure 16.4

The dilemma in the pole vault is that it makes very high demands on the neuromuscular system and can thus be very stressful. It also takes a num-ber of serious competitions for the athlete to stabilise every element of their technique and, most important-ly to determine the most effective grip height and the stiffness of the poles they can use.

Even when they are 'ready' they can get it wrong. For example at the 2001 World Championships in Edmonton, Dimitri Markov, an experienced com-petitor at world level, found himself having to borrow a pole from an oppo-nent to make his final clearances! He had moved beyond the biggest pole in his own bag. In the 2004 Games in Athens a shortage of poles possibly cost him a chance of an Olympic Title. However this time the problem was because the poles he needed were held up in transit to Athens. Even when the athlete does everything 'right' fate can step in!

Perhaps the most important concept is to REDUCE training loads to ensure that there is no stressful training over the last ten to 14 days before a major competition. Ironically this is precisely the period when many young athletes start training seriously.

CHAPTER SEVENTEEN

Conditioning for developing athletes

"What is technically desirable must be physically possible."

Launder 2002

With an event like the pole vault it is easy, perhaps understandable, for coaches to become obsessed with technique. However they must always remember that the great vaulter is not only highly skilled but also superbly conditioned, for the pole vault demands all round physical ability. It should be no surprise to learn that some of the great vaulters in history also had outstanding potential in the decathlon, nor that great decathletes are usually good vaulters.

For example Bob Richards, the Olympic Pole Vault Champion in 1952 and 1956, was also a three time American Champion in the Decathlon. In more recent times the American athlete Tim Bright moved from the decathlon to the vault with considerable success as did Alexander Averbukh of Israel, the 1999 World Championship silver medallist. Lawrence Johnson, World Indoor Champion in the vault in 2001, was also a very promising young decathlete. However even more significantly, early in his career it was suggested to Bubka that he should switch from the vault to the decathlon – fortunately he declined!

Like the decathlete, the good vaulter must be able to run, jump and throw. They also need great core strength to withstand the immense forces at take off, and to ensure that they can maintain the rigid body essential for transferring the kinetic energy generated in the run up efficiently into the pole. The vaulter also needs the body awareness of a gymnast as they interact with the pole after take off.

While an effective training program for an elite athlete must address all of these issues, the conditioning of a pole vaulter should first be based on the development of running speed, all round power, core strength and specific jumping ability. One of the biggest challenges facing a coach, is to determine the balance of a training program for any given athlete. There are no fixed formulae. The coach must call on their experience, expertise and intuition to determine the exercise and training loads each athlete needs

- At that specific point in their development
- At that point in the training cycle.

Ambitious coaches should discuss these important issues with other coaches at every opportunity.

So while a beginner in our system will do no specific conditioning work until we feel they are hooked, an Olympic calibre athlete may follow an intensive training program which will include many different elements of conditioning. As we suggested in Chapter 14, which deals with the process of technical coaching, every athlete has differing short term and long term needs. The coach must determine the training priorities for each athlete on the basis of many variables. These include their life/study/work commitments, their chronological age, their athletic age, their performance level and potential, the time available for training and the timing of their next important competition.

The principles of training

The first principle is that hard training does not necessarily bring success! In fact hard training, especially at the wrong time in the overall preparation cycle, can lead to a dramatic fall in performance. This is because hard training shocks and stresses the system.

Coaches must understand the notion of general stress. Modern life alone can be stressful; add the stress of study, especially during examination and assessment periods, of work and of personal relationships. It is easy to see that there can be a cumulative effect. Pile on hard training and/or tough competition and the level of stress can escalate to the point where it can lead to illness and injury, not merely poor performance. There must be careful planning to balance the training load with appropriate recovery and restoration sessions.

An additional stress on athletes of the highest level is the demands placed on them by sponsors and other interested parties. Bubka alluded to this in a presentation he gave at an IAAF Congress. He indicated that the situation arose when he had to use a sports psychologist to help him find the right balance between the many demands being placed on his time and his commitment to his sport.

Therefore the coach must balance out three forms of training

- Developmental training

- Maintenance training
- Recovery training

In the preparation of pole vaulters one of the critical issues is the balance between training with the pole, in all its forms, and conditioning. In South Australia we have been witnesses to, and sometimes involved in, a debate about the relative importance of these two elements. In our view one must never lose sight of the big picture, performance in competition in the pole vault. Everything else is a means to that end!

While each experienced coach will have their own philosophy of training they must never lose sight of this fact. Sometimes their own experiences as an athlete will influence their coaching philosophy as may the context in which they coach. For example Miro Zalar, coach of Patrik Kristianson of Sweden, does not include gymnastics in his program partly because most of his athletes already had a good background but also because facilities for training in gymnastics were limited in Sweden, where he was based.

Developmental training

Development training must 'shock' the system because it takes a very high workload to produce significant physical adaptation. This is where the term 'overload' becomes important. So –

- There must be a gradual increase in training volumes.
- The intensity is increased while the volume is decreased.
- The overall training load should be progressively increased.
- The training effect will depend on the quantity and intensity of the work done.
- Stable continued progress will require the repetition of the same exercises over an extended period.
- A range of exercises must be used to spread the training load.
- Speed and power should be emphasised when the athlete is fresh.

Technical training should ONLY be undertaken when the athlete is fresh. This is especially important when major changes need to be made to the athlete's technique.

Maintenance Training

Maintenance training involves lower volume and much lower intensity. This is because maintaining fitness levels is far less demanding than building them. By the time that athletes begin maintenance training they have already been in serious and often intense training for some months. It is essential to have a large variety of exercises to maintain interest and commitment.

The volume of technical training will increase; once again Speed and Power should be emphasised only when the athlete is fresh.

Appropriate recovery and restoration sessions

There is little doubt that this is one of the weakest aspects of 'Western' training methods.

Recuperation is often not viewed as an integral element of 'Training', but rather as an optional extra to be undertaken when injury or bad weather prevents 'real' training. At the highest level of performance recuperation must be given a high priority. Athletes must have access to spa, sauna and massage because restoration sessions must be given the same importance in the program as other aspects of training.

General exercises

Because of the nature of our program, conditioning as a separate activity is only gradually added as young athletes begin to commit more time to training. Running and jumping with a pole for sixty minutes or more is in itself a worthwhile whole body conditioning session.

As we suggested earlier, the place and importance of conditioning gradually evolves. First the warm up period is slowly extended; this is done by increasing the number of exercises, adding a range of running drills and then merging the physical warm up with the technical warm up. This also gradually expands with a gradually increasing range of exercises and drills with a pole. In our system, as soon as it is clear that young athletes have made a commitment to the vault they begin to extend their warm up with simulation drills with the pole. It should be noted that a visit to Formia will confirm that some of the best athletes in the world continue this pattern of planting drills from six or eight steps, first walking, then jogging, trotting and running. Initially they should be done with a simulated take off, but gradually include an increasingly powerful take off until the athlete is springing into the air to land on the free leg – before the pole tip is allowed to touch the track!

These simulation exercises combine basic technical development with the warm up which gradually extends into conditioning as the number of repetitions and the intensity of the work gradually increases.

Speed

Because of the intense neuromuscular demands,

pure speed can only developed through carefully planned and executed training. In essence it is only possible to sprint at maximum speed for less than four seconds. Training must therefore involve short bursts of sprinting and long recovery periods. The recommended pattern involves 6 – 8 repetitions of distances of 40 – 60 metres in the pre competition period and 20 –30 metres during the competition period with recoveries of between 3 to 5 minutes. 'Ins' and 'outs' are a popular variation. Here the athlete accelerates over a distance of 40 metres to hit a check mark, from here they sprint flat out for 30 – 40 metres, they then back off for forty metres before accelerating again to top speed for another 30 metres after which they gradually decelerate. After a 5 – 8 minute recovery they repeat this sequence once or twice.

While extensors of the knees and ankle are important it is the hip extensors that are critical to the athlete in the acceleration and top speed phases. It is vital to ensure that movement quality does not deteriorate as speed increases.

Other training modes

Clearly resistance training with low repetitions and high intensity can provide the strength base for the speed strength needed in sprinting. This can be done through a wide range of methods but as suggested below we still favour training with free weights. Other possibilities include
- Weighted vest running.
- Uphill running.
- Towing training.
- Water training.
- Plyometrics.

Young, ambitious vaulters must commit a considerable percentage of their training time to improving both maximum sprinting speed and optimum run up speed.

Both are highly 'technical' activities, so tightly focussed training is mandatory if worthwhile improvement is to occur. Remember that the challenge is to do simple things extraordinarily well.

Strength and Power

Although these are distinct aspects of fitness for the vault there is considerable overlap in the training methods for both. In the pole vault, power, which is a combination of strength and speed, is generally the dominant factor. However strength, pure isometric strength IS critical at the instant of take off.

The critical concept here is "Progressive resistance training" because strength can be developed

in many ways, not merely through the use of weight training. It will depend on the age, experience and performance level of the athlete involved as well as the coaching context, especially the facilities and equipment available.

Depending on these factors, a coach can choose from a range of activities. These include
- Gymnastics
  An all round gymnastics program may well be the best option for younger athletes if facilities and coaching expertise permit. In any case every coach should try to create a training area near their vault facility which should include a high bar, parallel bars and if possible a rope.
- Simple exercises using the bodyweight as the resistance.
  Examples include Press ups, chin ups, sit ups, hand stands, hand walking and various body bridging exercises.
- Medicine ball exercises especially in combination with a Swiss ball.
- Swiss ball exercises, properly and intensely executed, can make a major contribution to the development of core strength.
- Plyometrics. Even simple exercises like the standing long jump can be a valuable training exercise/field test for young athletes. However there are a vast range of jumping exercises which can be employed to develop leg power; any triple jump coach will have a fund of them.
- Weight training. This is the best, perhaps only way to obtain significant strength gains. With the 'commercialisation' of strength training many institutions have replaced their free weights with very expensive Variable Resistance or Accommodating Resistance machines. Despite the blandishments of the producers of this equipment, this is a mistake in our view. Free weights are better for producing sport specific strength and also power, especially when based around the dynamic lifts of Cleans, Jerks and Snatches.

Flexibility

Flexibility or suppleness as it is often called, is an important but undervalued component of fitness for pole vaulting. Apart from the importance of flexibility in minimising injuries in many aspects of training, shoulder flexibility can be critical to avoiding injuries at take off.

Endurance

While endurance would not appear to be important in this event it must be gradually improved as a vaulter develops. Mature athletes may be involved in long drawn out competitions on a regular basis during the competition season. While most athletes will build endurance naturally through extended jumping sessions in the pre season, those preparing to compete at the highest level may want to include specific endurance training in the early preparation phase of the training cycle. This could involve cross country running, Fartlek training or sessions of 8 –10 repetition runs of up to 200 metres both with and without the pole.

Cross training

Track and Field coaches should never forget that many other sports can contribute to the development of these physical qualities. There is a long tradition of general sport training in Europe. Alan will never forget a soccer game played by two teams of athletes in over thirty centimetres (one foot) of snow on the pitch adjoining the Warsaw University indoor training centre in January 1979! Basketball, European Handball and especially Volleyball are also superb activities for athletes during the preparation period as they introduce variety and fun while contributing to the development of aspects of fitness.

The broad nature of the training program of an elite pole vaulter is well illustrated by that of the late **Tadeus Slusarski** of Poland -1976 Olympic Champion – which is detailed below. Note that this is only provided to show the range of training a committed elite pole vaulter may undertake. It is not a program recommended for all athletes!

- Weightlifting Squat, clean and jerk, snatch, bench press, pull over, jumps with weight, fast jerk.
- Abdominal exercises. Scissors, leg raises, trunk raises, leg raises with medicine ball when hanging. In set – 10 repetitions: with ball 3 – 5 repetitions.
- Shot, Medicine ball exercises. Over the head forward, backwards, from right and left side, like hammer/from chest with half squat. Regular shot put left and right hand.
- Knee drills. High knee/low knee x 40 repetitions/ Goose steps 20 reps
- Special PV strength/Gymnastic apparatus. 4 different exercises on the rope. High Bar pull over after experiments to hand stand position; some on rings.
- Speed
- 20 – 60 metres with 20m run up with full speed; longer rest. No more than 30 metres together.

- Speed endurance. Once a week 100 – 200 metre runs, mostly as second accent of session. During competition season, 150 metres 2 times a week.
- Other kinds of running. On every work out 6 –10 strides and run compulsory easy technically 80 – 100 metres.
- Fartlek. Once a week in woods or park. Combination jogging, distance running, 100 –200 m, Jumping.
- PV technical elements. Plant every place when walking. Plant and take off when moving. Pop ups on pit, long jump with pole. Plant, rock back, extension.
- PV jumps with short, medium approach. With the bar at 80cm. Use elastic bar, "Bungy".
- PV jumps with full approach. Stands at 80cm to increase penetration.
- Acrobatics. Rolls, somersaults forward and backward on pit, flick - flack, trampoline.
- Hurdle drills. 6 Hurdles. Lead left/trail leg drills. Smaller hurdles 8/8, 5 metres apart – run three steps between.
- Jumping, bouncing drills. Jumping on grass, hopping, bouncing over 6 hurdles with different heights and distances. Long jumping.
- Sprint starts. Without blocks from different start positions. Regular starts with blocks x 10.
- Games. Basketball, soccer, volleyball x 20 minutes.

Bubka's training

The following is a SAMPLE week of Bubka's training; April 4 – 10 in 1988. Again the same comments apply; this is just a sample of the range of training Bubka did and only represents an example for a particular period in his training year. Not only would the nature and intensity of his training vary considerably during the year but it changed as he developed from a promising young athlete into the World Record holder with immense demands being placed on his time both as an athlete and as a significant sportsman.

Monday AM
1. 1 km jogging
2. 12 minutes exercises
3. Strength
    4x4 x 100kg clean
    4x4 x squat jumps x 25 kg
4. Technique
    Imitation exercises
    4 x Jagodin x 4 strides x 4 m grip x rigid pole
    6 x roll back x 6 strides x 4 m grip x rigid pole

4 x run up x 16 strides
4 x Jagodin x bent pole x 16 strides x 5 m grip
10 x total run up x 5.00m / 93 kg pole

Monday PM
1. 0.4 km jogging
2. 8 min exercise
3. Coordination
   Approx 300 m x 2 x 10m bounding; x 2 x 10m knee lifts
   2 x 10m resistance runs
   Vertical take off exercises. 4 x 40m take off with weights
   4 x 40 m take off with pole, 4 x 20 metres vertical jumps, 4 x 15m one leg jumps
4. Running
   4 x 100m x 12.5 seconds

Tuesday Rest
Swimming

Wednesday AM
1. One Km jogging
2. 12 Minutes exercises
3. Strength
   4 x 4 100 kg clean
   4 x 6 squat jumps x 25 kg
4. Technique
   4 x Jagodin x rigid pole x 4 strides x 3.85m grip
   3 x Jagodin x rigid pole x 4 strides x 4.10m grip
   6 x roll back x rigid pole x 6 strides x 4.10 grip
   12 x full run up x 5.00m/93kg x 5.00 grip

Wednesday PM
1. 0.4 km jogging
2. 8 min exercises
3. Jumping
   Approx. 200 horizontal and vertical jumps
   4 x 40m ankle jumps
   4 x 40m bounding
   4 x 40m resistance runs
   2 x 40m take off with resistance
   4 x 40m alternate jumps
   4 x 15m one leg bounding
4. Running
   6 x 100m "Ins and outs"
   25 x 25 m x 80/90% effort x 2 min rest.

Thursday AM
1. 2 hours gymnastics general preparation
   4 x 10m bounding
   12 x10m rolling forwards

Flying roll backwards into handstand with stretched arms
Floor
4 x rolls bwd/somersault fwd.
4 x backwards somersault
4 x flick flak in series
4 x Auerbach
Rings
4 x Swing into handstand
Trampoline
6 x somersault forwards – bend /stretched
4 x somersault with half and full turn
2 x double somersault
2 x somersault, forwards turn
Somersault backwards
Vaulting horse
2 x flip over from handstand
6 cartwheels
1 Tsukahara
Rings
4 x swinging into handstand
Parallel bars
4 x upwards swing into handstand
2. Strength
   3 x 4 hangs on rope with 15kg weight
   2 x 4m rope climbing- straight arms – 35kg weight
   2 x 6 reach overs with 40kg
   2 x 6 rope climbs with 35kg weight

Friday AM
1. 1 km jogging
2. Exercises
3. Technique
   2 x Jagodin rigid pole x 4 strides x 3.85 grip
   2 x Jagodin rigid pole x 6 strides x 4.15 grip
   2 x roll back rigid pole x 6 strides x 4.15 grip
   16 x full run up x 520/95 x 5.05 grip
4. Strength
   4 squat jumps from bent knees x 8 reps weights 80/100/120/140kg

PM
1. 30 minutes soccer
2. 200 horizontal and vertical jumps
   4 x 40m bounding
   4 alternate jumps
   4 x 40m hops
   4 x 20m one legged jumps
3. Running
   Pyramid work 100/150/200/150/100 with 3 to 4 min rest

Saturday AM
1. 2 hours gymnastics, general preparation
    10 mins running
    Fwd rolls
    Bwd rolls
    Back somersault
    5 x fwd somersaults
    5 x flick flak
    Auerbach
    Rings
    6 x upwards swing into handstand
    Trampoline
    6 x fwd somersault
    4 x fwds somersault with half and full rotation
    4 x Takahara
    Vaulting horse
    8 x handstand and sideways somersault
2. Strength
    4 x 3 handstands on rings with 10kg weight
    3 x rockback from L position on rings with 15 kg weight
    3 x 8 rockback on rings from pendulum with 15 kg weight
    3 x 4 metres rope climb with 15kg weight

PM
  Sauna

Sunday
  Rest

Note that this is just one week in a complex cycle of annual training; it merely represents the quantity and direction of training at that particular period ie between the indoor and outdoor competition periods.

While it is interesting to study even a sample of Bubka's training it may be more relevant for most readers to consider the information provided below. In their report on the Donetsk training centre where Bubka learned to vault, Kurschilgen and Pejic indicated that the frequency of training sessions increased from two a week for 10/11 year old boys up to seven a week for 16 year old youths. Note that at this age Bubka was already vaulting 5.10m!

That this is not unique is confirmed by the 1982 article, "Training tasks for young pole vaulters" by Jagodin and Tschugunov. This provides an insight into the differences between the Soviet approach to training young athletes and that common in the West – then and now.

Table 1

	No. of weeks	Sessions per week	Total Sessions
General physical training	11	5	55
Specific physical training	12	5	60
Summer training camps	8	4	32
Active rest	6	3	18
Competition weeks	14	4	56
Total	51		221

Table 2

	Year 1 13-14 yrs.	Year 2 14-15 yrs.	Year 3 15-16 yrs.
Training sessions a year	221	230	250
Vaults (less than 20m run)	500	550	650
Transfers to the pole	500	550	650
Vault drills-short run up	500	550	700
Vaults – over 20m run up	230	250	330
Sprints 20 - 50 m (K/m)	15	17	22
Sprints 70 -100m (Km)	40	45	45
Sprints over 100m(Km)	15	20	35
Gymnastics (hrs)	120	130	170
Comps. (vault/other events)	8/10	9/12	13/8
Strength training (Tonnes)	40	45	80

These figures also indicate a highly professional approach to the training of young athletes. However this level of professionalism is not surprising given that it is reported that there were 11,000 full time professional track and field coaches in the former USSR!

CHAPTER EIGHTEEN

Psychological preparation for pole vaulting

"Grant me the serenity to accept the things I cannot change, the courage to change the things I can and the wisdom to know the difference"

St. Francis of Assisi

Coaching and Philosophy may seem strange bedfellows but if coaches can communicate a balanced view of life to their athletes they will go a long way towards helping them resolve the many challenges they will face on the path towards perfection. Modern life is becoming increasingly complex, uncertain and unstable for almost everyone on earth, but especially so for adolescent boys and girls in the developed world. Young people are bombarded with images of perfection in life and in sport. They must resist the insidious threat posed by drugs, deal with the pressure of expectations in both sport and academics, work through the tortuous pitfalls of relationships, especially those with the opposite sex and sometimes they must even go against their local culture, and even the subcultures, if they are to succeed.

Before they can realise their potential in sport many youngsters may have to resolve any or all of these issues because even one can become a major distraction which drains away mental energy and the will to succeed in sport. Any sports educator dealing with young people must take a holistic view of their role if they really wish their athletes to succeed in life and in sport.

We believe there is an especially tight link between a coherent philosophy of life and the psychology of performance in the pole vault. This is because while the pole vault makes immense demands on the physical qualities of the athlete, it challenges them in another area – their mind! Along with the high jump, the pole vault in one of only two events where the athlete can actually see the target they face. Like the high jump it is also an event where the athlete almost invariably ends up failing. While these factors alone create a psychological challenge, the pole vault has an additional dimension – it is potentially dangerous!

Although it is rarely mentioned by athletes or coaches, there is little doubt that the normal human emotion of fear can impact on an athlete's performance. While few if any pole vaulters are driven from the sport by fear, there can be few who can honestly say that it has never affected them. In his novel "One door away from heaven" Dean Koontz wrote, "Fear is a poison produced by the mind, and courage is the antidote stored always ready in the soul." While this perceptive statement may be true is many aspects of life, in the pole vault courage alone may take you into danger.

We believe that the antidote to fear in the pole vault lies in a sound technique and progressive preparation. These are the foundations upon which confidence and performance are based. There is a link between fear and poor technique. While fear can be quite irrational it is often based in reality. The body/brain nexus is tight. If the brain is being told that a problem exists the body will react. So a vaulter whose brain is receiving messages – even subconsciously - that they are off balance, out of control and in danger, will not fully commit to a jump. Nor should they!

Clearly the first step is to ensure that an athlete has confidence in their technique and physical preparation. However the pole vault is a complex event, every element demands concentration. Competition, especially high level competition, brings another dimension to the challenge of pole vaulting. The athlete has to cope with a wide range of factors, many of which they can never control or influence.

These include

- Restricted or even no access to the competition venue for training.
- Limited training opportunities at the warm up track.
- Bad weather.
- Media intrusion.
- Other competitors – some playing 'mind games'.
- Friends and well wishers.
- Changes in qualifying procedures.
- Changes in competition times and conditions.
- A failed attempt.

All of these issues impact on the athlete's mind, sometimes to the point where technique and physical preparation are almost irrelevant at that moment. This means that we must prepare the whole person for competition! We would not leave the improvement of technique until the last moment nor ignore physical conditioning until the day of competition. Therefore we should not leave the athletes psychological preparation until then either!

There is a link between philosophy and psychology in the sense that athletes must become aware that no matter how important a competition is, it remains a sports competition! It is never a matter of life and death as some misguided coaches might claim. The athlete who knows that the sun will come up tomorrow no matter how well or poorly they compete, that their family will still love them and their friends will still be their friends will be better able to maintain their sense of perspective no matter what happens.

Anyone who understands anything about the personality traits of coaches and athletes knows that neither group will embrace sports psychology with great enthusiasm. The 'real' man doesn't need any help when the going gets tough because, as we all know, that's when the tough get going! You solve your own problems or die trying, as some do, unfortunately. This attitude is largely due to the fact that many coaches and athletes believe that 'sports psych" is only useful, if at all, to patch up or paper over problems once they have occurred.

However sports psychology can go far beyond this and can make a major contribution to an athlete's development in many areas of planning, preparation and competition. It is true that many experienced coaches have a working knowledge of sports psychology, but this is often intuitive rather than grounded in sound theory. There appears to be little awareness of the wide range of strategies a good sports psychologist can use to help athletes fulfil their potential and especially to prevent problems occurring in the first place. They can provide assistance in the areas of
• Goal setting
• Focussing
• Self talk
• Energy control
• Visualisation or mental rehearsal
• Developing self confidence
• Improving motivation
• Preparing for competition
• Dealing with pressure
• Post competition analysis
• Providing resources
In a book of this kind it is not possible to deal with all of these areas in detail. However we have allocated the next chapter to "Preparing for competition" and provide an introduction to three of the most important elements from a pole vaulting perspective below; these are "Goal setting", "Mental rehearsal" and "Dealing with pressure", below.

"Goal setting"

When asked, the majority of athletes will define their "goals" in terms of winning a specific competition; many youngsters will mention their dream of winning Olympic gold. This is understandable and reflects the prevailing cultural attitude towards sport where winning is seen as the only worthwhile objective.

The problem is that such an attitude can be counter productive. For example, if a climber spends most of their time looking at the summit of the mountain and not on making sure that every movement they make on the cliff face is carefully planned and precisely executed, they are unlikely to get to the top. To be successful they must focus on achieving a series of 'goals', some as simple as finding the next tiny crack in the rock to use as a handhold.

In the same way an athlete can bridge the gap between where they are now and where they want to be in the future by identifying each step they need to take. These steps become goals which the athlete strives to attain. They can involve virtually every aspect of training and competition. The fact is that every successful coach uses a 'goal setting' approach to training but it is usually informal and frequently an intuitive process which they take for granted.

The advantages of a formal "Goal setting" approach include
• It breaks the total task into understandable and potentially achievable components
• Both coach and athlete know precisely what they are trying to achieve
• It enables the athlete to better focus their energies
• It saves time
• Achieving planned goals can be a very satisfying and affirming process.
• There is motivation in striving for an achievable goal
• Confidence comes from successfully mastering challenges
• It can be a cooperative process which brings coach and athlete together
• Athletes may better understand how all elements of training fit together
• It can help them better appreciate the importance of specific training modalities
• Involvement in the process can help athletes 'own' their career
• Over time it builds a 'can do' mind set
The complexity of the pole vault, the wide range of training modes needed and the special demands of competing in this event means that

vaulters can benefit enormously from a goal setting approach. Each of these elements can be broken down into components which are then turned into 'goals'. These can include -

Goal setting for elements of technique

Some aspects of technique are objective. Run up speed, speed over the last five metres, take off differentials, grip height and pole stiffness are all measurable. Improving any one of those elements can have a major impact on performance so it is important monitor progression. In fact even coaches who do not use a 'Goal setting" strategy will often measure performance in those areas and compare them with established norms.

However, other aspects of technique are not easily measurable. Attaining a specific technical goal will often involve a subjective assessment by the coach. However even this process can be made more objective by using 'before' and 'after' videotapes to capture and define the improvements made.

Physical parameters
The Field testing approach detailed in Chapter Twenty can be employed to ensure that virtually every aspect of training can be turned into a series of goals. While goal setting is primarily individually based, there are established performance norms which correlate with predicted performance in the actual vault.

Competition skills
Setting non performance goals allows the athlete to 'win' in every competition. If they
• Get on to a bigger pole
• Cope with a head wind
• Compete well in rain or even snow – in places like Nampa in Idaho!
• Use a higher grip
• Deal with pressure
• Take off on every attempt – in warm up and/or in the competition
• Make third attempt clearances
With young or inexperienced athletes, the goal may simply be to improve their competition skills by following the routines detailed in Chapter Nineteen. For example it is not uncommon for novices who lack confidence to 'disappear' during a competition. Perhaps because they are intimidated by the 'professionals' – 'professionals' who may have been vaulting for all of six months, these young athletes often forget everything the coach is trying to teach them. Instead of

following the routines which will give them their best chance of a good performance they sit down and only emerge when they are called to jump – almost praying for the ordeal to end! Inevitably they fulfil their own expectations.

To prevent this the coach must recognise, reinforce and reward good 'competition skills' no matter what the quality of the actual performance on the pole. So every aspect of the routine for preparing to compete becomes a 'goal' to be achieved. In this way post competition analysis can be focussed on the way the athlete improved their competition skills and their technique instead of only on the athlete's performance.

To make the "Goal setting" process appear more real
• Write specific goals down
• Tick them off when you have achieved them
One implication of all of this is that the athlete should keep a training diary in which they record everything which impinges on their performance. This is essential for any athlete with long term aspirations because only by keeping a record of every aspect of training and of life will it be possible for an athlete to establish what training pattern works best for them.

While many who have a limited understanding of the true nature and purpose of sport will abhor this, we believe that it is possible to 'win' in many ways. So our purpose here is to suggest that goal setting should go far beyond the final target. Our beliefs have been driven by our long experience as teachers where our role was to encourage every child to develop whatever talent they had to the maximum, regardless of how they compared to others in the group. This notion underpinned the philosophy of the Five Star award scheme which was created in Great Britain during the 1960's and which evolved from the approach to teaching track and field developed by Alan at Dr. Challoner's Grammar School in Buckinghamshire. This approach has many advantages but the crucial one was that focussing on improving ones personal best, precisely defined the goal for every single child

Focussing

The ability to focus completely at exactly the right moment is a characteristic of all great athletes. Indeed it has been reported that many Olympic medal winners have been so tightly focussed on their performance that they did not realise that they had won! The key is timing! An athlete cannot stay switched on for the entire period from the start of the warm up through to

Figure 18.1 Bubka prepares for a critical jump.

their first jump, or even in the period between attempts. They must be able switch on at just the right moment and then switch off and relax until the time comes to focus for their next attempt.

An important part of this process is the ability to refocus after a setback or a distraction of any kind. The nature of the pole vault makes this is a critical skill. A vaulter can register a failure even when they have done everything right in the jump, simply because -

- They have chosen the wrong pole,
- The standards were incorrectly positioned
- The wind changed when they are halfway down the runway

Vaulters must therefore learn to immediately flush away any negative thoughts, to make the necessary changes and refocus for the next jump. In fact learning to deal with 'failure' is a vital step for any vaulter because even if they become the dominant vaulter in a region, State, Nation or the World it is almost inevitable that at some point they will fail!

Mental rehearsal, Visualisation or Imagery

Note that part of the first two paragraphs of this section are a repetition of ideas presented in the Chapter Ten. However the truth bears repeating.

While it is impossible to learn a complex physical skill without actually practicing it, there is considerable evidence to suggest that after a physical skill such as pole vaulting has been learned it can be reaffirmed and reinforced through a process called mental rehearsal. Given that all learning is done in the brain this is not as strange a concept as it may seem at first sight. In fact there is evidence to suggest that mental imagery can produce the same pattern of nerve stimulation as are produced when the vaulter actually performs the event. Mental rehearsal can both speed up and then reinforce any aspect of the learning process. This has many benefits; the first is that it allows the athlete to 'practice' during any time they have available away from the track, while the second is that mental practice is far less physically draining than the 'real' thing. Naturally mental rehearsal works best when the athlete is rehearsing the correct model!

The vaulter should therefore include visualisation of the event in their training. They can focus on a specific element of technique or they can run the entire performance through their mind. Of course the better an athlete knows their event the better and they can image and feel it, the more benefit they will gain from mental rehearsal. However the athlete must first clear their mind of the usual clutter so that they can focus on the important images they want to capture and practice. One way to achieve this is to use relaxation techniques. There are a number of strategies but one of the simplest is to listen to a relaxation tape for up to twenty minutes. While generic tapes are commercially available it is better to have one prepared especially for each individual athlete by their sports psychologist.

In sport, mental imagery is used primarily to help you get the best out of yourself in training and competition. Developing athletes who make the fastest progress and those who ultimately become the best, make extensive use of mental imagery. They use it daily as a means of directing what will happen in training, and as a way of preparing themselves for their best competition performances.

In the same way the procedure for imagery can be put on to a tape, and along with carefully selected videotapes of a vaulter's best performance, can be used whenever they wish to prac-

tice. This practice should not be restricted to the period immediately prior to competition. The more the athlete practices the skills involved, the better they will become and the more they will benefit. This is where a sports psychologist can be invaluable because they will usually have the time and expertise needed to produce media resources to assist the athlete and coach.

When athletes use these techniques just prior to a major competition, including the ultimate challenge, competing at the Olympic Games, they should also try to visualise the entire process of preparing for competition. They should rehearse the procedures they will follow from the time they get up in the morning through the meals they will have, their route to the warm up track, their warm up procedures, movement into the call room, behaviour in the call room, movement out to the competition area, check poles etc. One of the most valuable exercises an athlete can undertake is to visualise their movement from the cool but tense atmosphere of the call room out into the cauldron of the stadium.

Terry Orlick, a Canadian sports psychologist observed

"In sport, mental imagery is used primarily to help you get the best out of yourself in training and competition. The developing athletes who make the fastest progress and those who ultimately become the best make extensive use of mental imagery. They use it daily as a means of directing what will happen in training, and as a way of pre experiencing their best competition performances."

Visualizing the total experience in this way will help athletes prepare themselves for the pressure of reality. No matter how experienced an athlete is, preparing for an important competition can be a daunting experience. It is difficult to believe that the gladiators making their way out onto the sand of the Coliseum in Rome two thousand years ago would have been any more nervous than vaulters going into the qualifying round in the Olympic Stadium!

Mental rehearsal is also an important training method when an athlete is recovering from an injury which prevents them from vaulting. This is always a difficult time for the athlete who inevitably feels frustrated as they see valuable training days slip away. By committing time to serious mental rehearsal sessions they will not only maintain the image of performance, but they may be able to review aspects of their technique and begin to make anticipated changes in their 'minds eye'. Just the fact that they are doing something positive with their time makes this a worthwhile exercise but they may come out of this experience with a better understanding of what they must do to improve.

Part of the routine the athlete uses to prepare for every jump should include visualising a successful performance. Mental rehearsal supplements, but does not replace, other aspects of training. Again there is no mysticism involved. The athlete must learn how to use the technique and must purposefully practice it. The more realistically they can picture and feel their performance the more they will benefit from the process.

Self talk or 'Affirmation'

Many of us were exposed to the power of self talk as very young children when our parents read us the story of the little red engine. Continually telling himself "I think I can, I think I can – I know I can, I know I can"! - He reached the top of the steep hill that looked like beating him!

Only a children's story, but one which contains a fundamental truth. If we tell ourselves that we can do something there is a better chance we will actually achieve it than if we doubt ourselves. There is considerable evidence that self talk can help an athlete build and maintain their confidence in potentially stressful situations – like going into a major championship for the first time or when faced with a third attempt at your opening height!

Simple 'self talk' statements can include

I deserve to be here – I have trained hard and I am in good shape

I have been here a hundred times before this

I am tough enough to get over this bar

I enjoy this – when you make it on the third attempt the crowd roars

I always jump well in difficult conditions

One suspects that Bubka went through this process at the 1997 World Championships in Athens. After an amazing career he came into the competition with a season's best of 5.65 metres and failed his first attempt in the final at 5.70m! He skyed his second attempt and went on to win with a new Championship best of 6.01 metres.

The history of the event is full of such examples; from an Australian perspective, one of the most significant was when Dimitri Markov, facing a third attempt at his opening height of 5.75metres (18'9") at the 2001 World Championships went clear, and then went on to win with a personal best, and a new Championship record, of 6.05m.

All athletes should continually remind themselves of their previous best jumps and begin to assure themselves that they can make it. Henry Ford summed up the importance of positive self talk with the succinct phrase

"Whether you think you can, or whether you think you can't, you are always right!"

Handling pressure

It is clear that great athletes have something special. Sometimes it is their technique which is superior, sometimes it is their basic physical ability; however invariably the great ones are all mentally tough. Bubka's technique and physical qualities were outstanding but his almost icy calmness under pressure was exceptional. As an unknown twenty year old he was able to win the his first World Championship in 1983 in part by dealing with difficult conditions far better than his more experienced opponents. In 1988 he stepped onto the runway in Seoul with one jump remaining to attempt a new Olympic record height of 5.90 metres. Failure meant fourth position, a clearance meant Olympic gold!

As Petrov described it to Alan in 1992, when Bubka prepared for his final attempt in Seoul, he realised that for the first time that day, the prevailing head wind had dropped away and had been replaced by a small tail wind. He immediately stepped onto the runway and almost before he was called, began his run up. The video film of his jump shows him taking off under, a most unusual occurrence for him but the result of the tail wind. Consequently he had to make adjustments throughout the jump and in fact just missed the bar with his chest on the way down – but it was a clearance and a Gold medal!

In his final World Championships in Athens in 1997 he was in a similar situation. Maxim Tarasov had cleared 5.96 metres, a height Bubka had passed, so he was going to have to set a new World Championship record to retain his title. That jump has reached iconic status because although the bar was set at 6.01metres, Japanese sports scientists have calculated that Bubka could have cleared a bar set at 6.40 metres! Perhaps it is worth noting here that Tarasov made a basic mistake at this point. After going into the lead with his 5.96m; clearance his reaction suggested that he believed he had already won. When Bubka cleared the next height, Tarasov was psychologically devastated. He should have taken note of what his compatriot Victor Saneyev said on this issue years before!

Al Oerter, the greatest competitor in the history of the discus throw won four Olympic gold medals in succession. He was never the world record holder going into any of these competitions but set Olympic records at three Games, on two occasions he did this on his last throw!

Victor Saneyev won three successive Olympic titles - he had to settle for silver in his final Games in 1980 but his performances were amazing because they were in the triple jump – the most physically demanding of all the field events.

All these great athletes demonstrated their ability to focus all of their energies to produce great performances when it mattered. So they not only provide us with models of how to compete **but also how to prepare to compete.**

- They know how to get their bodies ready for a great performance
- They can deal with all of the distractions which attend a major competition, the media, expectations of family and friends, gamesmanship by other competitors, changes in competition times and conditions
- They can follow their normal routines under pressure
- They can focus on what is really important
- They never stop believing that they can succeed. Victor Saneyev's statement, "As long as I have one jump left I am not beaten", sums up this philosophy perfectly.

Related to this, great athletes have the ability to refocus after a problem, disappointment or other distraction. For example in the vault, a major change in wind direction after the competition begins can destroy some athletes while others take it in their stride.

Coaches can contribute to the process on a daily basis with simple truisms such as

- "You can only do your best".
- "Respect your opponents" – after all they love this sport as much as you do – they face the same challenges – learn what you can from them.
- "The past is the past, there is nothing you can do to change it."
- "You can only influence the future".
- "Your life begins in the next instant".
- "There are more important things happening on the planet today!"

CHAPTER NINETEEN

The competition process

"If you have one eye on winning, you only have one eye to watch your opponent's sword."

A guiding principle for Samurai warriors.

Training is only a means to an end! The true test of the athlete occurs in competition, where weaknesses in any aspect of their preparation, in their character or even their courage may be exposed. Indeed it is this factor which makes the pole vault a unique challenge and which draws a special kind of person to the event as an athlete or as a coach.

With most events in track and field the role of the coach ends when the athlete goes to the call room or onto the track before the competition. After this they may shout encouragement but there is little more they can really do to help their athlete perform. This is definitely not the case with pole vault. Our experience suggests that young athletes can benefit enormously from assistance during competition. Most youngsters simply do not have the experience nor the body awareness to know what changes to make to improve their performance, especially when their normal thought processes begin to freeze up under the pressure of competition. However as athletes mature they do have to take more and more responsibility for their own performance in competition. This may be a process which takes many years but we believe that the sooner it begins the better for both the coach and the athlete.

The implication of this is that one of the tasks of the coach is to teach athletes how to compete. However the process begins with the coach themselves learning how to cope with the competition process. This is not easy and Alan has seen arguably the greatest pole vault coach in history begin to crack under the pressure.

The coach

On the day of competition the coach must be 'ready'; calm, confident and apparently in control – no matter how nervous they may be! They must never allow their emotions to impact on the athlete. That said, only a true disciple of Zen could always stay in control under the pressures of high level competition

If the coach hopes to remain cool, calm and collected they must try to avoid stress in the lead up to the competition. The best way to do this is to use routines. It is easy to encapsulate many

fundamental principles and behaviours in an easy to understand set of routines. This reduces the uncertainty which comes from continual ad hoc decision making. 'Routines' ensure that
- The stress levels of everyone involved are reduced
- No time is wasted trying to locate items or bodies!
- Equipment is not left behind or lost
- Everyone knows what is going on – and when

We recommend using checklists where the coach ticks off each task as it is completed.

If the local officials will let them, on arrival at the competition area, the coach should -

Check the jumping environment
- Pad safety
- Stands calibrated
- Box OK
- Local rules
- Starting height – increments through the competition
- Weather conditions - now and predicted
- Wind – now and prevailing – variable or steady – head tail cross?
- Run up surface – Fast / Slow
- Pole rack – poles positioned – your athlete's poles there!!

The Athlete

The ideal situation is one where the athlete arrives at the competition physically and technically ready to give of their best. They should be "in the zone", under complete control of their emotions, focussed, relaxed yet aggressive, confident to the point where they actually enjoy the tension and look forward to the challenge of competition. While every athlete responds differently to the pressure of competition, it is possible for coaches to begin to prepare them by introducing their athletes to specific knowledge and routines as outlined below. Athletes should -
- Know the rules of their event
- Make sure that their poles get to the stadium and are available for checking, if this is necessary
- Check the taping of their poles and, if they use a sticky spray, check that their can is not empty

- Get to the track with plenty of time to spare before the competition begins
- Begin their general warm up at a specific time
- Follow the check in procedures for the competition
- Go to the vault area at the permitted time
- Make sure their poles have been brought out to the competition run up
- Know the number of competitors in the event? Will this affect their technical warm up?
- Define THEIR spot in the competition area
- Defend THEIR area with their equipment bag
- Determine where their coach is sitting – if they are there.
- Measure their run up as soon as possible – always place some kind of mark which cannot be moved, accidentally or otherwise, in addition to the markers which may be supplied
- Begin their vault warm up at a specific time; the sequence could be
  - Plant exercises with a pole on the track
  - Short run up vaults into the box
  - Full run ups on the track
  - Check full run up on runway
  - Full run up and take off
  - Full run up over a bar
- Know exactly how many short approach jumps they intend to take
- Make sure that they are not pushed out of the warm up sequence
- Ensure they have enough time for up to three full jumps – preferably at a bar with the stands at eighty centimetres.
- Select a pole they know they can take off with
- Decide on their starting height
- Know where they are in the jumping sequence
- Be aware of athletes who will pass the heights that they intend to jump; check this throughout the competition. If this is not done the athlete may find themselves being called before they expect.
- Check the windsock throughout the warm up and the early stages of the competition. This will help them understand the pattern. Clearly if there is a consistent head wind there is no point in waiting for a tail wind! On the other hand if the wind is variable, try and identify any pattern which they can take advantage of.
- Adjust their run up accordingly.
- Keep ready and alert through the competition, while staying as relaxed as possible in the circumstances.

- Begin to prepare three jumps out/select the correct pole/ check that it is taped.
- Make sure they are ready to go when the jumper immediately before them in the sequence steps on the runway.
- Continue to warm up with specific exercises, pole drills and run up work during the competition. But they must stay alert to what is going on so they never have to jump before they are fully prepared.
- Use mental rehearsal to prepare for the first jump.
- Focus on the jump.
- Block out distractions. It is vital that athletes learn to ignore the many distractions which can occur during a competition. Some of these distractions are incidental but some may be deliberate attempts by other competitors to destroy your focus.

Clearly mastering all of these elements will take years but we have provided this list to give coaches an idea of the detailed knowledge needed in just one aspect of their role, if they are to be fully effective.

The first jump!!!!

Getting it right, or at the least 'getting off' with the first jump in a competition is really important in the pole vault. An attempt where the athlete actually gets off the ground even if they do not complete the jump, can be immensely valuable to the coach. The coach can analyse the attempt, decide what the problem was and can often suggest relatively simple adjustments, ie lengthen/ shorten the run up, use a stiffer/softer pole.

On the other hand if the vaulter is not really up for that first jump and runs through without taking off, both coach and athlete miss out on critical information. Although this data may become available after the second attempt, there is now only one jump left – perhaps on a pole the athlete has never used before! Any experienced coach knows that that can lead to real problems. Novice coaches will rapidly learn that this is one of the most important and stressful aspects of coaching!

The "Run through"

This is one of the most common and frustrating problems in vaulting. The cause can be as simple as major wind change a few steps out or it can be the result of deep seated problems in technique. While the latter will only be resolved through intensive work to improve the run up, pole carry and plant, many other problems can be dealt with through a simple process of refocussing. It may be that the athlete is simply not very good at 'steering' over the last six steps.

Summary

This is merely an overview of what most coaches find to be the most difficult of all of the tasks they undertake. The bench coaching role is especially stressful and the old adage "If you cant stand the heat, stay out of the kitchen' certainly applies here!

CHAPTER TWENTY

Field Testing and Talent Identification

"There is something much more scarce, something rarer than ability. It is the ability to recognise ability"

Robert Halp

Field Testing, or Control testing as it is sometimes called, is an undervalued and often under used component of a coaches armoury. It is important to remember that in essence track and field is merely a series of physical tests which measure 'How Fast', 'How Far' and 'How high'. In fact the events which make up the sport as we know it are the survivors of a long process of evolution in track and field in which various 'tests' have been tried and discarded, while others have changed over time. For example, at one time a whole range of standing jumps was included in the Olympic program, while the 'pole vault' became a different event with the introduction of flexible poles and foam landing pads.

With this in mind it is easy to see that there are many possible 'tests', some very closely related to the 'real' tests which make up the sport of track and field. Coaches can take advantage of this fact and use "Field tests" in many ways to extend and improve their training program.

Field Tests can be used

• To assess or confirm an athlete's potential.
While performance in the actual event is always a good way to assess talent, there are good reasons why Field tests may sometimes be better indicators of a youngster's potential, especially those with very limited experience. This is especially true in the pole vault where any potential a novice might have is likely to be hidden by major technical faults. Along with little or no opportunity to warm up and the stress inherent in competition, this will often make it difficult for a beginner to record a good performance. In this situation only the eye of an experienced coach can see the diamond in the rough stone.

• To demonstrate to a child and their parents that they do have great potential.
This is especially important when the 'athlete' has apparently failed! Even more so when most of the youngsters we would like to recruit are already involved in other sports, often at a relatively high level. Unless a coach can demonstrate, rapidly and objectively, that the child has REAL potential, it is difficult to convince parents - who often have little or no knowledge of track and field far less the pole vault - to encourage the young athlete to commit some time to it.

In a single session of field testing it is possible to show the family that the youngster has the potential to reach State or even International level. If their performance in these tests can be compared favourably with established 'norms', this approach is even more likely to be effective in getting them to at least pursue the event along with their other sports.

• To help athletes identify their best event.
Many athletes take up a particular event and then never try any others. Unfortunately this may reflect the interest and expertise of their first coach so an athlete may be locked into one event when they have greater potential in another. This is often the case with the pole vault where many athletes with great potential never ever get to try it because they are committed to the sprints or long jump. The tragedy is that many of them could take State level talent in those events and convert it into International performances in the pole vault. A series of positive results in Field tests may be one way to encourage athletes with international aspirations to look at a change of event.

• To help a coach monitor an athlete's physical parameters.
When used in this way they are often referred to as "Control" tests. While the pole vault must always be seen as a 'Whole', it is based on the discrete elements of running, jumping and throwing. Each of these components needs to be periodically checked and improved because as we continually state "What is technically desirable must be physically possible". Given the tight correlation between long jumping and the vault, it is clear that the former provides the basis for a range of tests. Figure 20.1 shows one approach to recording the test data in a format which immediately indicates and athletes relative strengths and weaknesses. It was included in Nikonov's articles 'Women become pole vaulters' published in 'Modern athlete and coach'. This is yet another example of the

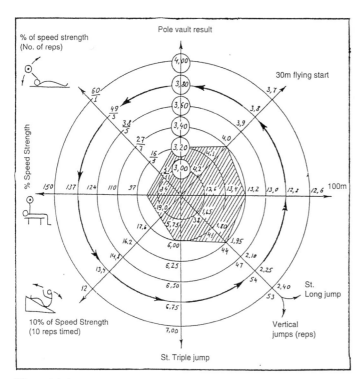

Figure 20.1

wonderful resource that Jesse Jarver's magazine, has been for Australian coaches.

• To provide motivation during the long dark months of winter.

While it is possible for athletes to compete in the 'real' event at this time, poor conditions and lack of readiness may lead to depressing performances. In addition there is always the very real risk of injury in this event when an athlete is not fully ready.

Field tests can be used as "Indirect competition" and as athletes see their performances in the tests improving they become like decathletes chasing points. The main value is that they can more readily see the value of their training and begin to smell the scent of success.

Another approach can be used when groups of athletes, even athletes with different specialities, train together. Here it becomes "Direct competition" where athletes compete against each other in field tests which are common to several disciplines. This usually engenders a real commitment to perform especially when sprinters and jumpers discover that the throwers can beat them in many tests of power and speed.

• To give athletes an opportunity to develop their competition routines and skills.

Taking part in a diverse range of field tests in either a 'direct' or 'indirect' competition mode can give athletes many opportunities to develop a

whole range of psychological skills including relaxation, focussing and refocussing

Athletes must learn to focus their concentration when it matters. During competition there are a thousand distractions – even hearing one's own name over the stadium loudspeaker system can have a negative effect. As with many aspects of human behaviours some individuals seem to blessed with this talent from birth but the vast majority of athletes must learn this 'psychological skill'. Most importantly they may learn that a good or even a great performance can be achieved on any attempt, even the last.

• As predictors of performance in the real event.

This is especially important in the lead up to major competition. While this will usually be both athlete and event specific, a coach working with an experienced athlete will begin to see which tests correlate best with competition performance. Sometimes there is an unusual relationship. For example the great Victor Saneyev, three times Olympic Champion in the triple jump used his results in the overhead shot throw as the primary indicator of his readiness for a good performance in his event. Experience had taught Victor that there was a close correlation between these two apparently unrelated activities.

• To provide a training effect.

The reduced technical demands of field tests means that the athlete can concentrate on producing a dynamic physical performance. Since they are usually approached with the intensity of a true competitive effort, athletes will often produce effort and movement qualities not always achieved even by highly motivated individuals in their ordinary training mode.

Good Field tests
• Require little equipment and are easy to organise
• Are relatively easy for athletes to learn
• Have elements in common with the real event
• Are standardised
• Have 'norms' against which progress can be measured

When field tests are used as "Control tests" the results can be recorded in many ways. One innovative approach is to record them on a template such as that shown in Figure 20.1. When the results of the athlete's control tests are plotted on the chart an athlete's strengths and weaknesses immediately become obvious and the training program can be adjusted.

Field tests can be derived from all of the basic elements of an athletes training.

- Weight training exercises are built in field tests but vaulters should be careful of striving for maximum lifts. Vaulters do not require the absolute strength levels of a hammer thrower.
- Sprinting any distance from 20 metres up to 60 metres with standing of flying start also provides a range of 'field tests'. Hand timing can be used but electronic timing is better
- Jumping tests. Long jumpers and triple jumpers employ a vast range of tests which are readily available in the literature. However we have found that the six stride long jump, twelve stride long jump and full run long jump are correlated with the vault. While the standing long jump is a simple exercise useful for identifying basic athletic ability we have found that it does not correlate closely with vault performances.
- Throwing Tests. Again there are a vast range of tests which are readily available. We have found the Standing 200 gm ball throw an interesting predictor of pole vault potential with young athletes while the Overhead Shot Throw is a good indicator of power and coordination. Throwing events provide an useful and enjoyable challenge for athletes at every level.
- Others tests can include a range of exercises in the gymnasium. We have found that a timed rope climb, half levers on the high bar and chinning the bar to be simple and useful.

Finally there is one Field test which has special importance in the pole vault because it relates to one of the critical issues in this book, the nature of the take off. This is a test used by some former Soviet coaches to assess a vaulter's take off efficiency. With a six step run up and a stiff pole, the vaulter gradually moves their grip height up as they take off to land on the pad. They should drive the pole forward but hang long behind the pole without rocking back. Eventually they can only just drive the pole to the vertical and get onto the front of the pad safely. The grip height is then measured and recorded.

Talent identification

In South Australia our policy with regard to recruiting athletes has had two distinct elements. On the one hand we never turn any youngster away. If they turn up and say that they want to learn to pole vault we look after them no matter what their potential may be. We do this for three reasons; the first philosophical, the second pragmatic and the third practical. With a group like ours, which must continually raise funds to buy poles, the larger our squad the better. However there is another reason this 'open' approach works for us. All children have friends! Even if the first athlete to arrive has limited potential, the friend they drag along to practice the next time they come, may be a potential superstar!

Our overriding philosophy is based on the notion of sport for all. We are therefore prepared to help anyone who wants to try pole vaulting. It should be noted that we never charge beginners for coaching even when parents offer to pay, as they frequently do. We believe that no child should miss out on the kind of life changing experience that pole vaulting can provide, simply because they cannot afford to try it.

As a sage once said "Philosophy does not pay the bills". So once our athletes are 'hooked', we expect them to pay an annual subscription to help purchase necessary poles. This naturally means that the more athletes we have the higher our income. Equally important it increases the number of parents available for the fund raising activities which are essential if a group such as ours is to survive.

The practical reason why we never turn youngsters away is that we learned early on in the history of our squad that talent is not always easy to identify!! We have had many youngsters with apparently little ability who subsequently reached good levels of performance. Dedication and commitment can paper over physical limitations in the pole vault as in other sports, as Simon Arkell superbly demonstrated. Figure 20.2 shows Simon on the way to winning the 1990 Commonwealth Games in Aukland, New Zealand. A dual Olympian who cleared a personal best of 5.80 metres in 1996, he was living proof of the importance of desire and determination. With better coaching early in his career he could well have been a 6.00 metre jumper.

However, we do believe in attracting youngsters with the potential to reach high standards. This is important for many reasons. The first is pragmatic. Agencies such as the Australian Institute of Sport or the South Australian Institute of Sport are only interested in supporting potential international athletes. If we want any assistance from them we must demonstrate our ability to produce athletes of this calibre.

Figure 20.2

Clearly the greater the initial potential, the easier this is.

A second reason why we need high level performers is that they become 'models' of both technique and training for the other athletes in our squad. Access to talented youngsters is important to a coach's psyche because even those of us who believe in sport for all still want to stretch ourselves as much as possible. The greater the talent of the athlete the further we will be stretched! Finally, it is only human nature to want one's efforts recognised, respected and even rewarded. In the real world only the outstanding performance of one's athletes will help achieve that.

Our approach is based merely on eyeballing youngsters as they compete in other events from the ages of 11 upwards. It bears no relationship to the formal Talent Identification Programs espoused, but rarely adequately funded, by sports administrators in Australia. So coaches simply go to watch as many junior competitions as possible, naturally focussing on the sprints and jumps, but most especially on performances in the long jump. This is because there is a very high correlation between long jumping and pole vaulting, even at the highest level.

The ideal candidate for the pole vault is a tall, slim long jumper with strong shoulders – which have ideally been developed through an involvement in the sport of gymnastics. In fact many youngsters come into pole vaulting directly from gymnastics, a sport which in Australia all too often exploits the dreams of young children, especially girls, along with the ambitions of their parents. As they grow too tall to be successful as international gymnasts - the goal of the majority of coaches in that sport it would seem, they are either ignored or actively discouraged by the coach who does not want to waste time on limited potential. Fortunately for us, when looking for another sport, these 'rejects' often choose pole vaulting. Unfortunately while most are brave and unafraid of hard training, not all of them are fast or even good runners. This can put a limit on their potential.

The simplest method of identifying talent is 'eye balling'. That simply means watching children run, jump and throw and assessing their size, shape, power. explosiveness, spring, rhythm, balance, their competitive spirit and their movement feel. This seems complex and it is, because it often takes considerable insight – even intuition – to see the potential diamond in the rough stone. Here it may be worth noting the story of the "Three spoons diamond" in the Topkapi palace in Istanbul, so called because its original owner, who clearly did not appreciate its true value, traded this priceless object for three wooden spoons! Clearly the task of identifying diamonds in the real world can be as difficult as identifying them in the pole vault!

While performance in the actual event is always a good way to assess talent, there are good reasons why Field tests may sometimes be better indicators of a youngsters potential, especially those with very limited experience. This is especially true in the pole vault where any potential a novice might have, may be hidden by major technical faults. This, along with little or no opportunity to warm up and the stress inherent in competition, will often make it difficult for a novice to record a good performance. In this situation only the eye of an experienced coach can see the diamond in the rough stone. Unless we can demonstrate, rapidly and objectively, that the child has REAL potential, it is difficult to convince parents who often have little or no knowledge of our sport, far less this the pole vault, to encourage the young athlete to commit some time to it.

Recruiting

Identifying talent does not guarantee that you have a recruit. The kind of athlete vault coaches are looking for is likely to be good at many other sports – indeed many will already be involved in other sports. In the South Australian "Context" these are likely to be sports with a much higher profile than track and field so it is hard to wean them away from them. This is why we include a large proportion of 'competition' with the athlete jumping over soft bars in our teaching process.

We also sell the challenge and excitement of the event as well as the fact that athletes can take their athletic potential much further in the pole vault than they could in other events. We provide examples of young vaulters who have represented their country at World Youth level who could never have won a medal in any event at State level in track and field.

Despite our success we have to sell our program. To do this we first sell ourselves as caring professionals and then we present the history of our group. Many parents like the thought of their child winning National Championships or even representing their nation, if only at youth or junior level, and we can easily demonstrate our success in helping young athletes to achieve these goals

CHAPTER TWENTY ONE

The relationship between stiff pole vaulting and flexible pole vaulting

"The take off point should be immediately below the top hand or at a point up to 6" or so behind that spot, but never in front of it."

Father Coultard. 1950

One of the most significant influences on the development of our ideas was an analysis of the techniques of some of the great vaulters of the stiff pole era. This provided the final key to fully understanding modern technique. Coming to this understanding required a paradigm shift in thinking, never easy for any of us. Readers may also have to go through the same process, which may challenge many of their fundamental beliefs, if they are to understand the implications of the ideas we are presenting below. They may also want to discuss this issue with David Butler of Rice University in the U.S.A. because he has become a thorough student of the history and evolution of the pole vault.

Vaulting with a 'stiff' pole

We appreciate that the poles of the 'stiff' pole era did in fact flex up to three feet. However vaulters using stiff poles could not **store** energy in the pole. They therefore had to put as much energy as possible into the vaulter/pole system at the instant of take off **and** most importantly, they had to continue to put energy into this system for as long as possible throughout the vault! They did this by -

- Driving the pole forward at take off
- Taking off "out" or at least beneath the top hand, NOT "under"!
- Springing up at take off
- Applying the principle of pendular oscillation once they had left the ground.

Figure 21.1, reproduced from Page 280 of "Athletics" by G Pearson, shows the great Cornelius 'Dutch' Warmerdam at the point of take off. It is important because it shows not only that he is taking off 'out' but that he is driving up and forwards with his whole body. The comments which describe this aspect of his technique -

"Take off foot a little behind the hands, shoulders shrugged well up to pole, vigorous knee lift – the bold upward forward movement is in every line of the body"

are also significant. Apart from the 'shrugging' action of the shoulders this could well describe the take off of a modern vaulter.

Taking off 'out'

Stiff pole vaulters never wanted to take off 'under' because they knew it would kill the all important swing after take off. For example Father Coulthard writing on the technique of stiff pole vaulting in 1960 states -

"The take off point should be immediately below the top hand or at a point up to 6" or so behind that spot, but never in front of it."

He goes on to say -

"Taking off too close, ..., will whip the vaulter off his feet and force his legs up too early into the swing which in turn takes him past the pole on the way up and destroys its momentum."

Springing at take off

'The Reverend' Bob Richards, a dual Olympic Champion from the stiff pole era, said that his ability to hold a high grip was because of his spring at take off and that he sedulously practiced the high jump because of this.

Another athlete from that period, subsequently recognised as an authority on this event, Richard Ganslen, said

"The springing take off deserves serious consideration and all vaulters should experiment with it. Specifically the springing take off helps the take off velocity and swing and aids the vaulter in changing his pure linear velocity to angular velocity."

Figure 21.1

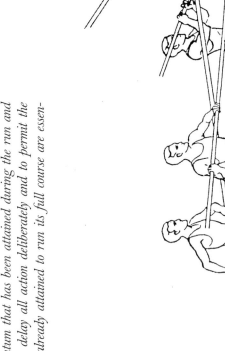

Figure 21.2

Pendular oscillation – or the 'Swing'

Because energy could not be stored in a 'stiff' pole, the vaulter had to continue to put energy into the vaulter/pole system after take off to keep it moving forward. They did this by employing a long extended pendulum whip of the whole body around their hands. Figure 21.2 shows Bob Richards, dual Olympic Champion executing this long swing to perfection. An important element of this so called 'swing' was that the best athletes tried to extend the take off and to fractionally delay the commencement of the swing. Anyone who has watched gymnasts on the high bar or trapeze artists in a circus will appreciate the timing of this movement and the energy it can generate.

In his excellent book, "Modern track and field", first published in 1953, J. Kenneth Docherty wrote

"The all important function of the swing is to maintain the body momentum that has been attained during the run and take off. To delay all action deliberately and to permit the momentum already attained to run its full course are essential."

He goes on to quote Bob Richards

".....the swing is the most important part of the vault and the difference between a good and a poor vaulter is the ability to swing correctly. The secret lies in holding your pull up until the legs have gone by the pole".

On the same topic Dutch Warmerdam stated

"There is a definite delay - in the swing - to take advantage of the velocity which has been developed during the run up. If the vaulter delays momentarily, the body moves forward, the arms extend, the legs swing up automatically as the grip of the hands on the pole stops forward progress."

He went on to say

"So the vault becomes a giant swing carried on and on - ."

and

"Novice and expert alike will profit in coordinating their efforts into one action of a giant swing"

In summary, the best vaulters of the stiff pole era tried to

• Spring up and forward to DRIVE the pole at take off

• Take off 'out' NOT 'under'!

• Execute a long, but fractionally delayed, swing of the whole body with extended arms

Once it had passed the pole they then shortened the body to speed up the angular rotation necessary for the body to swing up rapidly.

These elements were stressed by all good coaches at this time. This becomes clear when one studies the ideas of H.N.Ozolin, a vaulter during the 1930's, who became a very perceptive and influential coach at the Moscow Institute of Physical Culture. Father Coultard illustrated some of the drills Ozolin employed which were "designed to acquire a hang and to keep the take off well out". He went on to describe how Ian Ward, a British record holder of this period, used the same drill "to increase his hang and delay his swing".

The relationship between 'stiff' pole and 'flexible' pole vaulting.

Our analysis of both stiff pole and flexible pole vaulting leads us to believe that the factors which were important to good technique with a stiff pole are as important now as they were then. Similarly many of the faults we try to avoid now are the same faults that coaches and athletes tried to eradicate over fifty years ago. Fittingly it was Bubka himself who tied everything together for us when, at the clinic held in conjunction with the 2003 World Junior Championships in Jamaica, he said

"Before the fibre glass pole, pole vaulters put their focus on moving the pole, then, when the flexible pole appeared many people put their focus on bending the pole. The pole (should) bend as a result of the speed and mass of the jumper, therefore, it is more important to concentrate more on moving the pole towards the plane of the bar, rather than being aware of bending it."

The matter of fact way in which he spoke indicated how basic and deeply embedded these ideas were for him. However his views should come as no surprise to those who have heard Petrov's catchphrase "Move the pole always".

To help readers fully appreciate the implications of Bubka's words and to help them better understand the relationship between stiff pole and flexible pole vaulting, we have broken this statement into three elements so as to deal with each in turn. Note that we have made minor changes in order to ensure that Bubka's ideas are presented as clearly as possible.

1. *"Before the fibre glass pole, pole vaulters put their focus on moving the pole .... (*Now with the fibreglass pole) *it is* (also) *more important to concentrate – on moving* (it) *towards the plane of the bar, rather* (than trying to bend it). "

In this sentence he is emphasising a critical element of technique common to vaulting with both stiff poles **and** flexible poles, namely driving the pole forwards at take off without making any overt attempt to bend it before the vaulter leaves the ground.

The dramatic photograph in Chapter Five of Bubka, immediately after take off in his World Record jump of 6.00 metres (19'7") in 1985, clearly shows this. The pole is still essentially straight, even though Bubka has already left the ground. It is also clear that he has taken off 'out' with a powerful springing action.

2. *"The pole (should) bend as a result of the speed and mass of the jumper"*

This simply re emphasises the importance of the 'free' take off in modern vaulting.

3. *"When the flexible pole appeared many people put their focus on bending the pole."*

There can be little doubt about Bubka's antipathy towards this misguided emphasis nor about its accuracy. The following statements by experts at the time the flexible pole came into common use confirm this.

For example Aubrey Dooley, whom Kenneth Docherty believed "might very properly be called the pioneer (1956) of fibreglass vaulting" certainly concentrated on bending the pole, not on moving it. Richard Ganslen, who had watched him in person and on film for four years states -

"The first observation the spectator makes of Aubrey is the fierce manner in which he bends the pole. This bending of the pole is not a natural consequence of a normal swinging take off, but a deliberate effort on the part of the vaulter"

And

"At take off he pushes the pole toward the pit with his lower hand, which actually prematurely bends the pole. (Ordinarily a pole does not begin to bend until the vaulter swings past it). This push stores some of the energy of the run and Dooley then drives straight ahead."

Father Coultard also writing about Dooley's technique says

"It is possible, as Dooley does, to take a wide grip, push with the lower hand and pull with the upper and hold the bend longer until you require it – 'storing the whip'.

Finally on this topic, when Docherty summed up what he saw to be the advantages of the flexible pole he wrote

"The driving action forward at the take off must be accentuated in order to get an optimum bend and therefore propulsive force out of the pole."

What is fascinating about this is that while these authors were spot on with their analysis of good stiff pole technique, they clearly did not understand the fundamentals of vaulting with a flexible pole. Had they simply continued to apply the principles of stiff pole vaulting to the newly arrived flexible poles many of the problems which still bedevil the vault might have been avoided!

Even a cursory observation will confirm that many present day athletes still appear to have an obsession with bending the pole before they take off. This has lead them down a path towards dead end techniques based on the myths and misunderstandings detailed in Chapter Twenty Five and it has probably contributed to many of the injuries associated with pole vaulting. In addition, this rush to exploit the recoil potential of the flexible pole has prevented many coaches and athletes from appreciating the other major advantages that it brought to the event.

It is for this reason that we believe that coaches are unlikely to understand the full potential of the flexible pole - until they stop thinking of it as a flexible pole! We appreciate that we have introduced this concept earlier but we believe it is suf-

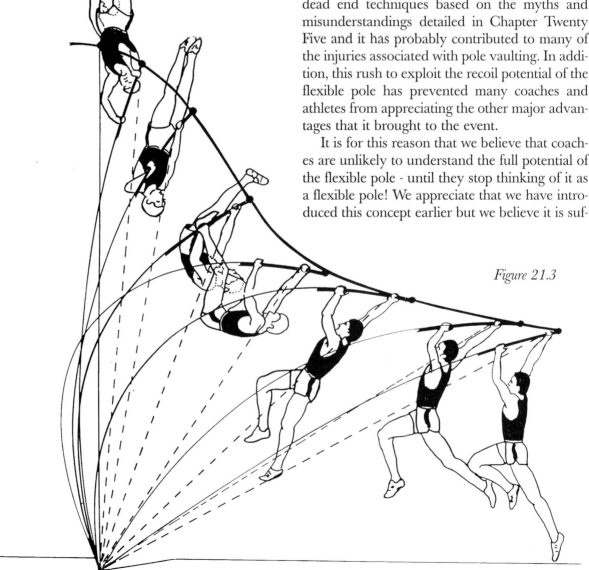

Figure 21.3

ficiently important to be dealt with again. Instead they should think of it as an infinite series of straight poles, initially decreasing in length to maximum pole bend and then returning to its full length. This 'variable length straight pole' is of course the CHORD of the flexing REAL pole as shown in Figure 21.3. From a biomechanical perspective this invisible chord (Cpole), shown as a series of dotted lines, becomes the real pole (Rpole).

With this in mind it is possible to apply the principles of effective straight pole vaulting directly to vaulting with a flexible pole. The modern vaulter should try to drive the pole forward as powerfully as possible at take off and continue to do so throughout the vault. They do this by

- Generating great controlled velocity in the run up.
- Taking off beneath the top hand or 'out', never 'under'.
- Ensuring an upspringing take off.
- Driving the pole up, high and forward at take off.
- Making no attempt to deliberately bend the pole at take off.
- Executing a long whipping swing to keep the vaulter/pole system moving forward and to put more energy into the pole.
- Using the forces generated by a specific method of inverting the body to maintain the bend in the pole fractionally longer.

These principles underpin the technical model we presented in Chapter Six. Here it should be noted that there are subtle differences between the techniques of the best female jumpers and those of the best men. This is because the different heights achieved by the two groups correlate with different temporal and rhythmic parameters and this feeds back into the technical model they employ. In fact our analysis suggests that there are progressive if subtle changes in the technical model at every level of performance.

CHAPTER TWENTY TWO

The structure of the run up for ambitious young vaulters

"The pole vault begins with the first step…"

Vitaly Petrov

The run up and take off determine the athlete's potential performance in all of the jumping disciplines. It is Because of this we have assigned this entire chapter to a discussion of the run up in the pole vault. The first point to be made is that the run up is a controlled sprint;. The second is that there is a close relationship between an elite athlete's speed at take off and their final performance. This emphasis on speed at take off is deliberate. There is little point in running forty metres or more to generate maximum speed if the athlete decelerates over the final five metres!

In fact there is little point in running any distance at all if the athlete is out of control, off balance and so unable to take off effectively. This means that the **every aspect of the run up**, from its length and its structure to the actual technique of running, **should be determined by the need to ensure a powerful upspringing take off from precisely the right spot.** One only has to consider the problems elite long and triple jumpers have in hitting the take off board accurately and consistently to understand how difficult this task is. For the vaulter there are additional challenges. They must

- Be able to accelerate to high speed while carrying and controlling a long pole,
- Reposition the pole from the carry, into a good position for the plant and take off
- Ensure that the pole tip hits the back of the box - which is positioned over four metres or more away, at exactly the right instant to coincide with the take off.

To consistently achieve this the vaulter must deal with three factors

- The first is mechanical and the easiest to resolve. It only requires precise repetitive practice to develop a structured and consistent run up which ensures that they arrive close to the correct take off spot at maximum controlled (optimum) speed.
- The second factor is perceptual. Unlike the long jumper who has an obvious and clearly marked 'foot' target, the vaulters 'foot target' is an unmarked spot on the track and the target for the pole tip is almost invisible until late in the run up. No matter how hard athletes

work on improving the run up, it will still vary slightly from one vault to the next. Research suggests that the greatest variation occurs in the initial phase of the run.This means that athletes need what is termed a 'Steering' capacity to enable them to make the minute adjustments necessary to ensure that from six steps out they hit the take off spot accurately. This 'steering' process begins approximately five to six steps out and is driven by the perceptual cues the athlete picks up, intuitively, as they approach take off. Some athletes seem to be genetically gifted with this ability while others are not.

More research is needed in this aspect of the vault. Our interest in it was sparked by a young athlete, Keiron Modra, who although legally blind, jumped 4,45 metres (14'6") as a sixteen year old to win an Australian Schools Under 17 title in 1985. Unfortunately in his next competition he missed the box completely and we had first to withdraw him from the competition and then gently suggest that he give up pole vaulting. He went on to represent Australia in three Para Olympics and to win gold medals in swimming and cycling.

An additional, but rarely mentioned, problem is that it seems likely that vaulters pick up perceptual cues from the front wedges of the pole vault pad. When they move to a pad with a different structure they have to reorient their perception and this can cause problems. Fortunately for most vaulters there is a range of tolerance from their normal take off spot which still enables them to take off, even if it is unlikely to ensure a great jump.

- The third factor is the psychological state of the athlete – their level of arousal as they step onto the runway.

When different climatic conditions, such as rain, head winds or cross winds, are added to an athletes variable arousal levels the problem escalates yet again! It is clear that great attention must be given to the run up, so that the vaulter is in a position to control as many of the – controllable - variables as possible!

Petrov has been quoted as saying that the pole

vault begins with the first step. We believe that it begins before that when the athlete chooses both the width of their grip and the positioning of their hands on the pole. A relatively narrow grip is critical to achieving a high plant, while the positioning of the left hand under the pole is important in ensuring control throughout the run up. It is also an important element in controlling the pole as it is lowered and it also contributes to a fast efficient plant. This is yet another confirmation that everything from the grip on the pole, the run up - from the very first step – the initial high pole carry, the pole drop, the increased cadence over the last 6/8 strides and the pole plant are inextricably linked and each phase must be carried out properly.

While running is a natural activity, sprinting is not! Good sprinting requires a series of accurate, balanced movements in which maximum power is applied against the ground in a very rapid sequence. It requires incredible coordination to produce the explosive but controlled movement sequences of arms and legs while at the same time stabilising the core muscles of the trunk and maintaining high levels of relaxation in the non working muscles. We believe that sprinting is as 'technical' in nature as any aspect of track and field.

As complex as sprinting is, running fast while carrying a long pole introduces an extra dimension. When a 5.00 metre pole is held vertically it weighs approximately 2.8 kg (6.5lbs). However when that pole is lowered to the horizontal, its weight appears to increase enormously. This is because of the torque forces involved.

If a vaulter is forced to counter these torque forces they invariably compromise their running posture and their balance. The most common symptom is the athlete leaning back and 'running on their heels'. This inevitably creates further problems as the athlete prepares to plant the pole and take off because it is virtually impossible to take off effectively when leaning back. Equally important is the fact that any loss of rhythm or balance during the last six steps, no matter how small, may cause the athlete to slow down or even run through without taking off.

There are four possible solutions to this problem. However all but one of these lead to other problems.

1. Use a wide grip. This can lead to an inefficient plant. For example even athletes of the calibre of 1984 Olympic Champion, Quinon and 1996 Olympic Champion Galfione, were disadvantaged by using a wide grip because this lead to a less than optimum pole/ground angle.

2. Carry the pole with the left hand touching the hip. While this relieves the torque problem to some extent, especially if the athlete is not gripping high, it causes real problems during the plant. This is because the top hand, positioned well behind the body, has a long way to travel to get into a high position above the head at the instant of take off. This method almost inevitably leads to a late and low plant.

3. Run the pole tip along the ground. This solution was suggested as long ago as 1978 by a Hungarian coach working in Canada who anticipated that increasing grip heights would lead to the torque problem outlined above. He even designed special easy sliding pole tips made of Teflon to facilitate his method. To date no elite vaulters have chosen to use it, perhaps because while it eliminates torque forces it cannot exploit them, as appears to happen with the fourth and most effective solution detailed below.

4. The majority of well coached modern vaulters, both male and female, use the fourth

Figure 22.1 Lobinger of Germany shows that it is possible to vault 6.0 metres while making basic mistakes!

Figure 22.2

However the most important aspect of the last method is that it enables the vaulter to run fast, gripping high on a big pole while using the relatively narrow grip which is essential if the vaulter is to maximise the pole ground angle at take off.

Of course a strong athlete who is gripping low on a light pole does not NEED to use a high carry angle; they can get away with both poor running technique and an inefficient pole carry. However if male athletes have the ability and the ambition to compete at world level they must be prepared to grip high, that is 5 metres or more and use poles 20kgs/44lbs or more above their body weight. In this case a poor pole carry will certainly have a negative impact on the vaulter's running posture and take off.

In the recent past some good vaulters, such as Phillipe Collet of France HAVE carried the pole almost horizontally for the entire run up. Others like Tim Lobinger of Germany, a 6.00 metre jumper, hold the pole very low and horizontal several steps out from take off. Figure 22.1.

Inevitably athletes such as these are used as examples to support the notion that "There are many ways to skin a cat", in other words there are many different ways to jump high. We would simply respond that they may have jumped high but Bubka, Tarasov and Markov have jumped much higher and achieved better competition results using the method we are suggesting.

Running posture

Even when the pole is carried efficiently the centre of mass of the vaulter/pole system moves forward. To maintain balance and control and 'stay tall' as they accelerate to maximum speed, the vaulter needs to execute the claw strike of the foot slightly further ahead of the centre of mass than does the sprinter. This leads to a slightly more upright posture and a more exaggerated knee thigh drive characteristic of the initial phases of Bubka's run up which were shown in Chapter Six. Maxim Tarasov demonstrates an

solution. Here the pole is carried at approximately 70 degrees to the horizontal at the start of the run up. **Figure 22.2 shows former Olympic Champion Maxim Tarasov at the start of his run up.** The tip is progressively but slowly lowered until the athlete is six steps from take off and then dropped smoothly as the plant is initiated. This method minimises the torque forces throughout the early stages of the run up and appears to exploit these same forces in the final phase as the athlete attacks the box. As Petrov stated in 1985 *"…when increasing speed and the gradual lowering of the pole there appears an additional thrust that forces us to run more quickly with an increased stride rate".*

Figure 22.3

Figure 22.4

even 'taller' running position in Figures 22.3 and 22.4.

It is clearly vital to stay tall and balanced through to the take off. This means that the vaulter has to deal with the forces which begin to act on the body as the pole is lowered and prepared for the plant. Figure 22.5 shows Tarasov running fast, relaxed and with the pole under complete control.

Lowering the pole

When the pole begins to drop in preparation for the plant and take off, the problem changes. Now, whereas many vaulters bring the pole to the horizontal and run with it like this for several strides, our target technique is based around a 'moment free' lowering of the pole where the pole only **passes through** the horizontal as it rotates about the fulcrum of the front - left - hand.

Figure 22.6 shows Tarasov midway through the action of planting the pole.

It is during this phase that it is important for the vaulter to stay tall. The centre of mass must not be allowed to sink as the pressure from the pole increases. The power of the lower leg extensors becomes important because the less flexion there is, the greater the stretch reflex and the greater will be the concentric contraction during the driving phases, so keeping the hips high.

Petrov suggested that the increased stride rate (cadence) is CAUSED by the effect of the falling pole and should therefore happen naturally.

Anyone who has ever carried heavy cases down a staircase will recall the sudden increase in leg speed if the cases are 557 moved forward. It would seem that a similar process occurs when the pole is lowered in preparation for the plant.

Figure 22.5

Figure 22.6

We believe that this increase in cadence is so important to ensuring a good take off that we teach it and drill it from the moment an athlete makes a commitment to the vault. There are good reasons for this.

If a vaulter runs freely, their stride length will continually increase – as a sprinter does out to at least 60 metres. With each stride getting longer it is difficult for the vaulter to make the fine adjustments needed for an accurate balanced take off.

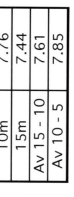

Athlete: Wendy Young
Date: 6/4/07
Time:

Activity: Competition Vault (2003 Nationals 1st at 4.0)
Result: Clear
Wind:
Temp:
Position: Side on to t/o mark
Frames/sec: 50
Shutter: 1/250

Pole Angle	38.1 deg
Trunk Angle	3.5 deg

The Graph of Speed of the Run - Up versus Distance out from the back of the the box is obtained using a LAVEG. This is a laser device that measures the distance the vaulter is away from the laser source at a sample rate of 100 times a second. Software is used to filter the data and prepare the graphs and summary information for coaching feedback.

Speed at Markers

Distance	Speed
5m	7.61
10m	7.76
15m	7.44
Av 15 - 10	7.61
Av 10 - 5	7.85

Maximum Speed

Speed: 7.94
Distance: 6.59

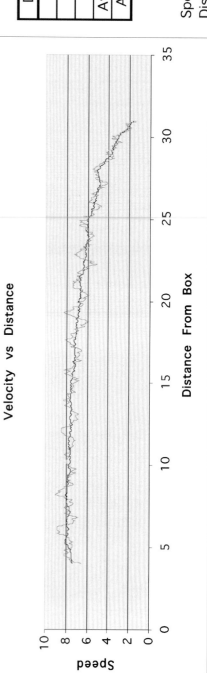

Velocity vs Distance

Speed

Distance From Box

Even worse, if they are hit by a headwind a few strides out, they will be forced to take even longer strides to reach their take off spot. At best this may lead to some loss of control and balance while at worst it may mean that the hips drop and the take off is compromised.

By 'changing gear' six steps out, the athlete keeps the hips high, finds it easier to control the lowering pole and has a greater ability to adjust their run up during this critical phase. For example if they are 30 centimetres out at their mid mark, each of their next six steps need only be lengthened or shortened by 5 cm for them to be in a good take off position. It also means that they are already 'changing down' and so can ensure the rapid increase in stride frequency in the last three steps, which is a characteristic of great vaulters. Finally we believe that changing gear six steps out encourages the vaulter to attack the take off.

Although it has received little attention, the Soviet method of moving the pole from the carry to the plant position attempts to match the drop time of the pole with the speed of the athlete. This is important to minimise torque forces, or even, as Petrov suggested, to exploit those forces

to increase both speed and cadence. The data provided by Nikonov and shown in Figure 22.7 shows that some athletes from the former Soviet Union including Olympic Medallists Bubka, Gataulin and Yegorov managed to accelerate during the final five metres while other vaulters did not. Nikonov asserts that the difference could be put down to the more effective plant techniques used by the athletes who continued to accelerate. We suspect that any study of vaulters around the world will confirm that few athletes manage to maintain, far less increase, their velocity over the last five metres before take off.

It is interesting to consider Bubka as a case in point. Figure 22.8 His check mark to begin the lowering of the pole was at 19.25m (Nikonov), with a take off point at 4. 25m from the box. This means that he ran 15 metres as the pole was lowered and he prepared for take off. If he was travelling at around 10metres a second it would take him 1.5seconds to cover this distance. Our small experiments suggest that if you stand holding a pole at 60/70 degrees and let it drop freely the fall time will be approximately 1.5 seconds! As Petrov said in 1985, "The speed of lowering the

Athletes	Run-up Speed (m/sec)		Maximal 5m Speed over 30m	Conversion Coefficient	Grip Height (m)	Performance (m)
	Penultimate 5m	Last 5m				
Bubka	9.78	9.80	10.73	0.913	5.13	6.01
Gatulin	9.25	9.43	10.50	0.898	5.05	5.90
Jegorov	9.17	9.36	10.57	0.886	4.95	5.85
Bondarenko	9.17	9.23	10.40	0.888	5.00	5.65
Bogatoryov	9.19	9.13	10.37	0.880	4.85	5.80
Spasov	9.20	9.06	10.35	0.875	4.80	5.70
Tshernyajev	9.14	9.04	10.46	0.864	4.75	5.70
Obizayev	9.12	8.96	10.44	0.858	4.75	5.65

TABLE 1: The influence of technical preparation to the pole vault performance.

Figure 22.7

(m)	Run-up Speed over last 10m (m/sec) — Check mark distances (m)					
	8.8	9.0	9.2	9.4	9.6	9.8
4.70	17.00	17.25	17.50	17.75	18.00	18.25
4.80	17.25	17.50	17.75	18.00	18.25	18.50
4.90	17.50	17.75	18.00	18.25	18.50	18.75
5.00	17.75	18.00	18.25	18.50	18.75	19.00
5.10	18.00	18.25	18.50	18.75	19.00	19.25
5.30	18.25	18.50	18.75	19.00	19.25	19.50

TABLE 2: Placement of check marks according to the run-up speed and the grip height.

Figure 22.8

pole must be synchronised with the vaulter's speed in the run up. One may easily control that rhythm when the vaulters speed in running with the pole is within 10 m/sec or is about the speed of a body falling freely."

As far as we are aware there have been no studies, empirical or otherwise, which establish whether this relationship continues when athletes are running slower than 10 m/sec but we have assumed that it does. Only informal experimentation will show a coach whether the suggested figures are appropriate for their athletes.Our experience suggests that they appear to be valid for our better athletes. However we believe that as soon as young athletes become committed to the pole vault we should begin to introduce as many elements of the "Advanced technical model" as they can cope with. So we encourage them to begin to master the run up structure outlined below and shown in Figure 22.7 along with the high carry angle and the associated pole drop so that they can develop the specific rhythmic structure required. A run up therefore has a 6/6 pattern, 8/6 pattern, 10/6 and so on.

Developing the run up

Once these principles are accepted it is clear that the pole vault run up must have a specific structure. The basic pattern is that run up speed is increased gradually with an erect body position and with raking strides, then as the pole is lowered to begin to prepare for the plant, the cadence is increased.

We believe that this establishes the importance of the final six steps when the pole is being lowered and run up cadence increases. We therefore think in terms of SIX plus six/eight/ten/twelve steps. Note that we do not commonly use the 'LEFTS' system common in the USA simply because three of our most successful athletes have been left handers for whom this would be inappropriate. However we do use it to help beginners build the structure of part of their run up.

Once the decision is made on the number of steps to be used, that specific run up should be practised from that point on. We also believe that the full run up used by each vaulter has a unique structure and rhythm. This means that the full competition run up must be continually practiced and improved; with committed athletes this means throughout the whole year.

This practice can follow a logical sequence of
- Practicing the run up on the track with no markers.

- Using a fixed starting point, run up and noting the provisional six step cue and take off points.
- Running up to plant into a towel – adjust the run to establish six step and take off point.
- Running up to plant into a sliding box – confirm check marks.
- Moving to the vault runway; check markers.
- As above and take off – this is where the 'Jump and hold' drill is invaluable.
- Check run up speed with a Laveg or a video camera.

Running technique with and without a pole can be improved through the use of specific drills. Because there is ample material on sprinting in the literature we do not intend to deal with this issue in great depth here. However it is worth making the point that while there has been some debate about the value of such drills our experience confirms that they can be used to make significant improvements in sprinting, both with and without the pole. Improvement requires a balance between drill emphasis and speed emphasis – each drill must be taken seriously with the athlete focussing on correct execution from the beginning. There are three ways to assist transfer of motor skill from drills to fast running. The athlete should -
- Understand the relationship between drills and actual running
- Begin a drill slowly with complete concentration on the specific technical aspect to be developed. Gradually accelerate, thinking about the specific technical element to be practiced. As the rhythm is established, the athlete must consciously relax particular parts of the body in turn.
- Accelerate towards full speed and then focus on specific elements of good running technique.

Although we may have previously challenged it, experience has taught us that Petrov's dictum "The pole vault begins with the first step of the run up" is in fact true. Like most coaches we used to focus on the last few steps before take off, essentially the plant and take off phase. Only gradually did our focus shift further and further back until we really did begin to take notice of that first step. There we discovered a whole range of previously unnoticed problems. Athletes who skipped into the first step were varying by as much as thirty centimetres in this first movement. While we realise that some very successful coaches prefer a skip or short run into the first mark we believe that it is better to control as many variables as possible and begin the run up, as did Bubka et al, from a still position.

We became aware of another problem when one of our most talented athletes drifted into a pattern where, before she began her run up, she took most of her weight back over a flexed leg. This caused her to begin her run with her hips low, a problem which was often carried through to take off. The solution was to ensure that she stayed tall on the right leg as it moved back and then to make sure the right knee was brought up on the first step, as if to touch the lower hand on the pole.

Finally it is important to appreciate that there is no point in improving run up speed unless the athlete has the technical ability to exploit that speed and, most importantly, their body can cope with the shock of an explosive take off.

CHAPTER TWENTY THREE

The Plant and Take off for ambitious young vaulters – and their coaches?

"… a pole vaulter is born in the last steps of the run up"
Petrov

The primary objective of any ambitious athlete who has begun to master the advanced technical model, should be to try to exploit higher grips and to use the stiffest possible poles. To do this safely and effectively they need to be able to generate and direct the energy needed at take off to drive the pole/lever towards the vertical. At the very least, this requires a fast run up and a powerful upspringing 'free' take off in which the hands are driven high to maximise the pole ground angle.

This means that the athlete must be able to run fast while controlling a long lever, using a relatively narrow grip. In turn this requires an initial high carry angle of the pole. The downside is that this high angle carry can make the plant a more complex process - to the extent that many coaches prefer to accept the disadvantages of a low pole carry to minimise any problem. We have no doubt that this attitude will seriously disadvantage ambitious and talented athletes.

As we suggested earlier, there is little point in an athlete accelerating to top speed over forty metres only to decelerate over the final five metres.Unfortunately this is precisely what many athletes do! While there may be several reasons why this occurs we believe that a poor planting action is the most common cause. This appears to be confirmed by Nikonov who uses the data shown in Figures 22.8 and 22.9 to suggest that the athletes who continued to accelerate over the final five metres were able to do so because of their superior planting technique.

While loss of speed becomes increasingly important as athletes progress towards the highest levels of performance, a poor plant leads to serious problems for athletes at any level. The most obvious of these is 'running through' instead of taking off. Coaches often view this problem as evidence of 'lack of moral fibre' but we believe that the athlete is only responding naturally to intuitive feedback from their body which 'knows' that an off balance take off will lead to injury or worse. Unfortunately instead of doing the intensive work needed to improve the plant, many athletes rely on the exhortations of their 'friends' to override the sensible messages their brain is giving them and so continue into danger.

Many of the problems associated with a poor plant include
- A low pole/ground angle at take off
- An off balance take off
- An inability to spring up

As is always the case with the advanced model we are presenting in this book, each element of technique fits together as part of a totally integrated whole. So the ideal characteristics of an effective plant are –
- It is a part of a coherent and integrated technical model.
- It flows from the structure of the run up.
- The athlete continues to accelerate through to take off.
- The pole is moved from the carry position to the plant efficiently with no loss of control or balance.
- The pole is positioned for take off before the touchdown of the take off foot.
- It permits a free take off.

1. The integrated technical model.
The point continually emphasised throughout this text is summed up by Petrov's statement -
  "The run up and pole plant in the box should be seen as a single integral movement: one must not think that the pole vaulter's plant begins directly before the box."
2. The structure of the run up.
Without the built in increase in cadence as the pole lowers it will be difficult for the athlete to control the pole and position it for the plant.
3. Accelerating through to take off!
This bears repeating! There is no value in the athlete running 40 metres to build up speed and energy - and then to let it fall away as they move through the most critical 5 metres before take off.
4. Moving the pole from the carry position.
As Petrov suggested, the 'Plant' begins with the first step of the run up. Many elite vaulters do begin a gradual but slight lowering of the pole from its initial high carry position from that first step. However the 'active pole drop', for want of a better term, usually begins six steps out from take off as the athlete hits the

cue mark which also signals the beginning of the change in running cadence. Over the next three steps the pole tip drops from its high carry position to approximately head high, rotating smoothly around the fulcrum of the left hand. During this phase the left hand itself moves down slightly with the lowering of the pole. This is all straightforward and obvious; now comes the difficult part!

The problem is how to get the pole tip moving down to the box without lowering the left hand any further! The reason for this is simple. If the left hand drops to get the tip down, the mass of the whole pole is now low and it must be lifted into the plant with a long pull push action. This is mechanically inefficient. However the photograph of Lobinger, a 6.00 metre vaulter from Germany, in Chapter 22, confirms that it is possible to vault high even when making basic mistakes.

The alternative method, which we recommend, is to keep the left hand as high as possible, and to rotate the tip down towards the box by starting to raise the top end of the pole! This is initiated by 'rolling the wrist' of the right hand up. Figure 23. This action initiates the plant proper and begins as the athlete moves onto the right foot, three steps from take off. Executed

the Petrov way it creates a three and a half step plant!

The rationale is simple. If we want to have the pole in position for take off just before the take off foot touches the ground we must begin the planting action early. We also want to ensure that we do not drop the left hand – and the pole – to the level of the hips.

We realise that there is continuing debate about when the 'plant proper', ie the movement of the pole tip down toward the box, should begin. Even Gunther Tidow in his excellent paper in "New Studies in Athletics" hedges his bets, and merely reports that some athletes use a two step plant while others employ three steps. However the method described above is in our view the most efficient and effective method of planting the pole. At the very least it should eliminate a late plant, an important consideration given that a late plant will lead to a host of problems through the rest of the jump.

It is important to remember that important as the 'plant' is to effective pole vaulting, it is only a means to an end, that is to put the pole into a position to make an explosive upspringing take off.

Figure 23.2 shows Tarasov moving onto the right foot two steps out. He is perfectly under

Figure 23.1

Figure 23.2

control and the pole is in an excellent position so that he can move his hands up with the pole rotating smoothly around the fulcrum of the left hand. Figure 23.3. This moves the tip down in preparation for the plant in the box while the hands move up ready for take off Figure 23.4.

It is perhaps not surprising that many of the myths associated with the take off. As suggested earlier, the change from the stiff pole to the flexible pole led many athletes into the trap of focussing on bending the pole at take off and not on driving the pole upwards and forwards. However that change took place over fifty years ago so it is astonishing that debates continue to rage, even on the Internet, over the relative merits of a springing take off vis a vis running off the ground or deliberately taking off flat. We can only hope that this chapter will resolve this issue once and for all.

Figure 23.3

An effective take off flows from an accurate, balanced run up and an efficient planting action. It should be a powerful driving 'upspring' in which the pole is driven up and forward with a powerful extension of the whole body. We have little doubt that if coaches and athletes accept the notion of an infinite series of straight poles from take off to maximum bend, it will be easier for them to develop an effective take off.

The ideal take off is one -

- **Where the pole/ground angle is maximised.** The importance of maximising the pole ground angle at the instant of take off often gets lost in discussion of pole vault technique. This is unfortunate because it is a critical factor in moving the pole forward and then initiating pole bend. As vaulters grip higher on stiff poles it becomes **the** critical factor.

- **Where the take off foot is actively whipped down and back to the ground** in what we have termed a "Claw/strike". While it is impossible to prevent some flexion at the knee joint at this point, vaulters should try to keep the take off leg straight and rigid.This is important because the key to an effective take off in all the jumping events is to generate a high ground impulse in minimum time. As Petrov says

"The vaulter TRIES to place his leg straight and rigid but under pressure of speed and body mass the leg bends, and then throws the vaulter up."

Figure 23.4

- **Which is "Out" rather than "Under".** In his 1985 presentation Petrov argued for a take off point directly under the top hand. However it appears that more and more elite vaulters are taking off 'out', because this facilitates a 'free take off' or a 'pre jump'. Note that it is the position of the foot relative to the top hand at the moment the athlete leaves the ground which is important, not where it first touches down.

- **Where both hands are driven up as hard and as high as possible. The athlete should have the feeling that this high punch of the hands continues after take off.** It is here that a relatively narrow grip is an advantage.

- **Where the body is rigid from the top hand to the take off foot.** This is important because all of the kinetic energy generated by the run up and take off must be transmitted to the pole through the top hand. Unless there is a tight connection between the top hand and the rest of the body, energy will bleed away as it is absorbed in the shock of take off.

Despite the critical importance of this aspect of technique it rarely seems to be emphasised enough either in technical training or in physical conditioning.

Anyone who has coached top class shot putters will understand the importance of this concept, as will those who have analysed the killing blows of the martial arts or the classic knock out punch of a boxer. All three involve the transmission of force to a single point from a momentarily rigid body platform connected to the ground.

- **In which the heel of the free leg is driven up to the buttocks** as the take off leg strikes the ground. This movement is vital because
  1. It ensures that the body holds a strong 'dish' position which enables it to absorb the shock of take off
  2. The powerfully punched knee/thigh is now 'blocked' so that the energy of that drive transmits vertically into the body.
  3. It ensures that the hips are not dragged forward to collapse the rigid body system.
  4. It helps minimise back problems.
- **Which is a powerful driving upspring** where the take off leg and ankle are fully extended at and immediately after take off. Coaches will do well to remember that to the French and the Italians this event is "The jump with a pole" and to the Germans it is the "Pole high jump". It is only when the athlete JUMPS at take off that it is possible for them to approach their full potential. Remember how this point was emphasised in the discussion of stiff pole vaulting.
- **Where the lower hand is carefully positioned** - to allow the bottom arm to relax as the top hand hits the pole. This is one of the more subtle but vital elements of this technical model.
- **Which is completed before the pole tip touches the back of the box**
- **Where the pole is straight at the instant of take off**

All of these elements were illustrated in Chapter 6.

These last two characteristics define one of the most revolutionary, and certainly the most controversial, of all of the innovations Petrov introduced in his original paper presented at the European Coaches Congress in Birmingham in 1985. There he said

- *"And only on concluding the take off should the vaulter transfer smoothly into support …."*
- *"During the plant the pole ………….. bends under the effect of the vaulter's speed and body mass ….."*
- *"The vaulter's task is to drive the pole at take off as much as possible and to give himself a FREE TAKE OFF with transfer at the end into a smooth plant of the pole."*
  "If we perform a free take off we can feel the pushing action of the whole body and we can transfer the speed of the run up and take off". But this angle must be achieved with a complete extension of the body and mainly, keeping that short difference between the full extension of the body and the tip of the pole reaching the end of the box."

It is clear that few if any coaches understood what he was saying at that time. This may have been because of the problems in translation or because of the revolutionary nature of the concept, a concept which many coaches still do not accept.

However it is just possible that some of the confusion has arisen because the term "A free take off" has never been precisely defined – at least in the English language! In an attempt to clarify this issue we have attempted to define both the "Free take off" and its logical extension "The Pre Jump" and to explain the major advantages of both concepts in this chapter.

A 'free' takeoff occurs when the toe of the jumper leaves the ground at the instant the pole tip hits the back of the box. The most obvious indicator of a free takeoff is that the pole is still straight at the instant the vaulter leaves the ground. This is in complete contrast to the methods still used by many modern vaulters.

The theoretical rationale for the "free take off" is simple and logical. No matter how a pole is planted, the instant the tip touches the back of the box, the vaulter/pole system must begin to decelerate. This is because the kinetic energy from that system becomes potential energy stored in the flexing pole.

The rationale for the 'Free take off' is as follows
- No kinetic energy generated in the run up should be lost before the vaulter leaves the ground.
- No energy should be wasted trying to bend the pole before take off.
- A pole flexes as the result of the kinetic energy generated by the vaulter at take off.
- The greater the kinetic energy at the instant of take off, and the greater the pole ground

angle, the easier the pole will bend.

- Therefore the pole should not be 'loaded' until the instant after the vaulter leaves the ground.

In the first place it is completely logical to assume that if an athlete is trying to jump over a bar positioned high in the air that they should as far as possible direct their forces at take off towards that target. Secondly, assuming that it is properly directed, the more energy the vaulter can put into the pole, the higher they will be able to grip and the stiffer the pole they will be able to use. Of course there are other factors which impact on this, especially the ability of the vaulter to 'hit' the pole at the correct angle with a 'rigid' body as indicated above.

We believe that Bubka took the concept of the 'free take off' even further. Again this is illustrated by Figure 5.7, a photograph of his take off for the World Record clearance of 6.00 metres in 1985. This shows that he has LEFT THE GROUND BEFORE the pole tip has hit the back of the box! **We have called this extension of the free take off a "Pre Jump".**

While recognising the limitations of our analysis it is possible to use simple geometric principles to estimate some critical distances. Our calculations show that Bubka's toe was approximately 8 to 10 centimetres behind the perpendicular from the top hand and 5 to 8 centimetres above the runway at the instant the photograph was taken. The pole is still straight which indicates that he has lost little or none of the kinetic energy generated in his run up. Of equal significance, he has increased the pole/ground angle by up to five degrees compared with a toe tip take off.

Clearly the pole does flex up to ten degrees, but this appears to us to be localised around the left hand. We believe that the incipient bend here is caused by the inertial forces acting on the flexible pole as Bubka punched both hands high in the take off and is not the result of the pole tip touching the back of the box. This would seem to be confirmed by the fact that the right arm is still 'covering' the right ear and has not been driven back by the forces which would be initiated the instant the pole tip touches the back of the box.

Inevitably there will be ongoing debate on this issue. However at the clinic in Jamaica on July 20th 2001 Bubka made his vision of the take off crystal clear. In response to a direct question from Alan he said

"In pole vaulting the crucial factor is how to transfer energy to the pole, through the complete body of the vaulter: the arms, shoulders, hip, back and legs. But if the pole begins to bend while the vaulter is yet on the ground, it is impossible to

transfer the energy; all the energy is lost and goes to the box. The point is. How to achieve this? ***The free take off is a very short period of time, we can say no more that hundredths of a second, going from the end of the take off and the moment in which the tip of the pole reaches the end of the box. But this short time makes a big difference that allows the competitor to greatly improve their results."***

We make no apologies for repeating this quote because we believe that Bubka was describing a 'Pre jump'. This is not surprising because the concept of the 'pre jump' is easy to justify on theoretical grounds. Apart from encouraging an aggressive plant which seamlessly melds the horizontal velocity of the run up into a springing take off, there is another major benefit especially for jumpers gripping above 5.00m (16'5'). At every level of performance it is important to maximise the pole/ground angle at take off because the greater this angle is, the easier the pole will bend. When athletes use very high grips, maximising this angle becomes even more important. Based on the above photograph, our calculations suggest that Bubka has increased the pole/ground angle by up to five degrees compared to a toe tip take off.

Describing a "Pre jump" as distinct from a Free take off, Bubka said

"When you can do it (pre jump) you can increase the angle of the pole in relation with the ground."

Since even Bubka believes that taking off before the pole tip touches the back of the box is extremely difficult to do, it is clear that it is not possible to pre jump every time. However it is also clear that even an attempt to pre jump will produce a more efficient take off, especially if the jumper continues to drive the arms up through the pole after they have left the ground. We see a free take off as a failed pre jump!

There is considerable anecdotal evidence to support the concepts outlined above. For example, two German coaches, Thomas Kurschilgen and Franc Pejic visited the Donetsk pole vault centre in 1988. In their twelve page report they noted

"The take off must be free, similar to a long jumper with the arms held high. Only immediately after leaving the ground is the resistance in the box noticeable; only a free take off enables maximum acceleration of the pole and jumper, creates a high take off speed for an effective transmission of energy."

In her "Kinematic analysis of the women's pole vault" Stephanie Grabner quotes Keller who says

"During the take off the vaulter on the one hand tries to create a vertical impulse to straighten the pole without a reduction of the horizontal velocity

and on the other hand to try to achieve a favourable take off position to transmit their energy to the pole".

She goes on to quote Petrov

"To fulfil this demand the athlete should strive for a free take off with only a small loss of energy and ensure that the pole plant does not take place before they have broken contact with the ground."

Klaus Bartonietz and Johann Wetter indicated that one of the three major elements of their target technique is

"At the finish of the take off the pole is not yet bent ('free take off'), only when the take off foot leaves the ground has the pole full contact with the back of the box and starts bending".

Note that Bartonietz is arguably the leading track and field biomechanist in the world.

Dr. Jean Claude Perrin, formerly National Pole Vault Coach of France and personal coach of 1984 Olympic champion Quinon, reported that

"European Jumpers are actually jumping into the take off about 30cm further back than what has

been regarded as the ideal spot vertically below the top hand". As a result of the changed takeoff action the vaulters are actually in the air, or off the ground before the pole hits the back of the box."

While many modern athletes demonstrate a free take off, to date there has been little visual or force platform evidence to confirm the Pre jump take off. Interestingly the official IAAF film from the 1986 World Junior Championships in Athens does show and describe a pre jump take off in which Lessov of Bulgaria leaves the ground 1/100ths of a second before the pole tip hits the back of the box. To quote the IAAF commentator verbatim

"Lessov of Bulgaria (taking third place) left the ground 1/100th of a second before the pole tip hit the back wall of the box".

The last word must be from Sergey Bubka. In his response to a specific question from Alan he said,

"It (the Pre jump) is a crucial factor, but at the same time, it is not easy to achieve. During my career, I was able to do it some times."

CHAPTER TWENTY FOUR

Ambitious young vaulters and the swing into inversion

"Many athletes seem to view the swing as simply a way of moving the body from take off into the rock back"

Perhaps because of the complex relationships involved, another advantage of the flexible pole is often ignored. In Chapters Eleven and Twenty One we indicated that the 'swing' was a critical element in effective vaulting with a stiff pole. The figures of Warmerdam and Richards show this conclusively. However in the transition to the flexible pole this was another aspect of technique which tended to be ignored as the focus switched from moving the pole to bending it.

The progressive shortening of the pole means that the movement path of the hands is extended as shown in Figure 24.1. This increases the amplitude of the swing and means that the athlete has more time to put energy into the pole. It is easy to carry out a simple experiment which will help anyone understand the notion of ampli-

tutde and the positive effect it can have on the speed of the whipping action of the left leg and foot. Simply take a rope or string with its bundle of keys at the end and swing it around as we suggested earlier. Once the keys are swinging in a circle, move your hand forward. Immediately the speed of the keys will dramatically increase. This is what happens to the vaulters foot when the amplitude of the swing is increased.

Many modern vaulters use some of this extra time in the milliseconds after take off -
* to continue to drive the take off leg back,
* to create a slight flexion at the knee,
* - which enables the athlete to begin a long accelerating swing of the leg,
  - - in an action very similar to a powerful soccer kick,
  - - - which extends all the way to the point where the Vaulter pendulum passes the Chord of the pole.

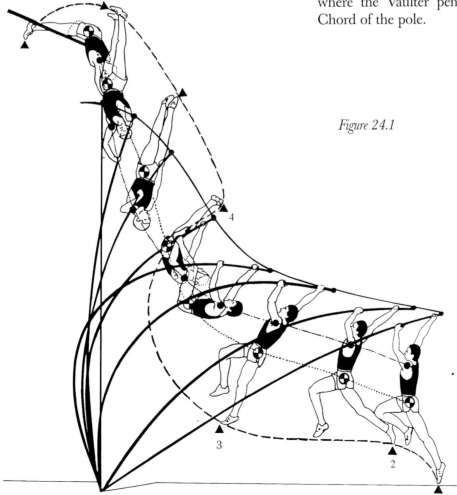

Figure 24.1

This becomes obvious when you look at the path of the left foot in Figure 24.1. It travels in a long whipping movement from Point 2, immediately after the driving extension of the take off leg and ankle have been completed, and continues on until Point 4 when the athlete's legs are covering the pole.

This phase of the vault is important because it provides skilful athletes with the opportunity to put an enormous amount of energy into the pole, while at the same time moving the body into the optimum position to exploit the recoil. It is also here that the effects of previous mistakes in technique can be magnified and life threatening situations may be created.

This can happen when

- The athlete attempts to move into a vertical position too soon after take off, without first driving the pole forwards and up. This raises the centre of mass of the vaulter/pole system and further reduces the angular momentum of that system. The pole stops rolling forward and the athlete is now suspended above the box.
- The take off is 'flat' and towards the pad instead of up through the pole.
- The pole is quickly compressed into a low bend instead of flexing naturally as the vaulter hits it.
- The vaulter is gripping too high in relation to the quality of their run, plant and take off.
- The vaulter is using a pole which is either too soft or too stiff.

The 'swing'

We have already emphasised the importance of a balanced and controlled run up, an early and accurate planting action and a high free take off.

Now we want to clarify the importance and mechanism of the swing into inversion. We suggested earlier that an obsession with bending the pole rather than moving it, has meant that other important advantages of the flexible pole have been ignored. This certainly appears to be the case with 'the swing', which was critical to effective vaulting in the stiff pole era but appears to have been neglected in the transition to flexible poles. As a result, many young athletes seem to view the swing as simply a way of moving the body from take off into the inversion.

The change in emphasis from 'moving the pole' to 'bending the pole' at the beginning of the fibre glass era may be one reason this happened. It is also likely that the word itself contributes to this lack of understanding, because the term 'swing' does imply a rather passive movement. However even 'swing' is better than 'hang', or even

'hang/drive', terms used in recent years to describe this phase of the vault, because they imply almost complete inaction. **In an attempt to better define this action we use the term 'whip'.**

To put as much energy into the pole as possible the modern vaulter uses a 'whip' of the extended trailing leg after a driving take off. This long whipping leg action begins from as far back as the left foot is driven back at the instant of take off. It continues until the instant it begins to transfer its energy into the hips when the body passes the chord of the pole. Perhaps the best analogy is that the vaulter is trying to kick a soccer ball positioned on the chord of the fully bent pole with the instep of the take off foot. The problem with illustrations, as with Figure 24.1 above, is that they show a dangling left leg – Point 3 – when in fact the left leg is whipping forward and upwards much faster than any other part of the body is moving!

The amplitude of this whip is significantly extended because the Chord of the pole progressively and rapidly shortens. This is yet another aspect of modern technique which has neither been appreciated nor understood. If all coaches and athletes clearly understood the importance of the whipping pendulum swing of the trailing leg they would surely never allow their athletes to take off 'under'; they would also insist that athletes 'finish the take off' on every jump so that the take off leg is in position to initiate the 'whip'.

Whatever the reason, many athletes and coaches do not seem to understand the immense contribution this phase can make to putting energy into the pole, a process which should continue **throughout** the vault, not merely at take off.

Here it is worth recalling the words of 'Dutch' Warmerdam

"There is a definite delay - in the swing - to take advantage of the velocity which has been developed during the run up. If the vaulter delays momentarily, the body moves forward, the arms extend, the legs swing up automatically as the grip of the hands on the pole stops forward progress."

Compare these words from the 1940's with these which were written in 1986 -

"The athlete begins the hang phase, assisted by his high take off speed that allows sufficient time for the execution of this phase" and "relaxes in the hang somewhat his left arm and keeps the takeoff leg trailing in order to delay the upward swing. The swing, making use of the pause and the pre tension of the trunk muscles, is wide and powerful."

They come from the analysis of Bubka's 6.01m World record in Moscow in 1986, by Yagodin and Papanov.

They go on to say

"The so called 'wide swing' in Bubka's record vault begins with a lead leg action that has a horizontal velocity of 15.6m/s and a vertical velocity of 12.5m/s."

This confirms the notion of an accelerating whip like swing. It is interesting to note that when this whipping action is analysed on film, the movement of the foot is often blurred.

While this whipping swing of the trailing leg is vital to good vaulting it is dependent on all of the elements which precede it. So its' effectiveness is enhanced by -

- A narrow grip: Remember here the very narrow grip used by 'stiff' pole vaulters. which permitted a long pendular swing of the whole body.
- A pre jump which maximises the energy put into the pole at take off.
- A take off which is high and "out", because this facilitates pendular oscillation in the desired direction.
- A take off which is finished with a powerful extension of the take off leg.
- The take off leg driven back into a fully extended position after take off and then slightly flexed at the knee to set up the initial kicking action.
- A 'steel elastic' bottom arm.
- The chest driven up and forward 'through the shoulders'.

All of this leads to the creation of a pre stretch of the muscles of the body from the arms to the toe of the extended take off leg. Figure 24.2. With athletes using a higher grip, this pre stretch is further enhanced by what German coaches have termed 'a disengaged left arm' but which should more appropriately be termed 'an elastic stretch', which allows the chest to driven up and 'through' the shoulders. This also changes the timing of the movement into the inversion and adds to the powerful whip of the fully extended take off leg.

Not only does this action put energy into the pole, but the long swinging leg also helps to keep the centre of mass of the vaulter/pole system low for milliseconds longer. This naturally causes that system to roll forward more rapidly.

Conversely any early pick up of the legs or the body will raise the centre of mass of the system so that any chance of the long pendular swing is lost. Even the early pick up of the take off leg alone can have a major impact.

Some athletes deliberately extend the free leg in an effort to keep the centre of mass of the vaulter/pole system low and to slow down the rotation of the body around the vertical axis. In our opinion what most vaulters gain from this action, they may lose in other ways. Many of these 'double leg swingers' anticipate the dropping of the lead leg at take off and so never jump up and through the pole; in many cases they are forced to follow the long swing with a rapid tuck in which the knees are pulled into the nose. This is far less efficient than the Bubka method which enabled him to put energy into the pole even while moving into the inversion to cover the pole.

This is evident in the technique of the Polish Champion Kolasa who executes a double leg swing soon after take off but who is then forced to 'tuck and shoot' which means he loses any real chance to put energy into the pole at this point.

Indoor World Champion, Igor Potapovich, was one of the few athletes who could nail the take off, drop the lead leg and still ensure the shoulder drop/hip drive instead of reverting to the 'tuck and shoot' method.

Dimitri Markov has a great take off, perhaps the best of modern vaulters and also drops the lead leg for an instant before pulling it back up into the classic Petrov/

Figure 24.2

Figure 24.3

Figure 24.4

Bubka position. However the slight slowing in the rotation of his body around the hands may be one of the reasons why Dimitri is unable to cover the pole effectively and rarely gets the vertical shoot characteristic of Bubka's best jumps. It is also possible that the drop and pull action Dimitri uses with the lead leg, may make it difficult for him to 'fix' his body, through muscle tension, into the most effective shape for the inversion.

The Inversion

The energy of the whip is carried on into the inversion which should be initiated as the centre of mass of the vaulter moves level with the Chord of the pole. It is at that point that the left hand/arm makes 'contact' or 'engages' with the pole. This slows the movement of the shoulders

and torso, and causes the energy of the swing to be transferred to the hips, pelvis and torso.

To increase the speed of the roll back, the vaulter breaks at the hips to shorten the axis of rotation and then uses muscle power to momentarily lock the body into an 'L' position. Figures 24.3 and 24.4.

The timing of this movement is critical. Too early and the vaulter kills pole speed but if they are too late they may be unable to get into position to exploit the recoil of the pole. If this movement is delayed, it will be difficult for the athlete to invert fast enough to fully exploit the recoil of the pole.

One of the major differences between athletes using the Petrov/Bubka model and those who do not, is that the latter often 'break' at the hips AND at the knees to go into a tight tuck. Figure 24.5. This means that they miss the opportunity to put energy into the pole as is possible with the Petrov/Bubka method. As Petrov said

"The vaulter should not try to bend his legs at the knee and hip joints".

It also becomes impossible for them to achieve the extreme vertical positions consistently demonstrated by Bubka on the front cover of this book.

In the advanced technical model we are presenting in this book, the vaulter changes body shape as suggest above and then tries to roll the pelvis upwards, with the left leg staying as

Figure 24.5

Figure 24.6

straight as possible, but with a slight flexion in the right leg. In this way they move into a position 'covering' the pole. Figure 24.6 As soon as this movement is completed, the vaulter drops the shoulders and then drives the hips vertically upwards. This movement, shoulder drop/ hip drive is yet another element of the advanced technical model demonstrated by Bubka throughout his career that has passed almost unnoticed. However it achieves two important objectives.

On the one hand the energy generated by the drop drive movement helps to keep the pole flexed slightly longer, so it rolls forward quicker. On the other hand the vaulter can position their body to take full advantage of the recoiling pole and so maximise the speed with which they are projected vertically. We have found that it is better for the athlete to simply think of driving the hips up from a stable position on the pole. The shoulders then drop back naturally.

As we suggested in Chapter Seven, even great athletes like Maxim Tarasov make mistakes in this phase. It appears to us that Maxim was unable to maintain the tight control of his pelvis as he began the inversion and so was unable to roll it upwards. This meant that although his legs came back to cover the pole, his hips stayed beneath the pole leaving him in a poor position to take full advantage of the recoil.

Coaches who want to better understand the way energy is generated throughout the whip into inversion, should take themselves to a playground which has a children's swing, the bigger the better! Simply get onto the swing and get it moving the way any child would, long legs swinging forward – flexed legs swinging back. They will very quickly generate the energy to begin to move the swing to the horizontal. When they are near this point and hanging on for grim death to the side chains, they should begin to drop their shoulders backwards and drive their backsides through the seat of the swing. They will immediately feel the surge of energy this action produces. Clearly this is not a perfect analogy but it will simply and easily confirm the points made above.

Again it is interesting to consider the words of Petrov who said,

"The rock back and upswing must be completed before the pole begins to straighten…,the rock back and upswing on the pole is considered complete when the vaulter has managed to cover the arc of the pole with his hips and legs; while the legs somehow serve as a continuation of the upper end of the pole".

and

"Covering the arc of the pole with his hips and legs, while the legs somehow serve as the continuation of the upper end of the pole". It may be better to think of covering the bent pole."

This delays the recoil of the pole, maintains the bend fractionally longer and lets the vaulter/pole system move forward more quickly. It allows the athlete to get into the best possible position to exploit the recoil of the pole.

Figure 24.7a

Figure 24.7b

"The rock back should be done by simultaneously shifting the body parts – legs up shoulders down." This puts the athlete into position to ensure that the energy of the recoil is directed almost vertically through the centre of mass of the vaulter who "also straightens upwards along the pole".

While Petrov talks about "The throwing back of the shoulders", this is better thought of as a cue for athletes rather than an accurate description of what they really do. In fact this vertical position is achieved by the athlete driving the hips and legs above the shoulders which only appear to be moving down relative to the rest of the body. There is little doubt that Bubka put even more energy into the pole during this phase to give himself even more time to position himself for the recoil. Figures 24.7a and b show a simple exercise to help develop this phase of the vault. However again it must be stressed that there is little point in working on this element of technique until all the preceding elements have been mastered to a reasonable level.

CHAPTER TWENTY FIVE

Myths and misunderstanding in the pole vault

"If vaulters believe any of these myths they are limiting their potential and may be putting themselves at risk every time they take off"

The complexity of vaulting with a flexible pole has lead to an ongoing search for the ideal "Technical model". Until now, sports science has contributed little to our understanding of this event and has mainly been limited to describing what many athletes **do**, rather than developing clear guidelines for what they **should** do. What is astonishing is that many sports scientists appear to be unaware of the advantages of the technical model employed by many of the great vaulters of the former "Soviet School", including the incredibly successful Sergey Bubka. Equally surprising is that few students of the event appear to understand the link between the major technical elements of the great vaulters of the stiff pole era such as Warmerdam and Richards and that employed by Bubka.

As a result there has never been a definitive statement of all the advantages which the flexible pole brought to pole vaulting, far less a clear explanation of how to exploit it's **full** potential. This has lead to a situation where the technique of vaulting with a flexible pole has often been driven by the whims of individual athletes or coaches and where myths and misunderstanding have had a greater impact on technique than science.

A fundamental misunderstanding about the most effective way of causing a pole to flex has lead to many of the problems observed at every level of performance around the world. While this **is** a complex issue, it is surprising to discover that many coaches still believe that the vaulter should attempt to bend the pole as much as possible before leaving the ground. Amazingly, some still believe that the best way to bend the pole is to actively pull down with the top hand and push up through the pole with the bottom hand! What is astonishing about this particular misunderstanding is that it can possibly be traced back to the erroneous ideas and methods of vaulters like Aubrey Dooley, whom J. Kenneth Docherty credits with being the pioneer of fibre glass vaulting in 1956!! Of course the pole **will** bend, and bend an incredible amount, but at the cost of an effective take off and problems throughout the jump.

Unfortunately sports science may be one reason why this myth is perpetuated. In the fourth edition of his text, "The biomechanics of sports techniques", the late Dr. James Hay wrote

"If the athlete drives upward and forward across the line of the pole, the magnitudes of the parallel forces are relatively small and their tendency to bend the pole is minimal. On the other hand, if the vaulter drives forward into the pole, the magnitudes of the parallel forces and the resulting bending of the pole are correspondingly greater."

The first sentence argues against the notion of a free take off which has been a critical element of the technique of many of the leading vaulters since 1983, while the second reflects the erroneous ideas and methods of the very early pioneers of fibre glass vaulting. Note that Dr. Hay's book was reprinted in 1993, ten years after Bubka had clearly demonstrated that the athlete should not attempt to bend the pole before they leave the ground and eight years after Bubka's coach, Vitally Petrov, publicly advocated a "Free take off" in which the pole is not flexed, and therefore not loaded, until after the athlete has left the ground.

There is little doubt that this particular misunderstanding has prevented many athletes from achieving their full potential, but there are other myths and misunderstandings which have also impeded progress in this event.

The myths include
* Grip as high as possible
* It is better to use a wide grip because it makes it easier to control the pole
* Run as far and fast as you can
* It doesn't matter how you run, as long as you run fast
* The angle the pole is carried at is not particularly important
* Taking off 'Under' is all right – it is easier to bend the pole that way
* The position of the free leg at the instant of take off is not critical
* Get yourself into a vertical position on the pole as soon as possible after take off

What makes some of these 'myths' really dangerous is that they contain a germ of truth! Great athletes do grip high, they do run far and fast, they do try to invert rapidly after taking off.

However they do each of these things in the context of a total technical model where the perfect execution of one phase leads into the perfect execution of the next phase.

When young athletes unthinkingly base their technique on any or all of these myths it is unlikely that they will ever fulfil their potential. Even worse they place themselves at risk every time they jump.

The myth of gripping high

It is true that athletes should aim to grip as high as possible, **but only after they have mastered the fundamental elements of the basic technical model, and can take off with control!** In other words they should already have an accurate run up, a reasonable plant and can swing their hips above their shoulders.

Coaches are often tempted to push an athlete's grip up before they are ready, simply because it seems like an easy way to pick up extra height. Even if it works, the result may be to delay the athlete's long term development because gripping higher may make it difficult, if not impossible, for the athlete to maintain the positive rhythm of the jump. Even worse, the athlete may risk injury if they are unable to drive the longer lever through to the safety of the pad.

A wide grip

Most vaulters will find it easier to carry a long pole using a wide grip, because it helps them counter the torque forces generated when they run with a low pole angle. **Unfortunately this is a trap** which can lead to major problems at take off and on through the rest of the jump. With a wide grip -

- If the top hand is above the head at the instant of take off the bottom hand must be extended almost horizontally forward. This leads the athlete into a flat take off and an early bend of the pole. The late George Moore, President of Pacer American and pole vault aficionado, wrote an article warning of the dangers of this method more than thirty years ago.
- Conversely if the front arm is correctly positioned, the top hand is now well behind the head and low. This also leads to problems. First it reduces the pole ground angle but even more importantly it prevents the athlete from hitting the pole with the rigid tall 'dish' position so critical to good vaulting.

Figure 25. 1 shows 1984 Olympic Champion Quinon of France. While he is doing many things very well it is clear that he has been unable to maximise the pole ground angle! It

Figure 25.1

is interesting to compare this position with that of Tarasov at take off in Chapter Seven.

Running too far and too fast

All things being equal the greater the speed with which the vaulter arrives at the take off point, the higher they will jump. However in pole vaulting as with driving a car, the faster you are travelling when out of control the bigger the crash is likely to be. The key word is **optimum**, in other words the best possible controlled speed. It is the impulse with which the vaulter hits the pole that causes it to flex. Speed is only of value if it can be allied with a high plant and a 'solid' body.

The faster you run carrying a long lever, the more difficult it is to maintain control and balance, so danger lurks around the corner. Athletes are intuitively aware of this and unless they have a death wish they will often pull out of the jump at the last instant. Those with a death wish will continue and their out of control, off balance take off will feed a host of problems as the jump progresses. The critical question here is how far a vaulter needs to run to generate the speed they can control and use at take off?

In the 2004 Australian Olympic trials, 23 year Stephen Hooker cleared the Olympic qualifying standard of 5.65 metres from twelve steps (six lefts!). As a 19 year old he jumped 5.30 metres off ten steps (five lefts).

The pole carry

Beginners who use low grips and light poles can get away with carrying the pole horizontally in the run up. However, if they are ambitious and talented, vaulters must eventually move to higher grips and heavier poles. At this point they may find a poor pole carry restricting their development. One of the problems here is that there have been examples of elite vaulters, for example Phillip Collet of France, who employed an almost horizontal pole carry. One can only say that although he was a successful vaulter at that time he might well have been better had he used the method we suggest in this text. After all it has been used by the three highest vaulters in the history of the event to date, namely Bubka, Tarasov and Markov.

Our experience has lead us to believe that even beginners should be taught to carry the pole correctly when they move to a run up of twelve steps or more. Of course athletes may decide to solve the problem by using a wide grip but that only leads to the problems detailed above.

A poor pole carry can have a major impact on many aspects of technique. The longer and heavier the pole, the bigger the problem. This is because of the torque forces involved. Inevitably the athlete is forced to lean backwards and run on their heels in an attempt to balance these forces and this invariably leads to a poor plant and take off. Figure 25.2.

Taking off 'under'

While each of the myths outlined above can lead to serious problems, the most pervasive and dangerous is the notion that it is all right, even beneficial, to take off "under" ie with the take off foot placed ahead of the top hand. **This is simply not true!**

Taking off "Under" leads to a range of problems, the first of which is a marked deceleration of the athlete prior to take off. In his paper "Run up speed in the pole vault", Ulrich Steinacher (Die lehre der Leichtathletic" 1989) stated

> "An optimal performance can be achieved only when the vaulter/pole system executes a precise and correct planting movement with minimal velocity losses during the last three strides." He goes on to say "Considerable velocity losses can occur at the takeoff by running under. If the dynamic take off spot from a full run up is more than 60 – 70 cm

> ahead of the top hand, the velocity can be reduced by as much as 3.5m/sec and the support phase will last 0.14 to 0.16 seconds. A take off point 30 – 35cm ahead of the top hand will reduce velocity losses to 1.4 – 1.8 m/sec and the support phase to 0.12 to 0.14sec."

The energy thrown away at this point can never be recovered. This is serious enough, but it gets worse. Because every element of the jump is part of a coherent whole, a take off in which the athlete is "under" has negative effects on successive phases of a vault, to the point where it often puts them in danger.

- If we consider the body as a pendulum swinging around the top hand it is clear that while a take off which is 'out' naturally assists the forward pendulum swing of the body around the top hand, a take off which is 'under' has the opposite effect.

- It is virtually impossible for the vaulter to hit the pole hard ie with the body **solid** from take off toe to the top hand. Instead energy bleeds away as the badly positioned and 'soft' top arm is driven back and the lumbar spine sags forward.

- Athletes who take off "under" can never optimise the pole/ground angle, a crucial factor in effective performance.

- It is difficult for the athlete to "finish the take off" with a driving extension of the take off leg. So typically we see vaulters who are 'under' being 'ripped' off the ground and so unable drive the pole up and forwards. Inevitably the take off is flat, with the vaulter travelling forwards and the pole bending prodigiously. Sadly while the athlete is often projected to a great height, the pole does not roll towards the pad and the vaulter may find themselves projected vertically upwards into a dangerous position directly over the box. Invariably they achieve a great height but

Figure 25.2

come up short and finish up crashing down on the bar with no hope of a clearance. Even worse, they will often be encouraged to repeat the same mistakes by well meaning but ignorant friends and sometimes by their 'coaches' who only 'see' the height reached but not the result of the jump.

- If the vaulter does not finish the take off, they are unable to set the take off leg up for the long whipping swing which puts more energy into the pole.
- This in turn reduces their ability to initiate the upwards roll the hips to 'cover' the pole.
- There is no chance of a "Free take off", with all the advantages this can bring
- If athletes take off 'under' on a regular basis they risk ongoing back injuries.

The 'Tap'

One of the biggest mistakes athletes can make is to rely on a 'tap' at take off. This practice, where the coach or another vaulter stands alongside the take off point and gives the vaulter a push in the back as they take off, should never be used. It allows the athlete to paper over a major weakness in their technique. It can lead them to believe that they are capable of gripping higher in competition than they can safely handle. While it is unlikely that anyone has done an objective study of this issue we suspect that athletes who habitually rely on a tap in training and in their competition warm up are more likely to no height than those who do not. They are also more likely to be injured.

The position of the lead leg at take off is not crucial

This particular myth is dangerous because although it seems relatively unimportant, the action of the lead leg during the take off is vital. Many athletes do not understand this and they can be seen checking their foot after a jump, with the lead leg pushed forward and with the foot directly under the knee. At take off this action tends to pull the hips forward and destroy the strong body position they should be aiming for. It also means that they lose the vertical impulses that could be gained by driving the heel of the free leg up to the buttocks. To confirm this element of technique the reader has but to look at the images in this book!

Rock back as soon as possible

It is important to try to get back to 'cover' the pole as fast as possible – but not at the expense of finishing the take off! While this may seem

to be playing with words there is a critical and perhaps life saving distinction between the two. This is because an athlete who tries to invert as soon as they leave the ground after a poor take off, is risking injury. One only has to consider the Metronome to understand that if the weight is moved up on the lever it must slow down and eventually stop pivoting around the base.

The athlete **should** swing up rapidly, but only after driving the pole forward with a powerful springing take off. This puts energy into the vaulter/pole system and ensures that it will continually move forward towards the pad.

Common misunderstandings

Apart from the myths detailed above there are other elements of poor technique which are often misunderstood. These are:

- Picking up the knee of the take off leg immediately after it leaves the ground
- Continuing the swing of the whole body after it has moved past the chord of the pole.

While the first problem is very common and easy to spot, the second is quite rare and often can only be seen when viewed in slow motion.

Picking up the take off knee – that is flexing the take off leg at the knee and or hips, at any point before the athlete swings to the chord of the pole is a reflection of previous mistakes and the precursor of future problems. Interestingly it can be seen in the later stages of the swing of World class vaulters like Gibilisco and Hartwig; indeed with the latter it is never completely straight during the swing and we suspect that this may have cost this great athlete the few centimetres he needed to move to second on the all time list. Unfortunately we believe that it may have stemmed from a take off which was under.

All this confirms that the athlete has not 'finished the take off' with a driving extension of the take off leg, a key element in effective pole vaulting. Unfortunately as is often the case in this complex event, the problem expands because pulling a flexed take off leg forward prevents the athlete from making the long whipping swing of the take off leg. At the same time this action slightly raises the centre of mass of the vaulter/pole system and so slows it down. Combined with a high grip this again creates a potentially dangerous situation, especially for vaulters of limited experience.

The second problem, the continuation of the swing of the extended body past the chord of the pole. is a problem of timing and of body awareness. To appreciate the problem one must first understand what the athlete should do! The powerful whipping swing of the body around the top hand is a critical component of the advanced technical model. However as soon as the extended body of the vaulter has swung to the chord of the pole, it should begin to flex at the hips so as to shorten the axis of rotation and thus speed up the swing. This is important because it enables the athlete to cover the pole before it begins to recoil.

However some athletes do not begin to 'break' at the hips at this point as they should, but continue to rotate the extended body around the top hand after they have swung past the pole. This means that the rotation is much slower, they never 'cover' the pole while it is still flexed and so lose much of the benefit of the recoil. Many athletes still eventually manage to achieve a good vertical position on the pole and the real problem remains undetected – unless you keep a close eye on the differential between grip height and the height of the bar.

The final and perhaps most dangerous misunderstanding, is that there are no absolutes and that every athlete should develop their own unique technique based on their specific physical characteristics.

With all of this in mind it is worth noting that there is one aspect of technique which is still debatable. That is whether it is advantageous to drop the lead leg immediately after take off. There appears to be an obvious advantage of this 'double leg swing' in that the centre of mass of the vaulter/pole system is initially kept lower. However our observations show two potential disadvantages. The first is that many athletes anticipate the dropping of the leg, so it occurs too early and they fail to benefit from the driving punch of the free thigh – characteristic of all good performances in all of the jumping events. The second is that it is very difficult for the athlete to invert fast enough to cover the pole before it begins to recoil.

Summary

Any one of the myths or misunderstandings outlined here can cause problems, when two are combined there can be no doubt that the athlete concerned is not going to fulfil their potential; if more than two are involved they are putting themselves at risk every time they take off.

But the biggest problem of all!

The biggest problem is not that athletes limit their own potential, or even that they may risk injury, by basing their technique on any of the myths and misunderstandings outlined above. It is when they become reasonably successful doing so because they now become models for all the young vaulters in their region, state or nation. Local influences can be far more powerful than international ones in pole vaulting, as in almost every other aspect of life.

This will become an even bigger problem if the model presented by Bubka and used so effectively by Tarasov, Markov and Lawrence Johnson is not picked up by the next generation of male athletes – even though the two leading female vaulters in the world at present, Isinbyeva and Feofanova, do employ it.

The notion that "There are a thousand ways to skin a cat" seems to pervade pole vault coaching even though any taxidermist will tell you that this is simply untrue! However it provides coaches with a convenient way of justifying an approach where the athlete is allowed to do pretty much what they like and there is no attempt to objectively analyse what they are doing. It is worth posing the question "If every athlete builds their own individual technical model how can a coach determine what is right and what is wrong with their technique?" However this view certainly makes it possible for coaches to go along happily in the belief that they have nothing to learn from anyone else!

Of course it is possible to jump 'high' despite technical errors. But how high is 'high'? When a local athlete jumps 6.00metres it is easy to forget that Bubka jumped 6.00 metres in 1985! In track and field terms that is almost prehistory! It is also conveniently forgotten that he could have pushed the world record to 6.30 metres and more, had the need to secure the financial future of his family not slowed his progression down. It is also forgotten that the next two highest vaulters in history, Tarasov 6.05metres (19'81") and World Champion, Markov 6.05 metres along with World Indoor Champion Lawrence Johnson 5.98metres (19'6"), all used the same technical model as Bubka - that developed the great Ukrainian coach Vitaly Petrov.

The debate will go on because pole vault coaches of the 21st Century are like the professional fencing and vaulting masters of the 19th Century. To attract clients they all have to profess special knowledge and skills. It would not suit them to admit that there is a generic pool of knowledge about the best way to pole vault which is accessible and available to anyone who cares to become a student of the event.

APPENDIX A

Pole vault poles

It should be clear that beginners can learn to vault with almost anything that resembles a pole. Many great vaulters recall their early attempts at pole vaulting in the backyard with one of mum's poles for holding up the washing line or an old piece of plastic tubing. The only criteria are that the pole is not too heavy and not too big in diameter for young hands to hold – and of course that it will not break! Length is not an issue because any pole can be cut down to the 11' - 12' beginners should use initially. As we suggested in Chapter Eleven beginners should continue to vault on stiff poles until they have mastered the 'working model' of technique.

However any ambitious young vaulter will eventually have to move to flexible poles. While the introduction of flexible poles brought a new and exciting dimension to the vault, it also brought many problems for coaches. Even small squads of vaulters need a large range of poles of different poundages and different lengths. These poles must not only be bought, cared for and stored, they must often be transported around the country, and in our case around the world!

The most important characteristics of a pole are quality, durability and consistency. The latter is especially important; a vaulter must be certain that identical poles from a manufacturer will always respond identically and that any rating change in the pole will be reflected in its' performance.

Every pole has a label indicating its' length and "weight rating", which is the suggested maximum weight of a vaulter to use that pole safely. With UCS Spirit poles these specifications are engraved at the top of pole; the pole length, (both Imperial and Metric), 'weight' in pounds and kilograms, its flex rating and the date of manufacture are all detailed. Unfortunately these details are not always easy to read; to make pole selection easy with a large squad and to ensure that the correct pole is chosen for each jump, it is worth writing the key details at both the top and bottom of each pole in large numbers with a permanent marker.

Most manufacturers also include a warning that a pole should not be used if it is rated below the vaulter's body weight. In the USA many high school Federations do not allow athletes to compete on poles below their body weight. However the fact is that around the world, many athletes are forced to ignore this warning if they want to bend a pole; veteran vaulters and social decathletes are the usual culprits. They can often get away with it if they grip the pole below, well below, the recommended grip height which is approximately 30 centimetres from the top of the pole. Here the rule of thumb is that for every 6 inches the grip is lowered, the pole stiffens by around 5 pounds.

Steve Chappell of UCS Spirit states, "Due to the pole structure and glass reinforcement any variation above or below the vaulters weight could result in a high break close to the bottom hand. A grip to low could result in a break in the lower third of the pole".

Flex ratings

The "flex rating" of poles has the potential to cause immense but unnecessary confusion and angst among coaches and athletes. Two points may help to resolve this issue. In the first place the Flex rating of a pole is completely irrelevant to the vast majority of vaulters. This is because the stiffness of the pole is only one of a great range of interacting variables in every jump an inexperience vaulter takes.

Elite vaulters have stabilised virtually every aspect of their technique and so have almost all these variables under control. This means that they can take advantage of a slight increase or decrease of pole stiffness and so can benefit from knowing the flex rating of a pole.

However, inexperienced vaulters alter some aspect of their technique on every attempt and it is almost impossible to predict what pole they need from one jump to the next. This means that an element of gambling comes into the choice of a pole; what is certain is that changing to another pole with a slightly different flex is not likely to have any effect on their performance.

Clearly the question of what pole an athlete should use goes well beyond their bodyweight. It is a function of their take off speed, the quality of their plant and take off, especially the height of their hands at the instant of plant, how hard they 'hit' the pole, their grip height; all of these factors contribute to the 'impulse' as they take off.

One of the biggest problems confronting coaches is the relationship between poles of differing lengths. The accompanying chart produced by pole vault fanatic Jan Johnson of the USA, will prove immensely valuable. Note that although Spirit poles are not listed they match the data provided.

BEST FLEX POLE PROGRESSION AND RELATIVE STIFFNESS

MS STIC	PACER	MS STIC	PACER	MS STIC	PACER	PACER	PACER	PACER	PACER	PACER	PACER	PACER
		SKY		SKY		SKY	SKY	SKY	SKY	SKY		
						MS STIC	MS STIC	MS STIC				
10' 70												
10' 80	10'6 70											
10' 90	10'6 80	11' 70										
10' 100	10'6 90	11' 80										
10' 110	10'6 100	11' 90										
10' 120	10'6 110	11' 100	11'6 90	12' 80								
10' 130	10'6 120	11' 110	11'6 100	12' 90								
10' 140	10'6 130	11' 120	11'6 110	12' 100								
10' 150	10'6 140	11' 130	11'6 120	12' 110	12'6 100	13' 90						
	10'6 150	11' 140	11'6 130	12' 120	12'6 110	13' 100						
		11' 150	11'6 140	12' 130	12'6 120	13' 110						
		11' 160	11'6 150	12' 140	12'6 130	13' 120	13'6 110					
		11' 170	11'6 160	12' 150	12'6 140	13' 130	13'6 120					
						13' 135	13'6 125	14' 115				
		11'6 170	12' 160	12'6 150	13' 140	13'6 130	14' 120					
						13' 145	13'6 135	14' 125				
		11'6 180	12' 170	12'6 160	13' 150	13'6 140	14' 130	14'6 120				
						13' 155	13'6 145	14' 135	14'6 125			
			12' 180	12'6 170	13' 160	13'6 150	14' 140	14'6 130				
						13' 165	13'6 155	14' 145	14'6 135			
				12'6 180	13' 170	13'6 160	14' 150	14'6 140	15' 130			
					13' 175	13'6 165	14' 155	14'6 145	15' 135			
					13' 180	13'6 170	14' 160	14'6 150	15' 140	15'6 135		
					13' 185	13'6 175	14' 165	14'6 155	15' 145	15'6 140		
						13'6 180	14' 170	14'6 160	15' 150	15'6 145		
						13'6 185	14' 175	14'6 165	15' 155	15'6 150		
CHART ASSUMES 1' = 20LBS TILL 15' LENGTH						13'6 190	14' 180	14'6 170	15' 160	15'6 155		
							14' 185	14'6 175	15' 165	15'8 160		
							14' 190	14'6 180	15' 170	15'6 165	16' 160	
							14' 195	14'6 185	15' 175	15'6 170	16' 165	
								14'6 190	15' 180	15'6 175	16' 170	
								14'6 195	15' 185	15'6 180	16' 175	
								14'6 200	15' 190	15'6 185	16' 180	
								14'6 205	15' 195	15'8 190	16' 185	
									15' 200	15'6 195	16' 190	
									15' 205	15'6 200	16' 195	
										15'6 205	16' 200	
											16' 205	

Prepared by Jan Johnson 4/30/99

One athlete's perception of pole vaulting

It is often said that the teenage years are the hardest years of one's life. Fortunately, I passed through this rough period relatively unscathed, and I think this is largely due to my involvement with sport, in particular with pole vaulting. From the age of 11, when I first picked up a pole, to 18, when I gracefully retired, I spent a large proportion of my free time around motivated athletes and dedicated coaches. Whilst many girls from my school were experimenting with drugs and alcohol, I was at the track with a group of people who prized physical fitness, dedication and hard work. It helped me to realise that I didn't have to go to parties and pour alcohol down my throat to be cool.

The group that I trained with was very close knit. In many ways, it gave me a sense of belonging at a time when so many kids become lost. I made some great friends who, like me, wanted to be fit and healthy and had goals. I still played many other sports in high school, but I think doing pole vault had the greatest impact on my social development. I was constantly mixing with girls and boys of all ages and economic backgrounds, which was important for me given that I spent fourteen years at a private girls' school. Also, as I became one of the older members of the group, I took on responsibility for helping the younger kids and looking after newcomers.

I will always value my coach, Alan Launder, not only for his technical knowledge and coaching experience, but also for his ability to put life into perspective. I was a very driven athlete, and had high expectations of myself. It was therefore important to have someone to stop me sometimes, and help me see the wood from the trees. Jumping over a bar with a pole may seem, at times, like the most important thing in the world. But at the end of the day, it is what you get out of the experience that you will really cherish.

I spent 6 months living in France and training with a French coach and group. My whole trip was arranged through pole vaulting contacts. At 15 years of age, I was in a foreign country learning maths and physics in a language I barely understood, but I made the most of it. I returned to Australia with a much broader perspective on life, due to my experience of another culture, language and lifestyle. I was also more confident in my own ability to make friends and deal with life when things weren't going so well. Now I am fluent in French, and maintain contacts with many of the people I went to school with over there. This is one of the experiences that I will always cherish. In addition I have travelled to compete in the USA and the United Kingdom on pole vault tours and these experiences have contributed to my better understanding of the world I live in.

Another great experience was competing for my country. In 1999 I travelled to Poland as a 16 year-old to compete in the World Youth Championships. Apart from the pride of having represented my country, and the thrill of travelling with the Australian team, the pressure of competitions such as these prepared me for other challenges. Now I thrive under pressure. Competing at a high level taught me to deal with my nerves and bring out my best performances. I have confidence in my own ability under pressure, and in a way I think it is a self fulfilling prophesy.

The most important thing is that young people have a sense of purpose and belonging at a time when they are shaping the rest of their lives. The strong sense of community and mateship with my pole vault group was one of the most positive influences of my adolescence. I can look back now on 7 years well spent.

Jenny Lovell. 1/11/2004

Jenny is presently completing two degrees. The first is in International Law and the second in Modern Languages; she is already fluent in French, Italian and Spanish and will shortly begin an intensive course to learn German. In 2004 at the age of twenty three she was employed at Adelaide University teaching Economics, another of her areas of expertise.

As this book goes to the printer Jenny is undertaking a ten day walking tour in Patagonia.

APPENDIX C

An example of the Process of technical coaching

Taking off 'under' creates many problems for vaulters whether they do it intentionally or not. However if they want to bring their take off point "Out", the solution appears easy, simply adjust the run up. Unfortunately this deals with the 'symptom', it does not deal with the 'cause' of the problem! This may be rooted in a vaulter's limited physical parameters but it may also be the result of poor technique or perceptual errors, in their psyche or a combination of all of these. It may be that it just 'happened' as they learned to vault and has become habitual. Whatever the cause of the problem, the reality is that if an athlete is to change their take off point from 'Under' to 'Out', they may have to improve or even radically alter every aspect of their technique prior to the moment of take off.

Certainly vaulters who have been taught that only the final two steps are critical to a successful jump, will probably find it difficult to achieve an effective take off. This is because any loss of balance or control before that point, however minute, will be registered subconsciously by the vaulter who then intuitively takes off under, if only because it seems to take them closer to the safety of the pad. As in skiing and rock climbing, where the wrong thing often 'feels like' the right thing, this intuitive reaction only leads to further problems and greater risks.

The biggest problem is that to take off 'out', a vaulter must be both willing and able to jump up in a powerful springing action – summed up succinctly by the term 'Stabhochsprung' or 'pole high jump', used by the Germans. Athletes who have spent most of their lives taking off 'under' have often never learned to really jump. Instead they have been dragged off the ground by the pole. This can be clearly seen by observing the action of their take off ankle at and immediately after take off. Following an effective take off the ankle will be completely extended, with the take off toe pointed down; however when athletes take off under, the toe will invariably be pointed forward towards the box or even in extreme cases towards the pad.

Clearly before vaulters can take off 'out' they must learn to jump! While a few will never be able to change, most committed athletes can make major improvements by altering simple elements in their training – such as including regular sessions of long jumping and stiff pole jumping. In the early transition period, sand pit jumping is of immense benefit because it reduces the micro perceptual demands of planting the pole and allows the athlete to concentrate on jumping up.

It is highly likely that they will also need to include more long jumping in their training program along with a higher proportion of plyometric work. They may also wish to add very specific exercises for developing the rebound strength needed in the pole vault take off.

Of course if an athlete wants to enjoy the immense benefits of an effective springing take off they must first develop a structured and balanced run up in which the pole is precisely controlled and positioned for the plant and take off, with no loss of balance or control.

This will take commitment and hard work but it has an additional benefit – it will eliminate another major problem in the vault, namely 'running through' or aborting the take off. Often viewed as the result of mental softness, 'running through' is more likely to be caused by the athlete's intuitive, and accurate, realisation that they are not ready to take off so they sensibly pull out of the jump. Get the run up right from the first step and many other elements will automatically improve, including the position and effectiveness of the take off!

APPENDIX D

The evolution of the Adelaide approach

This book is the product of forty years of teaching physical education, coaching track and field and immense study.

The ideas in this book were not taken from the pages of other authors but came from a process we describe as reflective tinkering. Here ideas are tried and tested, accepted or rejected, expanded or diminished – all in the real world of coaching young athletes. Inevitably we made many mistakes along the way but gradually, working with our 'orphans', we developed what we believe to be a unique, effective and successful approach to developing pole vaulters.

While our own personal experience working with generations of young athletes has been the primary driving force behind the evolution of our ideas, there have been many other influences. So once a decision was made to improve pole vaulting in South Australia, Alan organised a seven week trip to Europe in 1978 to study with Tom McNab in England, Anton Krupsky in Leverkusen, Germany, Maurice Houvion in Vincennes, Paris and Andrzei Kresinski in Warsaw, Poland – the latter pair both coaches of Olympic Champions. A subsequent trip to France gave him an opportunity to study the methods of Dr, Jean Claude Perrin, coach of Olympic Champion Quinon.

However the seminal influence was meeting Vitaly Petrov and Serbey Bubka at the World Cup competition in Canberra in 1985. This meeting set us on a new path in a search for the truth about pole vaulting. Vitaly's ideas were revolutionary to the point of being outrageous to our blinkered minds. However we began to try to apply them and gradually his ideas made more sense to us. Subsequent meetings with him in Formia, Canberra and Adelaide added to our understanding, as did informal conversations with him during major competitions such as the World Junior Championships and the Olympic Games.

Not only this but we had the chance to meet with Sergey Bubka and begin to see this great athlete's perspective on Petrov's ideas. In 1990 for example, we had a two hour one on one session with him in Munich where Sergey answered all our questions openly. However even more revealing was his response to questions, of which at least five were from this author, at the clinic organised in conjunction with the World Junior

championships in Jamaica in July 2001. His answers are now in the public domain on the US pole vault education web site and should have gone a long way to silencing any coach who doubted Petrov's ideas.

Another important resource has been Australian track and field coaching magazine "Modern Athlete and Coach" edited by Jess Jarver. Because of his contacts in the USSR, Jess was able to spirit articles out of that country and publish them in English. Australian coaches therefore had access to material which was denied to other coaches, although much of it was subsequently published later in the USA. Naturally all of this added to our knowledge of Soviet methods.

However we were even more fortunate. In early 1991 a young Russian vaulter, Roman Botcharnikov came to live with us in Adelaide for three months. Roman was a disciple of both Petrov and Bubka and thoroughly understood their methods. As a 5.50metre vaulter he also tried to apply them. He returned to Adelaide in November 1991 and lived with and coached alongside us, for ten months, until we arranged a track scholarship for him in the USA. Clearly he was a valuable learning resource.

Then in 1996 Alan invited Alex Parnov, another Russian coach to come to Adelaide. He stayed for two years and it was possible to observe his methods as he worked with Dimitri Markov, Victor Chystiakov both world class vaulters, and introduced Tatiana Grigorieva to the pole vault.

Another Russian coach Sergey Mirishnishenko arrived in 1998 and stayed for two years before moving to Queensland to take up a coaching position we arranged for him. Finally Dimitri Markov, 2003 World Champion, arrived back in Adelaide with his family in 2004 and this has given us yet another opportunity to study his methods.

The idea of bringing together the knowledge and wisdom gained from all of these experiences gradually emerged after visits to the Reno pole vault Summit in 1999, 2003 and 2004. They crystallised after participation in pole vault camps for young athletes in Nampa Idaho and at UCLA in 2004.

The ideas in this book may appear revolutionary but they have worked for us. We believe that they will work for other dedicated coaches.

References

Boase G. "Relating training parameters to performance", Modern Athlete and coach" 29/2 April 1991.

Boiko V. and Nikolov J. "Something new in the pole vault", Modern Athlete and Coach 28/4 October 1990.

Botcharnikov R. "The continuous chain model in the pole vault", Track Coach.

Bubka S. "An athlete's view of limits and possibilities", IAAF Conference "Human performance in athletics"; limits and possibilities". Budapest. Oct 11-12. 1997.

Bubka S. "Round table with Sergey Bubka", Pole vault clinic, Kingston, Jamaica, July20 –21. 2002.

Burnett A. "The biomechanics of jumping; the relevance to field event athletes", Modern Athlete and Coach 39/3 July 2001.

Butler D. "The pole carry and active pole drop", The Pole Vault Standard, Fresno, 2004.

Czingon H. "A pole vault technique comparison." Die Lehre der Leichathletik, Vol 32, No9, 1993

Docherty J. "Modern track and field", Prentice Hall, Eaglewood Cliffs, NJ. 1953

Ferry B. "Modern pole vaulting", Tafnews Press, Mountain View, Cal, 1998.

Hay J. "The biomechanics of sports techniques", Prentice Hall, Eaglewood Cliffs, New Jersey 1993

Jagodin V. "What is happening in the pole vault", Modern Athlete and Coach 21/3 July 1983

Jagodin V. "Sergei Bubka above the bar", Modern Athlete and Coach 31/3 July 1993

Jagodin V. and Tschugunov V. "Training tasks for young pole vaulters", Modern Athlete and Coach 21/4 October 1983

Jagodin V. and Papanov V. "Sergei Bubka – 6.01") Modern Athlete and Coach, 25/4, October 1987

Koontz D. "One door away from Heaven" Headline Books, Euston Rd. London 2002

Kresinski A. "Pole vault conditioning" Modern Athlete and Coach 20/2 April 1982

Kruber D. and K. and Adamcyevski H. "Consideration for a revision of pole vault technique in Germany", Modern Athlete and Coach" 33/2 April 1995

Launder A. "The pole vault", Australian Track and Field Coaches Association Manual, 1986

Launder A. "The Pre jump – a revolution in the pole vault", Modern Athlete and Coach, 27/3 July 1989

Launder A. "The second Russian revolution in pole vault", Modern Athlete and Coach 39/2 April 2001

Launder A. and Gormley J. "The pre jump take off in the pole vault revisited", Modern Athlete and Coach 36/2 April 1998

Launder A. "To coach or not to coach? Modern Athlete and Coach

Moore G. "An analysis of the pole vault take off." The Jumps, Jess Jarver, Tafnews, Los Altos, 1981

Nikolov J. "What's new in the pole vault?", Modern Athlete and Coach 24/2 April 1986

Nikonov I. "Women become Pole vaulters", Modern Athlete and Coach P12 Vol 34, number 3 ATFCA Athelstone Australia

O'Brien P. "The Ionian Mission", William Collins and Co. Ltd. Glasgow 1981 P 70

Pearson G. "Athletics", Thomas Nelson and Sons, London W1, 1963

Perrin J. "Perrin on pole vaulting", Technical bulletin of Canada, No. 49, Summer 1988

Petrov V. "Unpublished paper", European coaches congress, Birmingham, England, 1985

Schon D. "Educating the reflective practitioner", Jossey Bass, San Francisco, 1986.

Steinacker U. "The run up speed in the pole vault", Modern Athlete and Coach" 29/2 April 1999

Stewart M. "The DimaSport pole vault conference". Modern Athlete and Coach, 41/2 April 2003

Tidow G. "Model technique analysis sheet for the vertical jumps", Part 3: The pole vault. New Studies in Athletics 1989.